How to Transform Your Grief into Bliss

SANTLAL SEJWAL

First published in 2021 by

Becomeshakespeare.com
One Point Six Technologies Pvt. Ltd.
123, Building No J2, Wadala Truck Terminal,
Wadala (East), Mumbai- 400037 Maharashtra, India.
T:+91 8080226699

This book has been funded by WORDIT ART FUND
WORDIT ART FUND helps deserving
Authors publish their work
To apply for funding, please visit us at
becomeshakespeare.com

ISBN - 978-93-90543-17-5

DEDICATION

I want to dedicate this book to my uncle, i.e. the younger brother of my father, late Mr. Jainarain Sejwal who loved me like his own son and my wife late Chanderpati Sejwal who supported me in each and every step throughout her life.

May their souls rest in peace.

ACKNOWLEDGMENTS

Though the book had been written during the past six years, its content is the reflection of my thoughts which have been developed throughout my life. I had started to collect the quotations in 1971 and now the total collection of such quotes is about ten thousand, out of which some have been used in the book. Such collections of quotations and important information is my hobby which now has become the part of this book. Thus, it can also be said that this book has been written throughout my life. Thus, I want to acknowledge everyone from the beginning.

In fact, human beings take birth with a clean slate, then each and every experience irrespective to pleasurable or bitter starts accumulating in the brains and in turn develop our personality. Therefore, I am very thankful to all the innumerable people dead or alive who have given me the opportunity to experience pleasurable experiences as well as those who pushed me toward bitter experiences. In fact, those who challenged me are the real motivators in my life. In the words of Winston Churchill, "Kites rise highest against wind, not with it." However, I am going to mention the name of only those who supported me especially to help me in higher education during my Army Service.

Some of them are:- Major Raj Kumar my OC in Sikkim, Lt Col G S Bahia my CO at Allahabad, Major A B Sibhal my professional *Guru* and Major S Gupta both were my OIC Technical Services Group in Faculty of Electronics (FEL) Military college of(MC) EME, Lt Col Tribhuavan Singh, Technical Adjutant in FEL MC EME. Without their supports, it would have been very difficult for me to complete my higher education, by going out of their way to help me. Naturally, without that education, no one could write on such a vast topic. Therefore, I pay my gratitude all to them.

Thanks to my neighbours Ex Maj Gen V K Passi, Mrs Poonam Passi, Ex Col V K Chaudary and Dr. Rita Singh also for encouraging me at the time of writing the book. Thanks to Estate Manager Mr Kamal and other staff, Mr Nain Singh, Mr Mukesh, Mr Rajender, Mr Jagdish and Mr Birender, of Rajesh Vihar AWHO Khurpatal for providing me general facilities during my stay at Khurpatal.

Above all, I am greatly thankful to my family members. First of all, my parents Late Randhir Singh and Smt. Shanti Devi who gave me opportunity to take decisions independently even at a very early age. This is the reason; I became mature earlier than usual. Thanks to my son Satyan, daughter-in-law Anju, granddaughter Tammana and grandson Ayan also who kept me free from family problems and provided tranquillity so that I may write the book.

I pay my gratitude to my both daughters Geeta and Pooja who allowed me to live alone at Khurpatal (Nainital) in a peaceful environment. In fact both of them are very much concerned about my comfort and health, thus, they were hesitated to send me at any new place alone. However, for writing on such a subject of spirituality, a peace of mind and such a tranquil place was very necessary. Thank you my lovely children.

I pay my gratitude to my granddaughter Swetcha who is also the admirer of the manuscript. She read it often and always encouraged me. She also helped me whenever there was any difficulty during the writing on the computer.

I am also thankful to my son-in-law Hari who provided me with many books from the Gold Coast Library when I was staying in Australia for a year otherwise many unique references could not have been mentioned in this book.

Last but not least my eight year old granddaughter Aria who wanted to play with me sometimes but understood the time I was busy in writing the book. Thus, even as a small kid; she has so much understanding that she understood whenever I told her why completion of the book is so necessary. So she deserves not only my gratitude but also my love.

I am very thankful to Become Shakespeare Publisher also especially Publishing adviser Rohan Patil who gave me offer for publishing the book, and Project manager Sameer Ambildhok who guided me regarding submitting the manuscript. Even they both waited due to lock down. I also thanks to other members of the project team Triputi Sawardeka, Pooja Datt and all others.
And I am very thankful to the readers as well. As, without your interest, this book remains at selves of book shops and libraries without fulfilling its destiny of inspiring the people of the world.

Finally, I pay my wholeheartedly gratitude to the Cosmic Forces/God which created the situations in my favour throughout my life otherwise I would not have been able to reach at this position of writing this book. Even the Divine's role is more than me in writing this book.

PREAFACE

According to statics of TV show *Satyamev Jayate* presented by prominent actor Amir Khan in 2014, the suicide rate in the world is 11 out of one Lac people yearly while in India it is 21 per Lac yearly. Between the ages of 15 to 29 the suicide rate in India is 35 per Lac yearly. Whilst According to a survey published in 2015 farmers' suicidal cases in India is 3.05 Lac for last 20 years from 1995 to 2015. However, after that period statics of farmers' suicidal case till Dec 2018 has not been available with the Indian Government according to the reply of a RTI.

Even the suicide rate in students is also increasing day- by- day in India especially due to wrong policies of education system. In every 55 minutes one student suicides in India. An online American magazine, *International Policy Digest*, in its November 2019 post, labelled India as the 'Suicide Capital of Asia'. This was in the response to a WHO report which cited that India had the highest suicide rate in the South-East Asian region in 2016.

The World Health Organization says that up to the decades 2020s, depression will be the second leading cause of death in the world so mental illness will be the second largest disease afflicting the world. Moreover, this prediction of WHO seems to be true on seeing the current rate of depression. Now about 20 per cent population of USA, about 25 per cent of Europe and 36 percent of India is suffering from depression. An article published by Guardian in 2016 stated that there were sixty one million antidepressants prescribed and dispensed outside hospitals in 2015 and the official figure have shown that the number of antidepressants given to patients in England has doubled in a decade. Whilst a WHO report published in 2018 stated that more than 300 million people of all ages suffer from depression.

Out of the depression cases in India about one lakh people suicide every year. Actually, the cause of depression and frustration is stress which is increasing day-by-day due to heavy competition and over-ambitiousness. Actually, suicidal case can be reduced for some extent by proper counselling but India endures 87 per cent shortage of mental health professionals. Even India spends only 0.06 percent of its health budget on mental health.

Though I am not a professional, I have faced many challenges and experienced several adverse circumstances throughout my life. In addition, I have experienced intense grief at the time of my wife's death. Anyway, I accepted each and every challenge boldly; tackle the adverse situations efficiently and cope with the grief successfully, and now live a peaceful and spiritual life. Thus, on the bases of my personal experiences, I have done my best efforts in this direction. Therefore, my main aim of writing this book is, to aware the common people about the stress and its effects; to teach them how to deal with adverse situations; how to cope with grief and how to live happy and spiritual life after recovering from grief.

Actually, grief is unavoidable but suffering is optional because suffering is merely a short of hypnosis. If you think you are miserable, you are miserable. If you think you can face crisis, you can face crises easily. Generally, you avoid facing the crises by one excuse or another and you have made your self-image accordingly. Actually, you are helpless only due to your inferior self-image which you have made yourself. Thus, these excuses cannot be eliminated until you will change your self-image. In fact, you and only you can change your self-image. Thus the miseries are not more than prejudice.

On the other hand, as and when you return in your original state from this type of hypnotism, you become happy. Mean to say, the sadness and gladness are only a mind game. Thus both these stages are only 'state of mind'. Therefore, first of all, you have to convert your inferior self-image into superior self-image. When you will start thinking positively you will find yourself cheerful.

In this context, Robert Louis Stevenson said, "The world is so full of a numbers of things; I am sure we should all be as happy as kings." Therefore, if you feel about yourself and think you deserve to be happy, you will resolve to create happiness wherever you go. Abraham Lincoln also said, "Most folks are about as happy as they want to be."

Anyhow, occasional grief comes to everyone but it can be handled. Moreover, you are not alone who experienced the grief. Actually, no one is special in this world that is spared by adversities. Rather everyone has to face it irrespective to wealth, knowledge, experience, wisdom, status, position etc. However, coping with grief is certainly depended on the personality of the individual.

Thus the book has been started with grieving process. In addition to define grief and grieving, how a griever can return to his or her normal activities is the content of the first part of the book. However, after coping with the grief, live a better life happily in this competitive and chaos world is also necessary. Therefore, suggestions about healthy lifestyle are described in the second part of the book. Third part of the book is associated with spiritual growth. Thus ways of attaining the bliss spiritually are described in the third and last part of the book. It can also be said that three concepts are combined in one book

Therefore, it will be more helpful for readers, if the book will be read in the order in which it has been written. I also advise readers that they should read each and every sentence, phrase and paragraph very intensively. Even some portion may be repeated and the sentences which they consider important may be underlined. Then take a break after reading of each chapter, even it will be more beneficial if they practice the methods and suggestions mentioned in the book so that grieving may be completed in a natural way and healthy lifestyle can be adapted.

For avoiding the bulkiness of the book, I have shared only those experiences which have been considered essential according to the content. I used simple words and avoided the philosophical terms so that book may not become complicated. Even I avoided religious sermons and discourses in order to develop healthy life style and spiritual growth. Means, I do not insist to follow society's norms; religious dogmas; rituals; etc.

Rather, I emphasis on positive attitude and moral values in order to maintain healthy lifestyle while meditation and thoughtless awareness are advised to attain bliss. Anyhow, I think if God sent us in this world without any manual then none of us has any right to mandate such norms and dogmas for human being. Moreover, norms, dogmas, ritual etc. are constantly changing throughout eras. Thus every new society creates its own norms. Secondly, if the general instructions regarding human being would have so necessary, God would have attach the manual with each new born baby as we found attached with appliances by its manufacturer.

Thus, living process is the matter of individual's choice. Therefore, way of living the life should be left to the individual instead of imposing the dogmas, norms, beliefs etc. by any institution. So, I have only described some suggestions whichever I consider suitable according to the situations. Therefore, my views give freedom to the readers to develop their own beliefs rather than binding them in traditional chain.

Instead of traditional and theoretical views, practical concepts and ways are described. Therefore mostly content is bases on my personal beliefs, knowledge and experiences.   Additionally, the researches of some researchers and views of some scholars, philosophers, psychologists, neuroscientists and other experts of the field are also included so that readers may comprehend the content thoroughly.

I used capital M for 'man' in the book because here the word Man is used for whole human species rather than single male gender. Likewise I used capital N for 'nature' because I honour the Nature very much so I consider Nature as proper noun like God, Sun, Star etc.

Generally, definitions of typical words are ignored in such type of books in order to avoid academic paternity. However, I observed throughout my life that mostly terms which seem very familiar and easier, in fact, have some special meaning also when we go in details. Therefore, for avoiding the confusion, I defined such terms; even some have been explained in details so that readers may understand the term clearly. First of all, I would like to explain the term 'transform' which is used in the title of the book.

However, meaning of transform is somewhat different from its similar words such as—change, convert, alter, transfer etc. Thus, here meaning of transformation is not merely a change of situation or shifting from one position to another or transferring from one stage to another. Whilst transformation is like transcendence which has a power to be born new, to make a fresh start, to turn over a new leaf—to a second chance, no reference to the past.

Naturally, the journey from grief to bliss cannot be completed without transcendence because this process requires something new: - new attitude, new thoughts, new behaviour, new habits etc. Mean to say, this process creates new personality and new life. Actually, this is the real *punner janam*. Thus it is such a 'state of mind' where everything is fresh and new which is unburdened by agony, grief, suffering etc. forever. Therefore, this entry into bliss creates a new aura which is full of such a positive energy where each and every one feels peace, joy and intense happiness. That's why I used the 'term' transform in the title.

Anyhow, I tried my best to avoid the repetition of same concept in different chapters, but it might be repeated unknowingly due to only one reason. And the reason is that I want to convince the readers that life must go on how much worse the circumstances may be. We can learn from Nature which never stops irrespective to occurring calamities, disasters, pandemics etc. rather it goes on forever. Thus the Universe will be as it is forever whether you live or not makes no difference to the Universe and Nature. Sunrise and sunset will remain on time, seasons remain changing accordingly, and flourishing and flowering of plants remain continue in your absence. Even your absence from the earth cannot affect the world's activities. Therefore, live the life 'as it comes'.

Thus I am sure that after reading the book, readers will feel solace. Even they may lead towards spirituality and can attain Eternal bliss. Actually, we are all soul in human body and originally we are all spiritual but our soul is covered by world's dust. However, after removing the dust, we become clear and pure. Thus spirituality in the life of human being works for removing the worldly dust. However, spirituality is not to be imposed by outside but it is already within us. Therefore, for spirituality, we have to dive within ourselves rather than seeking it somewhere else.

Therefore, if I succeed to help the common people in coping with grief and developing healthy lifestyle, I will consider myself fortunate. At the time of writing my first book *Man Towards its own end*, I have written the book very fast. Mean to say, I was very crazy to complete that book. However, after its publishing, I realized that writing was much enjoyable. Thus I concluded that writing itself is a great reward.

It can also be said that performing any activity wholeheartedly with awareness is more enjoyable than the fruition of the activity. The theme of Bhagwad Gita is also similar to this concept which says, "Do your *karma* with wholeheartedly rather concerning about its fruition because your *karma* is only in your hand rather than its fruition".

Actually, journey is always more enjoyable than its destination. If we are hurry to complete the journey and travel very fast, we may miss the amazing sight scene on the way. Moreover, we regret on reaching the destination when we realize that it is not as beautiful as the scenery we left on the way of journey. Anyway, Life is also a long journey. Therefore, we should live the life moment to moment with full awareness rather than desiring to reserve the place in heaven or to seek Invisible Power. Thus to live life mindfully and enjoy the journey of life whatever comes in your way is the essence of the book.

Therefore, I have written this book very slowly. Now I consider writing as a source of joy and happiness. Thus I enjoy the writing just as drinking the tea sip by sip. Actually, I enjoy the writing so much that I remain unaware about everything including time. This is the reason, I also advise the readers to read the book intensively and slowly.

I hope that this book will be helpful in this endeavour. With the Grace of God, my sincere efforts and positive energy which are visible in this book, May the readers realize the bliss!

Santlal Sejwal

CONTENTS

Events recur in cyclical pattern: Happiness and sorrow are two sides of the same coin: What are grief, pain, suffering, and grieving? Chain reaction of suffering: What are happiness and pleasure? What are spiritual ecstasy, bliss and Spiritual Bliss? Sources of happiness: Sources of Spiritual Bliss/Eternal Bliss.

God always warns us through hints: Do not ignore God's hints: Nothing is coincidence in the Universe: The Universe is full of mysteries: Whatever happens in our life happens for our betterment.

Everything is impermanent in the Universe: Although

grieving is a hard and long process, acceptance of loss makes it easy: Suggestions for grieving: Acceptance of true feelings improves our overall well-being: Acceptance is the first step towards endurance: Endurance as means to happiness.

Chapter 4: Make adversity an opportunity 125-145

Events effect positively as well as negatively: Hardship is main source of wisdom: We ourselves create our destiny: Tragedy teaches us lesson: Consider the adversity as a challenge: Adversity as catalyst for improving the Personality.

Chapter 5: Release your emotions.   146-174

What are emotions? The effects of emotions on human beings: Meaning of suppress in the context of emotions: Why do we suppress the emotions? Impact of suppressed emotions on our body and mind: what is regulation of emotions and how to regulate them? How to release emotions?

Chapter 6: Absorb in the work   175-194

How does grief affect the work? How to cultivate interest in work: Dedication to selfless work brings happiness: What is *Karmyoga* and How to be a *Karmyogi* ?

Chapter 7: Transform the grief into spirituality   195-213

Grief changes the temperament of human beings: Unresolved grief may become clinical depression whic is more severe than grief: Grief as means to spirituality: What is spiritual Awakening? Grief may be catalyst for spiritual awakening: How does spiritual practice bring bliss?

Part II

What is forgiveness? Why is the forgiveness so difficult? How does forgiveness improve our well-being? Forgiveness enhances compassion and kindness: How to forgive?

What is gratitude? Role of religion in expressing gratitude: Spiritual aspect of gratitude: Expressing gratitude enhances our happiness level and overall well-being: Reason for ingratitude: How to cultivate a mind of gratitude?

What is ego? What are healthy ego and ego-strength, and their importance in human's life: Which type ego of should be controlled and why? How to control the ego?

Meaning of comfort zone: How does our brain evolve out of comfort zone? How do knowledge, understanding and wisdom enhance out of comfort

Meaning of unconditional love: What is compassion? How can love and compassion be developed? Impact of love and compassion on healing process: Grief as means to love and compassion: How do love and compassion transcend us?

Chapter 17: Live a purposeful life   426-448

The journey of life itself is a pilgrim: Happiness lies in small noble deeds: What goes around comes around: Those who take care of others, God takes care of them: Service is the gate-way of bliss.

Chapter 18: Enhance your intuitive ability 449-477

What is intuition? Psychological aspects of intuition: Spiritual aspects of intuition: Link between gut feeling and intuition: How to recognize and follow the intuitions: How to enhance intuitive ability: Importance of intuition.

Chapter 19:   Live in the present moment 478-497

Meaning of living in the present moment: Why is it so hard to live in the present moment? How-to live in the present moment: Importance of living in the present moment.

Chapter 20:   Practice meditation   498-527

What is meditation? How to practice meditation: Difficulties occur during meditation practice and how to overcome them: Meditation practice improves our personality and overall well-being.

Part I

In the first part of the book, in addition to definition of grief and grieving, main emphasis is given on accepting the loss of tragedy and enduring the pain of grief. After accepting the loss, returning to the normal life becomes easy. Otherwise half energy of the griever is constantly consuming for fighting against grief and only half remain for recovering from grief. Though recovery takes time, the duration of time depends upon the individual's personality. However, releasing the painful emotions is next step in the process of recovery.

Thus, instead of pretending to be bold and strong, grievers should release their painful emotions by one means or another otherwise they will bury in their unconscious mind. And these suppressed emotions will remain punching from inside forever. Therefore, role of emotions on human's health, and the methods of releasing the painful emotions are also explained in this part.

However, there are some other ways of returning to normal life have been also explained in this first part of the book such as—absorbing in the work; how to convert adversities into opportunities and transform grief into spirituality. However, recovery procedure required patience. As nothing is stable, every procedure how long or hard it may be, complete its process soon or later.

Each and every event is part of cosmic plan so whatever happens, happens for our betterment. Therefore, no need to interfere with cosmic plan thus this fact is also described in details.

In addition, some terms such as grief, happiness, ecstasy, bliss, and emotion etc. also defined in this part.

Chapter 1
Brief description of grief and bliss

"The person you consider ignorant and insignificant is the one who came from God that he might learn bliss from grief and knowledge from gloom"— Khalil Gibran

Actually, everyone in this world wants happiness. However, on seeing the faces of the people, it seems that very few people are actual happy. Anyhow, unhappy people are either seeking happiness somewhere else instead of its real source or they are unable to distinguish between pleasure and happiness. Thus such persons consider the pleasure as happiness. However, the pleasure gives happiness but temporarily because pleasure is just like the ride of roller coaster which gives nuisance after completion of the ride. Therefore, pleasure pushes us towards more sadness.

However, it is another matter that happiness is also linked with sorrow but in positive aspect rather than negative. Mean to say, the existence of happiness is existed only due to sorrow. Actually, every` positive side of anything is existed only due to its dark side. For example, the importance of light is due to existence of darkness; the importance of health is due to existence of illness; winning can be enjoyed only when we have experience the pain of defeating etc. Likewise, we cannot realize joy without experiencing the misery.

Thus, the ways of realizing the bliss also pass through the tunnel of grief. Mean to say, bliss cannot be realized without enduring the pain of grief. In other words grief provides the seed for germination of bliss. It can also be said that the grief is the means to attain the bliss. Thus the journey of bliss goes through the road of ups and downs of this duality phenomenon such as happiness-sorrow; joy-misery; frustration-enthusiastic; gloomy-cheerfulness etc.

However, no one can jump in the center of bliss from sky with the help of any parachute rather everyone has to cross this roaring river of grief. Therefore, it can be said that you can only realize bliss by doing your worldly duties instead of renouncing the world. Otherwise in jungle you will experience single face of the life while another face of life will be avoided. Thus you may miss the bliss also. Actually, without experiencing the life as whole, it is almost impossible to attain the bliss. Thus, live integrated life to gain thorough experiences rather than living in fragments.

Actually, the endurance is very important for spiritual growth because endurance is more than any formal spiritual practice. Therefore, instead of avoiding the pain, you have to face it courageously; feel it; live with it and bear it then only you can lead towards bliss. Moreover, first of all, accepting the tragedy is necessary otherwise pain will be too difficult to endure. Anyhow, after understanding how the events recur, acceptance of the consequences of any tragedy may become easy. Therefore, I am going to start the content with 'what is the pattern of event's recurring'.

Events recur in cyclical pattern.

Events recur at regular interval, often referred to as cycles. For example, there are solar and lunar cycles in weather. This phenomenon also seems to be true on observing the recurring cycle pattern off load and draught which disturb the day-to-day activities and destroy the life of common man. Natural disasters such as earthquake and volcano also recurring cyclical pattern. Human aggression too conspicuous in national and international wars occurs in cycles. Even global political system shifts in cycles such as democracy, aristocracy and monarchy and, when monarchy becomes tyranny, this cycle restarts from democracy and thus cycles repeat in the same form.

In addition, epidemic, pandemics, and pestilence which are direct correlated with mood, nervous and mental diseases also recur in cyclical pattern. Even other cycles that coincidences include variation in Gross National Product, wholesale price index, interest rate, period of general instability, economic turning points, climate geomagnetic storms etc. Also recur in cyclical pattern. Moreover, these factors are directly correlated with sorrow and happiness of human being. Likewise, these days stock market has very much influence on human beings or it can also be said that nowadays many people's happiness and sorrow depend on fluctuation in stock market.

Thus, we encounter with happiness and sorrow with the same pattern of ebb and flow. Therefore, accept the situation whatever it may be and have patience, this situation will also change after a stipulated period being a part of the cyclical pattern. Moreover, due to this cyclic pattern, sometimes we become happy and sometimes sad. However, it seems that the feelings of happiness and sadness are felt without any reason but nothing happen without any reason in the Universe. However, the reason of mood's variation remains beyond the comprehension of human being.

Actually, on seeing superficially, it seems that all events happen spontaneously. However, cycle of events would not cluster unless they were related by cause and effect or common cause. The cause may be the human's interference with Nature which in turn weak the field, resulting in terrestrial then solar and finally solar induced terrestrial effect.

The phenomenon of cause and effect is termed 'butterfly effect' in chaos theory. The butterfly effect means, flapping of butterfly's wings in Amazon rainforests can become the cause of origination of the tropical cyclone in Indian Ocean. It may take long time but the connection is real. Means, very minor change in one place can be the cause of major changes somewhere else irrespective to distance.

However, looking deeply into the cause and effect theory, it becomes even more evident that whatever we do here on Earth creates effects that go beyond the Earth. Actually, each and every single atom is connected with other atoms in the Universe. Therefore, Cosmic Forces affect both organic and inorganic in an invisible way which is beyond our understanding due to complexity of the phenomenon. Even our thoughts may affect the cosmic system due to their potentiality of vibration similar to light and sound.

However, this hypothesis has been proved by dozens of quantum physicists in 1980s. The researchers found in their experiment that an individual electron influences another electron exists somewhere else in the Universe irrespective to distance. Thus this phenomenon is termed 'nonlocality' by them. Thus the theory of nonlocality confirmed that no matter how far apart electrons are separated, a connection is always retained between them. Therefore, nothing is existed in isolation in the Universe and everything can affect each and every other thing.

Thus sadness, depression, sorrow, happiness, joy, etc. are also linked to other things of the Universe. Actually, no one can change the universal laws and everyone has to face whatever happens in one's life. Did we ever pray to God for sorrow? No, no anyone in this world wants grief but it comes completely uninvited. Though no one thinks for accidents, still they happen because they are part of cosmic plan. Thus, grief comes to us unsought. Therefore, instead of splitting the hair of any tragedy, accept its consequences however grim they may be. Actually, what is resist is persist so resistance only increases the suffering.

Actually, neither we can sustain happiness forever nor we can bear it for long period. George Bernard Shaw also said that human beings can bear happiness for a very short period. Therefore, after that stipulated duration of happiness naturally the turn of its opposite will come and the Cosmos completes this cycle like other cycles. Therefore, we should always keep the view in our mind that everything in this world is temporary and nothing is permanent including planets. Even Universe itself will demise one day. Thus neither the happiness nor the sorrow remains permanently. Therefore, we have to tune ourselves according to this cosmic law of impermanent.

Actually, the world is so organized divinely that every one of us always remains present at our correct place at correct time which is in fact in balance with everything else. The literal meaning of the cosmos is 'in order'. Each and every electron of the Universe functions in synchronized way. Thus whatever 'is' could not be otherwise. Therefore, we should accept the present moment 'as it is'. If we will accept each and every event as part of Divine's plan, we may reduce our grief to some extant otherwise we will increase our suffering.

Actually, Journey of life does not travel in a straight line. Rather it moves in zigzag way such as- we go down the wrong path; we turn back; we get lost in the way etc. In short, it can be said that life is full of obstacles. However, the life which does not experience problems and difficulties is not life at all but stagnant and stagnant is always stale and disgusting. There are misery, sorrow, and grief which we have to face in our lives. Simultaneously, we enjoy— happiness, joy and bliss in our life. Thus both are parts of this journey of life.

Swami Vivekananda also said that the goal of man should be not to seek bliss or avoid grief but to go to the root of it all and master the situation which is responsible of their creation. Thus, situations are created only for our change so that we may be accustomed according to their cyclical pattern. Ups and downs are also part of the cycle thus each and every situation will change sooner or later. Therefore, instead of annoyed, accept the each situation whichever comes to you and adjust yourself accordingly.

Happiness and sorrow are two sides of the same coin

Happiness and sorrow are relative terms instead of absolute thus both cannot be considered in isolation. Two people in similar circumstance are not found equally happy or unhappy due to differences in their ways of living. In a similar situation, some people are enough capable to face the tragedy while some others breakdown even finish their precious life on happening the similar tragedy.

For some people, happiness is only absence of sorrow while some others desire something special in order to achieve happiness. However, what is that special thing which they require for their contentment; even they themselves do not know. Thus positive traits such as happiness, joy, and rapture as well as negative traits such as sorrow, sadness, depression, misery etc. are only state of mind. Thus, state of mind entirely depends on individual's culture, attitude, thoughts and lifestyle.

Therefore, it is almost impossible to make any common scale that can measure the level of happiness and sorrow of all people as we measure the temperature of our body. It is another matter that each individual measures one's level of happiness and sorrow according to one's own scale. Thus we set our own index for sorrow as well as for happiness according to our own attitude. Therefore, every one of us has different scale of measuring our state of mind. Mean to say, everyone has its own measurement to measure one's sorrow and happiness.

However, this scale of measuring our state of mind is remains changing, as we move ahead in our life according to our life style. Mean to say, if we keep our attitude positive and adapt a healthy life style, our happiness level increases. On the contrary, this level of happiness may be decreased in the case of reversing the life style. Thus this scale which differ in each of us becomes happiness- level of the individual known as "happiness-set-point"

Just as there is a certain weight that feels natural to your body and which your body strive to maintain.

Likewise, your basic level of happiness is also set at a predetermined point. If something bad happens to you during the day, your happiness can drop momentarily but then it returns to its natural set-point of happiness level. On the same principle, if something good happens to you during the day, your level of happiness rises momentarily but, then it returns once again to your Happiness set-point. Thus, shifting the happiness-set –point either towards upwards or downwards is completely in your hands.

However, without facing of sorrow, we cannot recognize the happiness. Mean to say, if we have never experienced the sorrow, we remain unaware about the state of happiness when it comes. Even happiness comes and passes through us frequently but we could not recognize it due to our ignorance about happiness. However, after encountered with sorrow, we recognize happiness by remembering our past time when there was no sorrow in our life and, in fact, that state was itself a state of happiness.

Therefore, grief is also part of life, go through it and endure its pain because the pain endured by you can only lead you to the bliss. Gold cannot be purified until it is heated in furnace. Therefore, regard the pain as a means for polishing your soul and heightening your spirit. Thus grief is the main source from where the bliss emerges. Therefore, not only happiness but sorrow is also essential ingredient for spiritual growth. Actually, the period of suffering is not the time you have wasted rather it is good investment for your spiritual progress. This is the reason that sages and philosophers advise to endure the pain instead of avoiding it. Even sages themselves endure the pain deliberately throughout their lives.

However, happiness and sorrow of the life are like peak of the mountain and valley where mountaineers make their base camp. Therefore, instead of regretting in the period of grief, consider it as base camp where mountaineers take rest and make plan for further climbing so that they may climb on the peak successfully. However, you cannot climb straightway to the peak without taking rest in the base camp. Therefore, the importance of base camp in the lives of mountaineers is not less than their destination. Thus grief in the journey of life has equally importance as happiness.

Anyhow, instead of breaking down in the grief, embrace it as a means of motivation which encourages you to move on in your life. Thus the existences of happiness and sorrow are interdepend ent. Therefore, both are complementary to each other and cannot be seen in isolation. Actually, both are mingled in such a complicated way that both seem interwoven. Thus due to their interwoven nature, both are described in single chapter in this book rather than separate two chapters.

Buddha also explained this fact and said that the desire of happiness pushes you toward anguish. He further said, "As and when you become free from the desire for achieving the happiness, you also become free from the fear of misery". Mean to say, desire of happiness creates the sorrow but when you leave your desire and become content, fear of sorrow also comes to end. Thus happiness and sorrow are interrelated and both should be considered obverse sides of each other.

What are grief, pain, suffering, and grieving?

Actually, the origination of these hurting feelings such as grief, pain, misery, etc. is found in the scriptures of Buddhism. In Buddhism, '*dukha*' is the word which was used in ancient *Paali* language. Although the term *dukha* is still used in Hindi language, it is translated as 'anguish' in English language. According to Buddha, *dukha* arises from ignorance, from not understanding that everything in the Universe is unreliable, ungrasping and impermanent. Thus instead of accepting present moment 'as it is', wanting to be 'otherwise' is the root of *dukha*. Mean to say, *dukha* is the emotional disturbance of not seeing and accepting the condition of life as it exists. Therefore, nothing is granted and permanent in the world.

However, many terms are used in English language for the term *dukha* to denote it in various percepts. For example—response of emotional hurting or physical wound is natural and the emotional suffering of that hurting is termed 'grief'. Whilst, a sharp dull feeling or unpleasant sensation, resulting from a derangement of functions, disease, injury or hurt is termed 'pain 'and the term 'anguish' is used to denote severe pain. Therefore, there is no escaping from the pain rather you have to realize it throughout your life for one reason or another.

However, when you resist the pain instead of accepting it, suffering arises. As much as you resist the pain, you intensify it. In other words, when you resist the pain, it hit you with more intensity and the realization of that intensified pain is termed 'suffering'. Thus suffering is the mental response of any stimulus. However, we have no control on stimuli but we can regulate our mental response.

Therefore, suffering is nothing but simply a process of thought. Mean to say, suffering is the emotional relationship with interpretation and perception. However, we cannot change the events which hurt us mentally and wound physically but we can interpret them in another way and can shift our perception. Therefore suffering is optional.

In this context some other terms such as—sorrow, woe, misery, sadness etc. are also in use. However, all these terms are used as synonyms of grief so generally they are used interchangeably. Although, all these terms are used interchangeably, they denote different level of intensity of the pain. Mean to say, the level of feeling the pain is differed in each term. And the term grief is used to denote the highest level of pain. Or it can be said that in grief one feels very intense mental pain. Thus, grief is the emotional suffering one feels when something or someone the individual loves taken away. Actually, grief is natural response of the loss. In other words, grief is your emotional reaction to a significant loss.

Thus, any loss such as—death of loved one; relationship breakup; emotional hurting; serious illness; loss of financial stability; job's loss etc. can cause grief. In other words, grief is a term that is used to describe the indescribable, visceral heart break which is felt in the face of loss, the pain of that loss is so powerful that it requires much efforts and patience to return back to previous mental state. Thus, the more significant the loss, the more intense the grief will be.

Generally, the most significant loss is associated with the death of the loved one—which is often the cause of the most intense type of the grief. An article published in The American Journal of Psychiatry states, "Death is the most obviously permanent and extreme form of loss. "However, bereaved may not know what to expect following the death of a loved one. Anyhow, certain emotions and challenges are common for all the bereaved which have to be anticipated.

Therefore, anticipation of such emotions and challenges is necessary for coping with grief so that grievers may return to normal life. Thus 'grieving' is the process of emotional stability and life adjustment you go through a loss. Actually, grieving is not simply a feeling but a natural process you must go through in the face of loss. Loss comes in many sizes such as scratching your car in minor accident or death of spouse or kid. The grieving of some losses can be completed only within few hours while some others take many years.

Therefore, grieving is a personal and highly individual's experience .Actually, grieving depends on many factors such as— griever's experiences, culture, personality, life style, faith and nature of the loss. Although some experts talk about grief occurring in set stages, each individual grieves in his or her own unique way. Or you can say that grief has unique rhythm and texture for every individual. Therefore, bereaved require full spectrum of expression of grief. Thus grieving is a long and pathless process which goes its own way. This is the reason that grieving should not be rushed rather let it be completed in its natural way.

Actually, loss requires grieving to incorporate the loss into reality to your life so grieving is a slow and deep process of unconscious. However, grief and grieving involves many feelings such as—shock, disbelief, numbness, crying spell yearning for the deceased, emotionally overwhelming, bouts of anxiety, guilt, anger, illogical thinking pattern, desire for withdrawing, irritation, sadness, depression, shame, unusual dreams, trouble in sleeping and some other problems related to health. However, these feelings of grieving are explained in details in chapter three.

Anyway, grieving leads to healthy personal development and wisdom. Grieving stages are normal and healthy parts of grieving process. So, instead of taking few steps of grieving, it is better to go through all its stages one by one patiently. If you go through all the stages of grieving, its process will complete timely. Thus let the grief flower, bloom naturally so that it may wither completely according to natural grieving process.

When grief wipes itself away through natural grieving process, it takes all unwanted filth of harmful emotions with it. Thus the psychological vessel becomes clean and clear. Then quality of psychological nothingness is emerged. Then love and compassion gushes in this vacuum. This is the actual peace of state of your mind which leads you towards transformation. Thus, in order to obtain glorious personality and for attaining bliss, this transformation is necessary.

On the contrary, some people become impatient in coping with grief. However, their impatience pushes them towards more problems. To cope with the grief, they either try to ignore the grief by pretending bold or suppress the pain of grief by one means or another. However, trying to ignore the grief keep it from surfacing which becomes worse in the long term. Thus, instead of ignoring, face your grief courageously and cope with it actively so that you may return to your normal activities timely.

However, the persons who try to suppress the pain of grief by consuming antidepressant pills or drugs, it springs back as and when they stop the antidepressant. Thus deliberate efforts of eliminating the psychological pain intensify the pain; in fact, this pain takes the form of anguish in long term. Additionally, instead of coping with the pain through usual way, when grievers remain continue on antidepressant or drugs, they become habitual of them.

Then, grievers entangle in web of anguish and feel helplessness in breaking it. Thus they become chronically angry, depressed or frustrated. Even they may become suicidal, chronically withdrawn, and excessively anxious or resort to substance abuse or other self -destructive behavior. So this complicated type of grief has been termed unresolved or chronic grief. However, who experienced chronic grief usually require help of professional mental-health assistance.

Chain reaction of suffering

Generally, we want to get rid of sorrow and obtain happiness through materialistic things. However, as we proceed in this direction as we move one step towards miseries and one step far away from happiness. According to the Vedanta as we try to obtain happiness from external sources, our miseries begin. For example, we pursue the happiness through fulfillment of our desires and indulge in sex, alcohol and other pleasurable activities but our desires are remained unfulfilled. However, our desires fulfill for a while but they reappear with more intensity.

Therefore, instead of removing sorrow, such unfulfilled desires increase miseries. Thus we entrap in a net of miseries and a series of depression, and then frustration starts. Buddha also said that desire is the main cause of miseries. Anyway, miseries can be reduced some extent by reducing our desires while grief is associated with a loss emerges from the tragedy and a proper process of grieving has to be followed for recovering from grief.

Actually, in order to coping with grief, facing the tragedy with patience and acceptance of the situation is very important. In other words, if you calmly accept the tragedy and adjust yourself according to the painful situation, your painful situation cease to be painful and your tragedy cease to be tragic. Otherwise feeling of loss and helplessness may suppress your body's immune system and leave you more vulnerable to disease. Actually, our body follows our mind. Mean to say, if we are ill mentally, we will also become ill physically in one way or another. And the phenomenon also works vice versa.

Actually, tragedy is associated with various discomforts such as, anguish anxiety, aggression, stress, worries, etc. However, if you remain unable to cope with them, they become chronic grief and it seems that they will never come to end. Thus, due to law of attraction, bad days are followed by more bad days. Terrible things seem to be constantly happening. Most of time mood remains blue. Life becomes bore and often seems cruel. Interest in work is being diminished. Generally, grieved person does not want to talk to anyone, often spends time alone and remains busy in negative thoughts.

Thus, grievers create such a process of negative thinking that instead of coping with grief, grievers engage in the pattern of negative thoughts. Then grieved persons either take drastic step such as commit suicide or turn towards abusive substance and make their life hell. Problems do not come alone instead they bring more problems. Thus, depressed and frustration attract more irritating events because your thoughts determine your frequency. If you are in the condition of blue mood, you will attract more bad things because according to the law of attraction, bad situations which make you feel more depressed is transmitted back to you. Mean to say; whatever you are feeling now is the feedback of whatever you were feeling before few hours. The duration may be somewhat long but the phenomenon of transmitting of your feelings back to you is real.

Why accidents do happen with sad people frequently can be explained by the following law of attraction. Actually, we release our thoughts and feelings at particular frequency. Sad persons release their mental energy on such frequencies which match the frequencies of non-living things such as furniture, knife, debris etc. Means, these objects are also release their energy at the similar frequencies. Each and every matter of the Universe releases the energy irrespective of living and non-living. This phenomenon of releasing the energy can be observed in hot iron. Thus, due to similar frequencies of energy waves of inanimate objects like stone and between sad persons, attract one another and they strike with each other thus accidents happen. However, it would have been noticed by each of us that when we are in the state of anxiety or in blue mood, we hit again and again with inanimate things.

In addition, when we are remained depressed for long period, our painful emotions start accumulating in our unconscious mind. However, the accumulated painful emotions are also released by our unconscious in the Cosmos in the form of vibrations. Then they return to us from Universe with amplification and our suffering intensifies. However, this process of negative feedback may be continued for uncertain period. Thus, due to phenomenon of negative feedback, a chain reaction of suffering starts which push the grieved persons towards the dead end.

Anyhow, the chain reaction of suffering cannot come to end until we accept the loss of tragedy and complete the grieving. Actually, ending of the chain reaction depends on individual's attitude. If we become able to change our thought pattern, our frequency of releasing the mental energy will also change. Then negative feedback will halt and chain reaction of suffering will come to end spontaneously. Therefore, for breaking the chain reaction of suffering, it is necessary to get rid of the trauma. Thus after getting rid of tragedy, thought pattern may be covert from negative to positive thinking.

Anyhow, after emotional stability, the mind becomes somewhat quiet. However, calm mind release the energy on such frequencies which do not match with the frequencies of inanimate things. Therefore, due to mismatching of the frequencies of human beings and inanimate things, they do not attract one another and accidents may be avoided for some extent. Thus, bad happenings may be minimized and life turns towards somewhat bright side.

However, on same phenomenon as negative thoughts attract bad events so as positive thoughts attract good events. Moreover, once good events start happening, they will be followed by more good events each day. Moreover, it is the actual starting of good days. Then good days will be followed by more good days and series of happiness will start. Thus, the phenomenon of negative feedback will be replaced by a phenomenon of positive feedback. Then good days will be followed by good weeks;

good months; good years. Thus you may enter into the state tranquility.

Thus calm and quiet person always remains in such aura which avoid accident-prone situation. Once mind becomes calm and quiet, feedback of peaceful thoughts starts and you may attain bliss. Even you can attain Nirvana like Siddharth Gautam and can become Buddha. Actually, a blessed person is similar to lighthouse which can show the path to all other persons.

What are happiness and pleasure?

The terms delight, pleasure, happiness, joy, gladness, etc. are generally used interchangeably due to minor differences among them but the term happiness is in common use. However, what is the real happiness which generally remains elusive from human beings only few people know. Whether is it mood or attitude? Or is it simply a feeling? However, happiness is considered as emotion. Thus, being emotion, happiness can be only felt but its description is very difficult to describe in words. Anyhow, some psychologists, scholars, philosophers and sages have described happiness according to their own views.

Plato defined happiness in terms of harmony within the soul and equated it with the spiritual well- being of a truly virtuous man. Aristotle has also considered it in similar manner that happiness is not something which could be felt or experienced at a given moment. Rather, in essence, happiness is the quality of a whole life. Mean to say, a virtuous and good life is happy life.

Indian sages and saints also emphasized on ethics in order to obtain happiness. According to sage Patanjli, Man is happier when he is kind than unkind. He further said that he is happier who is content in whatever he has, rather than complaining how life is treating him. Whilst according to Sri Aurobindo, happiness is the natural state of humanity. He referred happiness 'as delight of existence'. Thus he also equated happiness with the virtuousness. Therefore, righteousness is very important factor in obtaining happiness.

Swami Vivekananda had also similar views about happiness and said, "The happiest is the person who is not at all selfish". He also advocated on renunciation of physical pleasure and said that real happiness is not in the senses but above the senses. Whilst according to Indian Philosopher J Krishnamurti, "happiness is a state in which one is unconscious. However, it is only later, when misery strikes, does one realize how happy one was".

Biochemist turned Buddhist monk Matthieu Ricard who has been declared happiest person of the world says, "Happiness is deep sense of flourishing, not mere pleasurable feeling or fleeting emotion but an optimal state of being so happiness is something to be found inside". He further says that happiness is an underlying state, much deeper and richer than any other state in our mind. Therefore, happiness neither can be weekend nor strengthen by external factors.

Sonja Lyubomirsky Professor in the Department of psychology at the University of California has equated happiness with positive well-being. She describes happiness as the experience of joy and contentment combined with a sense that one's life is good, meaningful and worthwhile. Whilst the founding father of positive psychology Martin Seligman has also similar views about happiness. He describes happiness as experiencing frequent positive emotions such as-joy, excitement and contentment combined with deeper feelings of meaning and purpose. Thus it implies a positive mindset in the present and an optimist outlook in the future.

However, Buddha believed that the end of suffering is itself happiness because relief of intense pain is not less than happiness. It can also be said that happiness is nothing but absence of sadness. Means, if you are not sad, you are happy.

However, happiness and pleasure are used interchangeably due to their hidden difference. Mean to say, on seeing superficially, both seem to same thing due to similar joyous feelings. Although in pleasure one experience more enjoyment than happiness, happiness is considered more valuable in human's life. Thus all seer and saints have been emphasizing on the term happiness rather than the term pleasure since ancient times.

Actually, pleasure is the pleasant physical feeling which gives satisfaction and enjoyment by an activity or any event which we enjoy such as- sexual activity, drinking, delicious meal, disco, dance party etc. Mean to say, pleasure involves in such enjoyable things which excite our senses to feel a pleasant state of mind. Thus pleasure is related to sensual enjoyment which depends on external conditions. However, as and when the external conditions come to end, the pleasure also disappears. Mean to say, pleasure cannot stand for last long rather it is transitory. And this is the reason that happiness is always preferred over pleasure.

Based on statistics, a psychologist at the University of South Carolina concluded that neither dreaming of a good love nor hoping for professional success led to the feeling or a state of happiness. It seems that pursuing such objections arouses a strong expectation that is bound to be disappointed by reality or can even lead us to set goals that are higher than the previous. While achieving goals brings an intense feeling of well-being that can be compared to pleasure, this quickly fades until it returns to the level of well-being that we felt previously.

What are spiritual ecstasy, bliss and Spiritual Bliss?

Actually, the term ecstasy issued rarely due to its mysteriousness. Mean to say, hardly anyone knows the nature of ecstasy. Actually, the term ecstasy is used to describe overwhelming feeling of happiness or joyful excitement. However, thorough explanation of ecstatic experience is almost impossible.

The reason is that when we experience ecstasy, we realize great exhilaration simultaneously and this state of exhilaration can be equated with the intoxicated state. Thus, in ecstasy state we remain in such intense pleasure, excitement and euphoria that we want to remain immersed in those joyous moments forever. Therefore, at that state ecstatic person remains in half-conscious state. In other words, in ecstatic period, we are so self-hypnotized that we feel only ourselves in the Universe rather than our surrounding world. Thus in such state neither we are in mood of any description nor we are in the position of any explanation.

Actually, spiritual seekers realize this ecstatic state for only few days during the journey of attaining Eternal Bliss. However, some of them realize it again once or twice but the intensity and duration of ecstatic state decreasing every time. Anyway, spiritual seekers are unable to give full description of ecstasy even after ending of their intoxication period. The reason is that they may have not remembered thorough experience of ecstatic state because at that time they were half conscious due to intoxication. Therefore, afterwards description of the ecstatic experience of any spiritual seeker either may be somewhat more or somewhat less than original ecstatic experience.

However, some *sufi-sants* experience ecstasy for long duration but they generally do not describe it to others because they avoid all type of discussions. Additionally, they do not want name, fame, status etc. rather they always live in their own world so that no one can disturb them. Mean to say, they prefer peace and solitude over any other thing of the world. Thus either the spiritual ecstasy itself is destination for sufi-*sants*in spiritual growth or they do not want move deliberately further towards final stage of self-realization. Actually, the spiritual ecstasy is prior stage of Spiritual Bliss.

In fact, this ecstatic state is really so wonderful and pleasurable state that no one will be wanted to leave this state deliberately. Even spiritual seekers return from this state by completion because the extension of its duration is not in their hands rather God decides its duration for each spiritual seeker. However, this concept seems unrealistic but it is true. Actually, spiritual ecstasy is a lower and less central realization. Thus some spiritual seekers are also mistakenly considered it Spiritual Bliss.

Anyhow, bliss is differed from all other delighted emotions including happiness. Actually, other delighted emotions are that we commonly refer to externally world while bliss is an experience pertaining to the soul and it is not related to the external stimuli. In life, we find that whatever makes us happy has the potential to make us unhappy while bliss is lasted indefinitely. Even there is difference between bliss and Spiritual Bliss. Therefore, bliss and Spiritual Bliss both are being differentiated here and are defined simultaneously. Anyway, Spiritual Bliss is next step of spiritual ecstasy and final stage in ultimate experience of consciousness so it is also called Eternal Bliss. Thus in the highest ascents of Spiritual Bliss there is no feeling of exhilaration. Therefore, spiritual seekers realize intense feelings of calmness and great delight because the vehement exaltation and excitement come to end.

Taittiriya Upanishad describes the bliss as an ascending series of levels of bliss depending on the plane of consciousness occupied by the experiencer so it is called 'the calculus of bliss.' Human bliss is starting point then the Upanishad reach final stage of bliss after going through eleven enhanced stages. However, the final stage is—"one's bliss of the Eternal Spirit". The bliss of Eternal Spirit is of course inherent in all creation, and when the seeker becomes unified with the Spirit, he also experiences this universal and all-permeating level of bliss.

Thus in Upanishad it is denoted with the three terms *Sat*, *Chit* and *Ananda*. Actually these are not three separate concepts. They are aspects, broken out into human terms—of Existence, Consciousness and Bliss, all unified in one experience. Thus the entire Universe is permeated with bliss, the inherent delight of existence.

Sri Aurobindo described the Eternal Bliss or Spiritual Bliss on the bases of Upanishad in his book *'The Life Divine'*. He described, "When spiritual ecstasy and peace cease to be separate entity and united as one state, a Supermind comes into existence which reconciles and fuses all differences and contradictions. Then spiritual seeker realizes a wide calm and deep delight of all-existence which is, in fact, first step of self-realization". Thus Sri Aurobindo termed Infinite Bliss to this self-realization because this calmness and this delight rise together, as one entity, into an increasing intensity and culminate in the eternal ecstasy and absolute peace.

According to Sri Sri Ravi Shankar founder of Art of Living, bliss is joy minus feverishness that is not temporal, it is not a few seconds, a few minutes, but something that lasts all the 24 hours—walking, talking, eating, seating, sleeping—that thrills, that joy, that vibration, that ecstasy, that peak experience lasting all the time that is bliss. Whilst Rabindranath Tagore said that bliss is something that can last longer than pleasure that can endure even through suffering.

Meena Om founder of *Pranam*, a Movement to establish Nature's Law of Truth consider the state of Spiritual Bliss beyond all type of emotions irrespective to positive or negative. Thus she describes its spiritual aspect and says, "Spiritual Bliss is not sorrow, it is not joy rather it is a state where you realize the truth of existence whole and complete, when you feel on with the Supreme Intelligence and no question remain".

Pramahansayogananda also equated Spiritual Bliss with a state of higher spirituality. He explained that Spiritual Bliss is a transcendental state of superior calm including within itself the consciousness of great expansion and that of—all in One, and One in all.

In brief, bliss is a tranquil state of mind where we feel extreme joy, elation and euphoria. Thus bliss is natural state of mind consisting total peace and harmony. Whilst, Spiritual Bliss is the state beyond emotions, final stage of spirituality where spiritual seekers get self-realization. It can also be said that in Spiritual Bliss/Eternal Bliss, spiritual seekers merge with God.

Sources of happiness

Actually, we look far away to seek happiness while it is always remain in our surroundings. We try to seek happiness in glamorous world while it can be attained in simplicity. Thus happiness can be achieved in small deeds rather than waiting for any bygone. However, we spent our whole life running from pillar to post for gathering materialistic things in order to obtain happiness but ultimately it comes to us unsought, when we become satisfy in what we have already.

However, we spend our whole earning on our family and relatives in order to obtain single moment of happiness but we ignore needy. This is the reason that we always seem gloomy. Actually, to spend money on the service of deprived is the actual source of obtaining happiness. Mean to say, our true compassion is very big source of happiness.

Anyhow, we try to seek happiness in Post, power, status, appreciation, wealth, fame, etc. but eventually we obtain it when we stop chasing all these things and achieve a state of peace. Thus contentment and peace of mind are the biggest sources of happiness.

Thus ways of happiness are mysterious. Actually, happiness follows its own way and has its own schedule. We cannot chase the happiness rather happiness itself will chase us when we will be comfortable with whatever we are at this moment. Therefore, instead of desiring to become someone else when we accept ourselves as it is, we realize happiness then and there. Additionally, we are always try to avoid the uncomfortable situation but when we embrace the situation whatever it may be, happiness comes to us spontaneously.

Whilst, according to American psychologists, the happiest people are those who manage to become totally absorbed in particular pursuits; whether this involves do-it-yourself projects, gardening, fishing or writing something. Focusing the mind on a thought or action leads people to forget themselves. Mean to say, they no longer think about the future or the past but only here and now.

However, happiness is difficult to grasp but it seems that the important source of happiness is to remain present 'here and now'. Mean to say, when we remain aware and immerse in the present moment, we may realize boundless happiness. This is the reason that much emphases has been given on awareness and mindfulness in Buddhism.

Here, I want to share my own experience which was happened many years ago. Often I go for morning walk early in the morning, those days I used to go for morning walk in an area of countryside. One day, when I was on the way, suddenly a scène on the middle of path attracted my attention. A cow was standing still and chewing the cud while her calf was sucking her milk. Both were seemed very calm and quiet and unaware of surrounding environment. A cool breeze was blowing and weather was very pleasant. There was still some darkness so few stars were still shinning in the sky. The overall environment was very peaceful. However, I realized that the scene should not be missed.

However, there was not something special to see but I felt intense delight on seeing the scene of cow and calf. Even I was so enchanted that I forgot everything, and instead of continuing my walking, I was standing still at that place for long time. However, I realized that I was standing there only for few minutes. Mean to say, at that time, I was so immersed in those joyful moments that even I was not aware about the time. The scene gave me so much delight that it is still fresh in my mind.

Anyhow, happiness can be realized everywhere if you remain in present moment. For example—stars strewn night; a bright full moon night; flowing water in any brook; a dancing peacock and singing cuckoo in spring season may fill you with lot of joy. Additionally, dark clouds of monsoon; cool breeze; rain; rainbow; waterfall; dew drops on grass and leaves; a flying butterfly; chirping of birds; and a process of producing foam by ocean waves striking with cliff may be also a source of happiness if you observe them with awareness.

Thus, every bit of Nature may be source of your happiness. The list of natural things which may provide you joys moment is endless such as—various colors of cloud wandering below the mountain ranges; snowfall; snow covered peaks etc. There are other lots of things such as tilling of fields by farmers by traditional methods; various type of crops growing in fields; drizzling scene; bullock carts; grazing cattle etc. can give us much joy when we watch outside from train's window at the time of travelling.

In addition, when train crosses through dense forests and hilly areas especially rainwater flowing down from the crevices of rocks may also enthrall us. Thus each and every moment of journey overwhelms us in such a way that even we forget the journey time. Though lot of time can be saved in the flight journey, I prefer to travel in the train in order to enjoy the scenery.

Actually, either we are remain in hurry or busy in thinking. Thus, live slowly and mindfully, and observe your surroundings. You will notice happiness everywhere and in everything. Even an innocent face of infant; naughty activities of a child and a smile of stranger may be source of your happiness. Mean to say, each and every activity and each moment can be a happiness moment if you remain fully aware of your surroundings.

The author of the book 'Power of Now' Eckhart Tolle has also similar views. He wrote that happiness is realized in present moment instead of past and future. According to him, joy is the dynamic aspect of 'being', when the creative power of Universe becomes conscious of itself, it manifests joy. Mean to say, you can enjoy any activity in which you are fully present, any activity that is not just a means and end but that comes from deep within you.

Famous Buddhist Thich Nhat Hanh also emphasize on mindfulness in his book 'Peace in Every Step'. He wrote, "The foundation of happiness is mindfulness. The basic condition for being happy is our conscious of being happy and, if we are not aware that we are happy, we are not really happy". Thus, it can be said that one and only one thing is required for realizing the happiness and joy, and that is awareness. Where there is awareness there is joy and happiness.

According to the Dalai Lama, cultivating positive mental states like loving kindness, tolerance, forgiveness, patience and compassion definitely leads to happiness. For living happy and joyful life, he emphasizes on inner discipline rather than external facilities.

Lowri Dowthwaite lecturer in Psychological Intervention at the University of Central Lancashire has also similar view regarding attaining happiness. She says that we should pursue happiness through kindness, justice and honesty.

I have experienced throughout my life that if we perform our duty sincerely and remain honest with ourselves as well as with others, happiness comes to us unsought. Therefore, there is no need to chase happiness rather do your deeds selflessly. Happiness is like a butterfly which when we pursue, it flies far away, and always remains beyond our grasp, but if we sit quietly, may alight upon us. So we should stop struggling to attain the happiness.

Generally, we count our troubles and ignore blessings but if we will start counting our blessings, we will notice that there are more blessings in our life than troubles. In other words, our attitude itself can provide us happiness. Thus seeing towards bright side of life is a big source of happiness.

Sources of Spiritual Bliss/Eternal Bliss

Like happiness, we seek Spiritual Bliss also in such places which seem to be sources of Eternal Bliss but they are, in fact, beyond the real source of Eternal Bliss. Mean to say, we seek Eternal Bliss in the houses of worship; sermons of preachers; holy places; scriptures; dogmas and in other rituals. However, we ignore our own soul which is, in fact, actual source of Spiritual Bliss.

In addition, we seek Spiritual Bliss in intellect. Mean to say, we try to attain it through knowledge, reasoning and thoughts. However, as much as we try to attain it through these medium, as much as far we go from the reach of Spiritual Bliss. On the contrary, Spiritual Bliss can be attained when there is no reasoning and no any other thought process. Mean to say, when our internal dialogues come to end, the Spiritual Bliss is attained spontaneously.

Thus to obtain the Spiritual Bliss, we have to attain the state of thoughtless awareness so that a vacuum can be created within us. Thus, this vacuum within us is real source of Infinite Bliss. Therefore, in order to realize the Eternal Bliss, absence of cognition is necessary. It can also be said that the tranquil state of being where there is no mind is perfect requisite state for realizing the Spiritual Bliss. Therefore, we have to create the vacuum within ourselves so that the Eternal Bliss may be realized.

Actually, we remain wandering throughout life in search of peace and bliss like musk deer that wanders here and there all around in the jungle in the search of the fragrance of musk. In this context, Sri Ramakrishna Pramahansa quoted, "Musk forms in the navel of the musk deer. Being fascinated with its scent, the musk deer run hither and thither. It does not know where the fragrance comes from. The musk deer searches the whole jungle in the source of scent which comes from its own navel".

Likewise Eternal Bliss is resided within our own soul however we try to seek it everywhere due to lack of our ignorance. Anyway, there is only one source of Eternal Bliss and that is within our own soul. Therefore, in order to attain the Spiritual Bliss, we have to look within our own soul and have to be ceased our internal chattering. Then only we will be able to create a state of tranquility where Eternal Bliss may be realized. However, the process of thoughtless awareness and spiritual practice for attaining Eternal Bliss are described in the last three chapters of the book.

Actually, after attaining the Eternal Bliss, we feel a connection with the Supreme Being, and Divine guides us in each and every step. Thus in this state of Infinite Bliss, we connect to such a healthy energy in which we start living effortlessly in the flow. Generally, we feel ourselves very fresh and light and every surrounding person seems very innocent.

However, the rising Sun and Stars in the night seem bigger and brighter than ever before. Thus we feel absolute peace and calmness in star strewn night. It seems that melodious music is coming from the chirping of sparrows and flapping of leaves. Thus Nature seems very fresh and each and every bit of Nature pleases our eyes. In other words, the whole environment becomes very pleasant and time seems to passes in slow motion. Actually, our mindfulness as well as our clarity is increased manifold.

Additionally, miracles and coincidences start happening in our life. Moreover, in this blissful state, it seems that we are living in paradise and our surrounding things have been created only for us. Actually, we are synchronized with the Nature in such a way that we feel ourselves axis of all surrounding things.

Chapter 2
Do not interfere with Divine's plan

"There are no mistakes, no coincidences. All events are blessings given to us to learn from".—Elizabeth Kubler-Ross.

Actually, no any event happens without reason and all happenings happen in the Universe according to certain invisible plan known as Divine's plan or cosmic plan. However, it is true that human beings have done much progress in science and technology. Even Man has reached on moon and is further planning to reach to the planets but human beings are still ignorant comparative to God. In other words, we are not so much intelligent that we can make better plan than God. Anyhow, human beings are in illusion that the world is governed according to their intellectual capabilities.

On the contrary, not only the world but the Universe is also governed by uncontrollable dynamic forces of the Cosmos known as Natural Forces or Cosmic Forces. Actually, we should consider ourselves fortunate being governed by

Cosmic Forces because the cosmic plan has been favoring the human species since origin of the species. Otherwise it would not have evolved in the first place. Thus, whatever happens in our life happens according to Divine's plan which is, in fact, one way or another has been planned for our overall progress.

Therefore, accept each event calmly by considering it part of Divine's plan. Additionally, it is also in favor of us that cosmic plan always remains invisible and beyond our grasp otherwise human beings remain engage in order to avoid the events. Thus every event has been already determined by Cosmic Forces ahead before the time of its manifestation. However, it is another matter that every plan unfolds slowly as its time comes according to the schedule of cosmic plan.

In this context, Albert Einstein also said, "Everything is determined, the beginning as well as the end, by forces over we have no control. It is determined for the insect as well as for the star. Human beings, vegetables, or cosmic dust, we all dance to a mysterious tune, intoned in the distance by an invisible piper."

God always warns us through hints

Cosmic plan, in fact, remains invisible and beyond our comprehension but God always gives warning before happening something big so that we may protect from incoming danger. It is another matter whether we understand the ways of warning given by God or not. Actually, understanding of warnings is entirely depends on our awareness. The ways of giving the warning are numerous such as— intuition, through dreams, hunches, gut feelings etc. and through other hints described in this chapter.

Anyhow, in first place, if we fail to understand the warning, God gives us hints more clearly. For example, some small events start to happen which, in fact, have some kinds of link with the big event that is going to be happened in near future. However, if we again fail to connect the link of small event with future happening, God puts some obstacles in front of us so that we may stop then and there from going towards that direction. Mean to say, God wants to secure us from consequences of happening which is going to happen in the near future.

Anyhow, the persons who stop their wrong proceedings after understanding of Gods hint, they are escaped from the serious consequences of incoming tragedy. Otherwise, no option has to be left for others except bearing the consequences. Means, Events happen according to their correct schedule of Divine's plan even God Himself do not interfere with cosmic plan. That's why, He always warns us from the incoming danger by one means or another.

You have also realized such hints in your life by noticing that whenever you want to go outside for accomplishment of some important work, you get these hints. In case of unfavorable circumstances, negative things start to happen and as and when you move towards your work, you encounter with the obstacles again and again such as—weather conditions may be worse; bus, train or flight may be late or cancel; frequent red signals on the road; traffic jam; road blocks due to agitation or sliding etc. However, you ignore such hints and carry on your proceeding to fulfill your purpose.

Anyway, as and when you reach your destination, you found that your purpose could not be fulfilled. Your time and energy have been wasted unnecessary in this effort. Whatever may be the formal reason but, in fact, your plan was mismatched with the cosmic plan. Actually, you did not know that circumstances are not favorable when you have taken first step but God knew all these things already. Therefore, God wants to stop you from that wrong proceeding and hints were given again and again in the form of obstacles and problems but either you could not understand or you ignored them.

Anyhow, I am not going to convince you that whenever you found any obstacles in your life, you stop then and there instead of overcoming the obstacles. I am very optimist but it is no use to waste your energy and time unnecessarily. Therefore, it is better to pay attention on God's hints and you should recognize whether they are hints of God to stop you or you are facing the difficulties as usual. Though, hints sent by God in the form of obstacles are difficult to recognize, they can be recognized if you remain aware. Generally, hints sent by God are found frequently and in series linked with one another because He wants to resist you. However, the details of the hints have been described in chapter eighteen thoroughly.

Thus before going to start any new project, you should pay attention on such God's signals. Anyhow, after their analyzing, you should execute your plan. Actually, these hints are nothing but silence voice of God so for listening the God's voice, you have to be always mindful. Otherwise these hints may be ignored by you unknowingly. Actually, ignoring of God's hints and continuation the proceeding in the same direction is like swimming against current in river. Therefore, it is necessary to know that whether the circumstances are favorable or unfavorable by recognizing the God's hints timely.

On the other hand, if your circumstances are favorable, all problems, obstacles, difficulties etc. is removed automatically. For example, you would not only get taxi or bus in unexpected way but you also find green signals on most of the crossings of the road. Even your train or flight in which you are going would also be at correct schedule. In other words, it can be said that everything seems to support you. Actually, now you are swimming in the direction of the current of water rather than against it. Thus, you consume less energy for any given project.

Thus the chances of the success of any project are increased, even almost guaranteed because now your plan is fully matched with cosmic plan. However, you do not know cosmic plan but if you get positive signals frequently, you may carry on your proceeding because now your plan is fully matched with cosmic plan. On the contrary, if your plan is mismatched to cosmic plan, you get negative signals so that you may drop the plan.

In addition, God warns us through small incidents which are, in fact, linked with big event. Actually, they happen only for reminding us that either we are on wrong track or at incorrect time so that we may rethink about our plan. If we pay attention on the clues and change our schedule or plan accordingly, we may secure ourselves from big happening. On the contrary, if we ignore the hints given through small happenings or unable to link the small events with unknown big tragedy going to befall on us in near future. Then big event which is going be happened in near future according to cosmic plan certainly hit us.

Even sometimes God resist us forcefully to protect us from the consequences of big tragedy. Thus by putting any unavoidable hurdle, God keep us far away from the place of big accident. Actually such hurdles cannot be ignored either being impossible to remove or due to related with emotional feelings. Actually, God want to save us by all means and there is no doubt that eventually, He successfully saves us because, in fact, we are unable to avoid God's will.

Do not ignore God's hints.

In the support of above hypothesis, information regarding the terrorist attack on Trade Center on Sept 11, 2001 in USA is described below.

After Sept 11, 2001, one company invited the remaining members of other companies who had been decimated by the attack of the twin towers to share their available office space. At the morning meeting, the head of security told stories of why these people were alive. All the stories were just little things. The reasons of their survival are as under:-

The head of the company survived that day because his son started kindergarten so he took leave from the office.

Another fellow was alive because it was his turn to bring donuts.

One of them missed his bus and could not reach office.

One spilled food on her cloths and had to take time to change.

One's car would not start and could not reach office.

One went back to answer the telephone.

One had a child that dawdled and could not get ready as soon as should have.

One could not get a taxi.

The one who struck everyone was the man who put on a new pair of shoes that morning, took the various means to get to work but before he got there, he developed a blister on his foot. He stopped at a medical store to buy a Band-Aid that's why he is alive today.

It means what happens in this world, happens according to Divine's plan which should not be interfered because it is better than ours. As I have written above that before occurring of big tragedy, little things start to happen as hints of God. Now from above information, it is concluded that whenever, we have to face any sudden unavoidable situation, adjust yourself accordingly rather than irritated. For example, if you stuck in traffic jam, miss a lift or an elevator, turn back to answer a ringing phone, spill tea or coffee on the clothes, car puncture etc., all such little things that annoy you, accept them calmly as considering the hints of God in order to escape yourself from unknown danger.

Thus, we should understand these hints timely and accept that everything in this Universe is governs according to the Divine's plan and we also must proceed accordingly. Actually, God wants to shift us at particular place at particular time. So instead of interfering with Divine's plan, involve in it. Involving in the cosmic plan means accepting each and every situation calmly such as—if morning seems to be going wrong; you woke up late in the morning; the children are going slow getting dressed; car keys have been misplaced and you are unable to search them; breakfast could not be prepared in time; bathroom is occupied by someone else or any such other problem which became the reason of missing your bus, metro or train.

Thus in such a critical situation, you should not frustrate or get mad because all such happenings are part of Divine's plan and are being happened by some incomprehensible reason. Therefore, keep in your mind that this is the way of God to warn us from incoming danger. Actually, the conversation's way of God is unique so instead of telling anything loudly He only whispers. Anyhow, it is up to you whether you are capable to hear God's message and act accordingly or ignore His whispering considering as unnecessary things.

You are moving in a particular direction according to your plan but suddenly you have to change your direction due to occurring problems mentioned above. However, initially you change your direction reluctantly but ultimately your turnabout goes in your favor. Thus Invisible Power not only turns the situation in your favor but Cosmic Forces assist you also in adjusting your path for future movement. Therefore, cosmic system tries to convince you that there could be a Bigger Power that can not only make better plan than you but He can compel you to follow that plan.

For example, if have stuck on the road then neither your car can fly which has been already stuck in jam nor can you clear that jam so you have to only wait for its clearing. In the same way, when train stops in the middle of jungle or deserted land due to some reason which is beyond the control of locomotive's driver, you have to wait till the train move. Thus neither you can push the train from behind nor can you compel the driver for moving the train. However, your car will move as and when the jam will clear and train will move as and when the reason of stopping will rectify and the driver gets green signal.

Therefore, do not irritate and frustrate on such happenings which is beyond your   control. However, no one knows what may be going to happen in future except God. Thus it may be possible that God wants to stop you in the middle of path because this delay may be in your favor being the part of Divine's plan. Therefore, it is the way of God to compel you to follow the Divine's pan. Thus be patient and instead of annoying, accept each situation with tranquility.

Nothing is coincidence in the Universe.

According to Albert Einstein, God does not play dice. Means, no any event happens by chance. According to him, there is no any coincidence in the Universe rather coincidence is God's way to Keep Himself anonymous. Actually, each and every event happens in this world happens for reason. It is another matter that we are unable to comprehend the reason. Therefore, we should neither search the reason of any event nor split the hair regarding its consequences such as—why did some persons affect while some others did not affect in the tragedy; why did someone die while another one escaped. There may be so many such questions.

Actually, happenings of the events and their consequences are part of Divine's plan which is beyond human's comprehension. Thus, analyzing of the event will only disturb your peace of mind. Only God knows the reason of all things. For human beings, grief is inevitable, if you will try to search out the cause of any tragedy, you will only increase your suffering. Even you will become mad but reason of any tragedy will remain beyond your grasp.

On the contrary, if we consider each and every happening as part of cosmic plan, we may reduce the pain caused by tragedy for some extent. Thus the events which are considered as catastrophe, disaster, accident, miracle, coincidence, etc. by human beings are only part of the Divine's plan. However, such words do not exist in the dictionary of God. Thus, it can be said that coincidences are nothing but necessary events for forwarding the existence ahead. That's why they have been included in Divine's plan. Mean to say, in the absence of such events, the evolution of existence may be hindered. After all, God is concerned about whole existence of the Universe rather than about only Human Species.

However, many unanswerable questions may arise in your mind such as:--Why do bad events happen to good people? Why do innocent persons suffer more? Why does the natural calamity occur in certain area and why did it affect certain persons? Why did my loved one pass away? Why did such and such incidents happen only to me? Why did the baby born mental retarded? There may be such innumerable unanswerable questions may arise in your mind. However, for peace of mind, let such questions as unanswerable.

In this context Buddha said, "Events are happened, deeds are done, consequences are endured, but no one does any deed, no one is doer". Mean to say, neither should we blame to any person nor to God for any tragedy. Therefore, no one can be blamed for any happening. Thus not only events are happened according to laws of Nature but their consequences are also determined by Cosmic Forces. Mean to say, how each happening affects whom and in what way—for better or worse—is only part of cosmic plan. Thus, instead of searching the reason, it is better to accept all happenings and their effects whatever grim they may be.

However, it is another matter that some persons explain these questions according to their own beliefs which they had developed in this world on the basis of teachings of the parents, teachers, religious gurus and other elders or on the basis of information mentioned in the scriptures. Anyhow, in both cases these beliefs are personal views of individuals. According to them, the tragedy is related with the human being's *karma* done in previous birth. According to this belief whatever is happened in this life should be accepted as written in our destiny. Moreover, according to them, our destiny has been already determined as and when we take birth in this world on the basis of our *karma* of our previous life and they believe that destiny cannot be changed.

However, On the contrary, I believe that it is only a medium of solace to grievers so that they can accept the tragedy happened to them and may endure the pain on the pretext of previous birth's deed. This hypothesis only helps the grievers for some extent in enduring the pain. Otherwise, neither there is any logic in this hypothesis nor any evidence of previous birth.

On the contrary, destiny has not been determined on the basis of *karma* done in previous life which is unchangeable but you are making your own destiny every day. Mean to say, your today's *karma* makes your tomorrow's destiny. In addition, as you go ahead in your life as you change it on the basis of the *karma* of your day-to-day activities. Therefore, what we are facing today is not the result of the *karma* done in previous life rather our today's destiny is determined on the basis of what we have done yesterday. However, how do we make our own destiny is described in details in chapter four.

Even events are not happened by chance. Actually, Natural Forces are working in a complicated way in order to occurrence of events and Man is only a part of the cosmic system. However, the share of Man in this cosmic system is only in fractions. Anyhow, the question arises, how does individual performs ones role on the bases of day-to-day *karma* to become the part of natural forces? Whether any living Entity sitting somewhere high in the sky who is maintaining the records of our *karma* or is there any other system for maintaining the records of our *karma*.

Otherwise in the absence of such system how can we participate in determining our own destiny on the bases of our current karma? Anyhow, the answer of this question is described in details in third part of the book which is associated with spirituality. However, it is true that the record of the *karma* of each and every person is being maintained properly in the cosmic system.

However, Man considers Himself different from other species, He is one of all species and each and every species of the Earth is undistinguished part of the Nature. It is another matter that due to favorable cosmic plan, the brain of modern Man evolved much comparative to cavemen. Moreover, due to this evolution of brain, Man is trying to surpass the Nature and considers Himself boss of every species even Man playing God. However, in fact, Man has no control over Natural Forces rather Natural Forces have control over Man.

Thus I admitted the belief of Einstein that God does not play *satranj* by using dice. Means, nothing is happened in the Universe by chance. Therefore, nothing is coincidence but certain invisible power is behind happening. However, you can say that God plays chess on chessboard by using the pawns and other chess pieces such as rook, knight etc. Moreover, all human beings are the only pieces of the chess in this cosmic play. However, on the chessboard no any chess piece knows where it will be shifted next time but players know well that next time which pawn has to be moved and where it will be put. Even players know about the movements about few more pieces which are going to be shifted in second or third steps.

Mean to say, human beings are only like pieces of chessboard and Cosmic Forces are the Players of this cosmic chess so people do not know about their tomorrow or day after tomorrow due to uncertainty. However Players of cosmic chess (Cosmic Forces) know when and where we are will be shifted further. Thus only God knows full details of all events and about their effects. Thus like pawns of chess, we have been shifting from one situation to another since our birth by the Invisible Players of cosmic chess. Actually, wherever we are required for executing the cosmic plan, we are shifted by Cosmic Forces at that position. However, after completion of certain plan, we are shifted again at another place being part of the next plan and this process is going on throughout our life.

Thus, we are only pieces of the cosmic chess and ultimately we are removed forever when we are no longer required on this planet. Therefore, from birth to death whatever we face is a part of perfect plan of Cosmos rather than any coincidence. Thus, we are only a means to fulfill the certain purpose determined for us in this cosmic plan. Therefore, changes are parts of life so accept all changes calmly considering them as God's will.

Moreover, William Shakespeare also considered Man merely stage actor in his play *Seven Stages of Man* who plays various roles throughout his or her life. Thus we are only stage actors in the cosmic play to perform various roles throughout our life.

Actually, we have taken our birth on this Earth for certain purpose. How may be we are intelligent, expert and experienced, our plan cannot be better in comparison to cosmic plan. So do not consider yourself more than actor. Therefore, instead of analyzing or searching the reason of any event accept the present 'as it is 'by considering yourself as actor of the Divine's play and perform your role with sincerity . The Bhagwad Gita also says that do your *karma* selflessly.

In addition, our future role will be determined in this cosmic play on the bases of the roll which is being performed by us today. The Invisible Director of the cosmic play is planning to write your role in His next play, and your current performance will be definitely considered in all next plays. Mean to say, what *karma* you are doing today will become your destiny which affects you in future. Therefore, ignore the belief that your destiny is determined at the time of your birth and it cannot be changed after its determination. Rather form new belief that your destiny is being constantly determined daily on the bases of your day-to-days deeds/*karma* and you are able to change it throughout your life.

Therefore, do your *karma* without analyzing the causes of events and their effect. Actually, God governs the Universe in mysterious way which is beyond human comprehension so nothing happens here by chance. However, the Universe is always governed on according to systematic cosmic plan and Man is merely a medium to execute this plan.

Actually, existence of Man is well synchronized and balanced with the Nature in the Cosmos. Even your single step out of this synchronization may push you towards chaos. Therefore, in order to seek more comforts, efforts of breaking the synchronized system only create more discomforts in your life.

However, at any certain stage of our life, every one of us realizes oneself helpless for solving life's problem. We confront with such questions which have no answers. We face such complicated situations which are difficult to overcome
.Moreover, in this stage, we are unable to do anything except self-pity. When we found darkness around us and reached at dead-end, we disappointed. Then ultimately we start looking toward Invisible Power named as God.

Then we turn to God and try to find out Him. Moreover, as we reach closer to God, we come to know that all happenings are beyond our control and part of Divine's plan. As and when we understand this fact of occurring of the events, we accept the grief as a part of life. Then not only the pain of grief becomes easy to bear but we feel inner tranquility also.

Therefore, we should keep in mind, if grief is part of cosmic plan, then its remedy will too available somewhere in the cosmic plan. Thus, the solutions which are beyond human's wisdom are always found at Divine's door. Therefore, only God knows the answers of all questions and solutions of all problems. Anyway, if we are unable to find the solution even after trying our best, we should have patience, leave it to God and wait because, in fact, the time of the solution has not yet come. When time will come according to Divine's plan, the solution will also come out from nowhere even without much effort.

It would have been noticed by all of you that a thing such as key, pen, watch etc. which has been misplaced in the house or working place remains lost in spite of searching thoroughly. Then you stop your efforts for searching it and engage in other activities. However, after some hours or some days, the lost thing is found suddenly somewhere in the place where it was misplaced. Thus problems are similar to lost thing so they will not solve before time how much effort you do. Actually, life is like puzzle blocks which do not fit at wrong position how much hard you try to fit them.

However, at their correct position, they insert in one another without much effort.

Thus, regarding solving any problem, if it remains unsolved even after trying your best, leave it as it is. It will solve spontaneously when its time of solving will come. Therefore, stop fighting with adversities and accept each and every situation as considering it as a part of Divine's plan and will of God rather than any coincidence. Anyhow, you cannot control the Natural Forces so surrender yourself to Supreme Power and leave everything upon Him because God never takes rest and always remains on work.

The universe is full of mysteries.

Actually, the Universe is full of mysteries which are still ungraspable to human beings. However, as you go deep for understanding these mysteries, you become more miserable. Even you will become mad but you cannot resolve these mysteries. Neither any saint nor any scientist could resolve these mysteries so far. Moreover, I believe that if Man will resolve these mysteries, He will finish its own existence from the Earth. The history is witness that whenever Man succeeded to understand about any mysteries of Universe, He had gone one step far away from Nature and one step near to His own end. I have explained much about this fact in my book of environment '*Man Towards its Own End*'

However Man has studied about planet, stars and galaxies but Heis still unable to know completely about Himself. Albert Einstein once said, "I suspect that my life has been waste. I enquired into the farthest of stars, and forget completely to enquire into myself—and I was the closest star! "Therefore, it is no use of exploring space and ocean until we explore ourselves. There is, in fact, a mini Universe exists within each of us. Therefore, only after knowing about ourselves, we can be able to know about the Universe.

Einstein further said it seems there are two Gods; one who reveals Himself and another is who hide Himself. Actually, there are no two Gods literally but God is such huge entity that cannot be realized whole at a time but in small parts. It can also be said that if we would have resolved any mystery, we confront with some bigger mystery than previous one and this process is going on forever. In fact, God never gives complete clues thus God always keep something hide from the grasp of human beings.

Actually, these mysteries of Universe are the basis of the existence of human beings. In other words, if these mysteries will resolve, Human species will also demise. Noble prize winner in physics Max Planck said, "Science cannot solve the ultimate mystery of Nature.........every advance in knowledge brings us face to face with the mystery for our own being". Therefore, it is better to remain the mysteries as they are. Thus, instead of entangle in mysteries, we should appreciate them and live each day as it comes.

Anyhow, the enjoyment of life lies in uncertainties. For example, when we watch neck to neck cricket match, we feel much excitement and enjoy each moment due to uncertainty. Actually, each stroke of batsman, stop our breathing for a moment to see whether it will go in favor of the batsman or against him. However, till the end of match result remains beyond our guess and we remain in uncertainty. Therefore, uncertainty is the key factor of our excitement and enjoyment.

Likewise, when we watch any mysterious movie, we remain excite to know what will be the next scene. Thus a turning story on each and every scene and its unexpected end enthrall us throughout movie. Actually, if there will be no mystery, there will nonexperience of awe. Mean to say, if everything is already known to us, we lose curiosity, excitement, amazement and enthralled of life. Then our life will become dull, bore and cheerless.

Additionally, if our future is known to us, the charm of living the life will come to end. Suppose we come to know that everything is well in future and we are secure in all aspects then we will stop our *karma*. On the contrary, if we come to know that our future is not well and we are unsecure then we will disappoint and trap in depression and frustration. In the both cases our life will become mundane and meaningless. Mean to say, we are living cheerfully, peacefully and happily only due to our uncertain future. Thus leave each mystery as it is; live each moment 'as it comes' and leave other matters to God.

Whatever happens in our life happens for our betterment

Actually, whatever happens in our life happens for our betterment. Therefore, ignore immediate effects of the happening, if they are unfavorable to you. However, the effects which seem unfavorable just after happening of the event will prove favorable to you in last-long. Even sometimes the same events which were seemed unfavorable at the time of their happening transform our life later on. However, gap may be somewhat long but this law of Nature is real. It is another matter that we remain unable to understand the reality of any happening at the time of its occurrence.

In this context, I am going to illustrate a small story. Once, a farmer has a mare. Then one day the mare ran away. The farmer searched everywhere but could not find his mare so he disappointed and became very sad. However, after few days the mare returned but not alone. A nice and strong horse was also accompanied the mare. Thus the farmer did not only get his mare back but he found a horse also without paying single penny. On getting the mare and horse, the farmer became very happy.

After all, now he is owner of two instead of one animal. The farmer's son was very fond of horse riding so he put the saddle on the back of horse and started riding. However, one day when he was riding on the horse, unfortunately he fell down from the saddle. On falling down from the horse, he became injured and his one hand got fracture. Thus, when the farmer got the news of injury of his son, he again became very sad. Even, he felt guilty that whatever happens happened due to his own greediness. Means, if he would not accept the horse, his son would not be injured.

Anyhow, after few days, a war has been started in the country. Due to shortage of soldiers in the army, a movement was started by army to search suitable young boys from villages so that they may become soldiers in the army. Thus a team of army officers visited the farmer's village also in search of young and healthy boys for recruitment in the army. However, the farmer's son could not be recruited in the army due to his fractured hand. Then farmer became happy again because he do not want send his son at front.

Eventually, farmer understood the hiding message behind the complete series of happening that his son was rejected from army recruitment due to missing of his mare in first place. Actually the farmer did not know earlier the positive message disguise in the missing of mare. This is the reason when he gets bad news in the context of his mere, he becomes sad but as and when he gets good news related this episode, he again becomes happy. Mean to say, farmer's sadness and happiness were related with the immediate effects of the events. Actually, last-long effect of the first event was beyond farmer's comprehension until revealing of the final effect.

Therefore, the events which we consider as bad in short-terms may prove good at long-terms. So whatever is happened in our life is happened for the good or bad, we cannot know until knowing its final effect. Thus the events which seem bad in first place may be good at last. As only God knows the cosmic plan so only He knows the reason of any happening as well as its ultimate effects on us.

Therefore, we should accept the fact that whatever happens in our life happens for our betterment.

Actually, life always moves in the direction of best. On the way, we may find some rough roads which are generally considered as obstacles. However, obstacles are made only for our safety. So each and every difficulty and adversity has a disguise message which takes us towards our overall improvement.

Thus every pain we go through brings us new vision of life and provides valuable experiences which leads us towards maturity and happiness. Therefore, do not interfere with cosmic plan rather adjust yourself accordingly. Anyhow, if we start believing in Divine's plan, we will achieve inner peace and contentment in our life. Ultimately, we will become able to enter into realm of bliss.

Chapter 3
Accept the grief and endure its pain

"Acceptance of what has happened is the first step to overcoming the consequences of any misfortune"—William James.

Actually, the term 'acceptance' is used very commonly in day-to-day conversation. However, after knowing its real meaning, it seems that acceptance is not as easy as we think. Actually, acceptance means you are willing to let things unfold in a way that differs from what you originally had in mind. Thus acceptance is just opposite from your expectations. On the other hand, it is almost impossible that each and every situation comes according to your expectations.

Thus we cannot halt any event to be happened whether we like it or not because happenings are beyond our control. According to ancient philosopher Epictetus, "When something happens we cannot control it, the only thing in our power is our attitude towards it, we can either accept it or resent it." Thus accepting the tragedy and loss created by it with inner tranquility is to rise above it while resenting on it is to be overpowered by it. Acceptance of the consequences of any event which cannot be changed brings happiness and joy while resentment brings sorrow and misery.

Though acceptance is difficult, the situations which cannot be changed should be accepted calmly. Actually, acceptance is not resignation rather acceptance means accept the life 'as it is'. When we push nothing and welcome everything, we move beyond our performances and we lead towards more possibilities. Thus openness is the fundamental base for a skillful response to life.

On the contrary, if you will struggle with existence in order to decrease the miseries, your miseries will increase rather than decreasing. Therefore, there is no need to struggle with natural conditions; no need to control the consequences which is beyond your control; no need to swim against the current of water and no need to do the efforts towards changing the present situation. Instead accept the happenings and their effects courageously whatever worse they may be.

Actually, adversities and difficulties have been associating with human beings since origination of human species. However, the nature and pattern of problems were differed in each era but problems had been never come to end till this scientific era. Even in this modern world problems have been increased manifold. Therefore, you have to experience them throughout your life. So, there is no other option rather than acceptance.

Everything is impermanent in the Universe

Actually, nothing is permanent in the Universe including Universe itself. The Universe has been expanding since Big bang (13.7 Billion years ago). However, after a certain time, it will start shrinking back up to the point of black hole and ultimately it will meet its demise. Throughout the earth's history—taxonomic groups emerged and extinct. According to scientists there have been at least five mass extinctions of life recorded in the earth's history since 500 million years and in each case, of course, the life recovered. Mean to say, everything emerges, survives for certain period and demises after its certain age. Thus nothing is permanent. Whether galaxy or microbe, everything has to eliminate sooner or later.

Everything is erasing in front of us but we cannot do anything except watching it with our eyes. Actually, neither it is coincidence nor magic rather demise is reality of life. Thus vanishing is essential truth woven in the very fabric of existence. Whatever exists now definitely will extinct when its accurate time of extinction will come. A thought arises and then next moment another one takes its place. Thus thousands of thoughts arise daily in human's mind. A mental image arises in our mind and then suddenly passes away and gives way to another one thus it seems that we are traveling in a train, and trees are going backwards.

Mean to say, as we are going ahead in the journey of life, many things, persons and places are left behind. So this moment gives the way to the next and so on… About this fleeting moment George Harrison English songwriter told the truth when he said, "All things must pass." Thus everything passes, no matter whether it passes fast or slow.

Actually, demise of a thing confirms on the day of its origination. For example, one's death is confirmed on the same day when one's takes birth. Likewise, our separation from anyone is also confirmed on the same day when we meet first time to the individual. Thus accept the separation of a person or thing with tranquil mind, whatever may be the reason of separation. Moreover, all of us are aware of this law of demise when we become witness of the death of our near and dear. It is another matter that we forget this reality afterwards.

Thus nothing is eternal in this Universe and everything is constantly changing.

Even when I examine myself and think about whether I am the exact same person as I was some years back. I notice that my muscles are going weaker; hearing power of my ears is declining; flexibility of my body is being reduced and my stamina is being decreased. On the other hand, due to my constantly learning process, my knowledge and experiences are being increased day-by-day. Thus not only my body but my mental faculty is also being changed constantly. Anyhow, it is not a mistake rather it is part of natural process of aging.

On the same law, our friends, colleagues, relatives and other family members are not same as they were few years ago. Their knowledge, moral values, attitudes, health etc. has been changed. The water in the river is not the same that was few moments ago. Thus everything is changing moment by moment so we are not stagnant. Rather we are changing constantly like flowing water. Thus everything in the Universe is either going up or going down but nothing is stable. Therefore we should not consider anything granted and permanent. Rather consider each and everything impermanent and accept each moment 'as it is'. Thus changing is the natural phenomenon. Then, why are we so reluctant to accept the situation as it comes? Actually, being a part of cosmic plan, this present moment could not be otherwise.

However, Buddha also linked impermanence with sorrow and perched this universal truth in his sermons that till human being will exist in the Universe, sorrow also will remain along with human being like a shadow. He also explained the reason of the sorrow and said that everything is impermanent and is constantly changing but human beings are clung with everything and the clinging with the impermanent is main cause of suffering. Therefore, when we cling with something hoping that things will never change, we generally get disappointment which push us towards frustration and depression.

Daniel J Siegel Author of the book *'Mindsight'* wrote, "Due to our mind clinging to the familiar to our established expectations, the feelings of disappointment, confusion and anger arise that create our own internal world of suffering. However, when we accept what we now have in place of the lost thing, we become able to cope with the grief". Mean to say, the grief of the thing which we have lost can be cope with only when we accept the things which we have now.

Thus desire of clinging with something forever is unreasonable expectation of life and this desire of clinginess is the main reason of our suffering. Thus, instead of clinging to the familiar, broad your perspective so that you can accept the change. However, our past is now only a memory so we should not think about our past. Whatever has been gone, gone forever and whatever has been changed, changed forever.

Therefore, accept the loss of tragedy which has been already happened and adjust yourself in ever-changing situation. This current situation will also change after stipulated time. Therefore, embrace the impermanence and accept each moment 'as it is' irrespective to good or bad. Anyhow, neither events will happen according to your expectation nor their effects will change because everything is being governed according to the cosmic law.

Although grieving is a hard and long process, acceptance of loss makes it easy.

Actually, grieving is a very hard and long process which requires courage, patience and time for its completion. However, grieving proceeds through stages and acceptance of loss comes generally at the end of its early stages. Initial stages of grieving, in fact, are natural and have to face by each and every bereaved one. The early stages of grieving generally consist of severe mental state such as—shock, numbness, disbelief, emotional overwhelming, spell of crying or wailing, anger, guilt, anxious, etc.

A study conducted at Yale University involving 233 people who had experienced the loss of loved one identified five key stages in their response, incomprehension, then grief and nostalgia, followed by anger and revolt, apathy and finally acceptance. This last stage generally starts six to eight months after the loss, but it is progressive and is not completed two years on average, have elapsed.

Actually, when bereaved are overwhelmed by grief, they think that they will never return to normal life in future that's why some of them try to commit suicide. However, the truth is just opposite because every grief has beginning and end however intense it may be. Grieving of spouse or kid is very hardest challenge to cope with especially when death occurs unexpectedly. Anyway, after a certain period of time, a situation appears where grief which seems intolerable comes to end.

Often bereaved either shock or become numb on unexpected death of loved one. Although crying spell of bereaved for deceased is very necessary so that painful feelings may be released. However, bereaved cannot even cry in this state of shock and numbness while some male bereaved avoid the crying deliberately. Actually, crying does not denote the weakness rather it is a natural part of grieving.

However, if bereaved think that they can protect their family by putting themselves on a brave front and they continuously act to be bold, then they are wrong. Whilst, some bereaved become emotionally overwhelmed and even feel much difficulty in breathing.

On the other side, denial occurs when death of loved one happens at front or somewhere else. This is the reason that dead body of deceased brings at his residence so that deceased's spouse, parents and kids believe on the death of deceased. Otherwise without seeing the dead body, the confirmation is almost impossible for them. So bereaved remain denying continuously the death of the deceased until they see the deceased's dead body. Even denial remains continue for some bereaved on unexpected death. In such cases, bereaved can't believe what has happened because actually they do not want to believe on such unexpected happing.

In this context, Swiss-American Psychiatrist an Author Elisabeth Kubler-Ross and co-author of book 'On Grief and Grieving' David Kessler describe in the book, "Denial and shock are natural in the first stage of grieving and for some extent denial helps to pace our feelings of grief. Otherwise to fully believe at this stage would be too much otherwise letting in all feelings associated with loss at once would be overwhelming emotionally".

Therefore, it can be said that there is grace in denial. The first stage of grieving, in fact, helps the bereaved to survive but it should also be remembered that sustainment of disbelief should not be stretch for long period otherwise it may push the bereaved towards mental health problem. Therefore, acceptance of death of the deceased is essential for bereaved.

In addition, pattern of sleep is also disturbed and bereaved generally experience sleeplessness during night. However, sometimes they suddenly wake up in nights due to occurrence of unusual or horrible dreams in their sleep. Thena period of erratic and illogical thoughts start occurring such as bereaved may imagine that the deceased can be heard or felt. This imbalance mental state may remain almost few days while sleeplessness may last for some more days. In this stage of grieving, bereaved do not want to live more because for them the world becomes hopeless and meaningless.

Anyhow, as the bereaved slowly lead towards acknowledging the impact of loss, bereaved experience anger that may directed at God, family members, relatives, friends or themselves even sometimes at deceased person. Moreover, bereaved may also feel irritation on those who give advice to them so they avoid everyone and want to live alone. Even bereaved feel regret thus they blame themselves, and find themselves bargaining with thoughts about what could have been done to save the lives of deceased. Bereaved can become preoccupied about ways that things could have been better and perhaps tragedy might be avoided. Actually these feelings are important because they are psyche's protective mechanisms.

Anyhow, the thought pattern of bereaved may remain changing constantly in the initial stage of grieving. Even at the time of conversation, generally they lost somewhere else. Mean to say, they are unable to focus their mind on certain point and their thoughts are racing generally going over the events surrounding of deceased's death. Moreover, bereaved may find difficulty to concentrate thus they forget the things. In addition, bereaved feel difficulty to fill up the legal documents regarding deceased death even sometimes their signatures do not tally with their own signatures in banks. However, it seems that they are performing their activities in hypnotism.

As the grieving move forward, bouts of anxiety start occurring. Sometimes bereaved seem relaxed while in the next moment they seem anxious. However, such bouts of anxiety and depression may last for long time. Finally grievers arrive at acceptance, having incorporated the loss in to their lives enabling them to return to the present an eye toward the future. However, grieving is not yet completed on acceptance of the loss but later stages of grieving certainly become easy for bereaved.

Actually, accepting depends entirely on individual's will power. Anyhow, it takes time to believe in reality that the happening which has been already happened, happened forever. However, timely acceptance is very necessary for living the remaining life which is not possible without will power. Actually, Acceptance is not a passively submission to the fate. Instead your today's acceptance may be proved so potential which may change your tomorrow's fate. On the contrary, lack of will power prolonged the acceptance for uncertain period which further affect the process of grieving.

Therefore, accept the situation that cannot be changed. However, first of all, we should understand the difference between what can be changed and what cannot be changed. An organization which deals with alcohol addicts have the following prayer for serenity: "God grant me the serenity to accept the things I cannot change, courage to change the things I can and wisdom to know the difference."

Regarding acceptance Peter Alexander MC Williams wrote in his book *Life 101*, "Acceptance is not a state of passivity or inaction. I am not saying you can't change the world right from wrongs or replace evil with good. If you don't fully accept a situation precisely the way it is, you will have difficulty changing it." Meant to say, it is necessary to accept the situation completely 'as it is' in order to know whether the situation can be changed or not. Thus, he prefer acceptance over the other things.

Actually, acceptance is such an important commodity which is very helpful in the improvement of the state of mind of bereaved. Therefore, some called it 'the first law of personal growth'. Thus, you should understand the realty that events do not necessarily turn out the way you want them. However, understanding of this fact leads you towards acceptance of tragedy and the loss created by it.

Acceptance, in fact, helps you remain calm and serene in the times of crises instead of becoming angry and upset. Thus, acceptance provides you peace of mind which is necessary for further stages of grieving. Therefore, every bereaved has to accept the realty sooner or later otherwise the grieving will never come to end.

Suggestions for grieving

Actually, grief is like a roaring river which is constantly flowing in griever's life until it resolves completely. Moreover, there is no particular path for following the process of grieving rather it makes its own way. Mean to say, there is no any particular pattern for grieving which may suit to all grievers thus everyone grieves differently. This is the reason if you seek advice on dealing with grief, you will likely find a myriad of ideas. Anyway, all further chapters of first part of the book are related to grieving, some practical suggestions for grieving are as under:-

Researches show that most people can recover from loss on their own through the passage of time if they have social support and healthy habits. No doubt that you want to be live alone but acceptance of the social support is also necessary. Even sometimes you may feel irritation at those who are trying to help you. Anyway, this is normal in the life of griever so without much regretting on your behavior, kindly let others know what you need at the moment and what you do not. Thus find a balance time with other people and time you spend alone.

Second most important ingredient of grieving is health. Actually, **you and only you** can take care of yourself and no one else. Thus watch your diet even you may consult your doctor about nutrition supplements. Author Bethany Frankel who has written many books on health commented about diet, "Your diet is a bank account so good food choices are a good investment".

In addition, for improving your overall well-being, workout is strongly recommended. Exercise can lessen negative emotions as well as you will get a break from incessantly thinking about your loss. Thus make a schedule for walking, jogging, yoga and meditation. Always remember, "Your health is in good hands—your own."

As healing occurs gradually so grieving takes time. There is no certain time frame for grieving. Some people start feeling well within months while some others take years in this process. Thus, length of grieving process is different for everyone. Actually, the grieving process is not a liner, but more often experienced in cycles. Grief is someone compared to climbing a spiral staircase where things can look and feel like you are just going in circles. Yet you are actually making progress. So have patience! You are not standing still rather you are moving in right direction. Thus speed is not matter but only right way is matter.

Although grieving is very painful at times, it should not be rushed. However, in fact, neither grieving can be forced nor hurried. Anyhow, those who make hurry and take shortcut; they subconsciously create defenses against the pain of loss by walling off parts of them. Escaping from grief, in fact, hamper natural process of grieving.   Thus they invite more anguish for themselves. Therefore, never misuse self- destructive escape such as alcohol or drugs. Instead whatever your grief experiencing, it is important to be pertinent with yourself and allow the process to natural unfold.

Additionally, reevaluate your priorities but if possible, avoid taking the big decisions too soon. Instead have patience and wait till you resume a normal routine. Taking a vacation and visiting some peaceful place may also prove helpful. Last but not least which is proved therapeutic for bereaved, "Keep alive the memory of loved one in the form of deceased's mementos, pictures and other belongings." Even telling the stories and events regarding feats of deceased may also console you.

Anyway, the intensity of grief starts diminishing and little by little sharp pangs of grief soften. So have patient! Take one day at a time, move at your own pace and know that the pangs of grief do not last forever. However, even years after the loss, they may resurface when certain memories arise unexpectedly. Mean to say, at special occasions such as-anniversaries, wedding functions, festivals etc., you may still experience a strong sense of grief. Actually, human beings are naturally resilient, considering most of bereaved can endure loss and come to the point of emotional balance and can focus once again on day-to-day activities.

Acceptance of true feelings improves our overall well-being.

Actually, our half energy remains consuming in fighting with grief and only remaining half is utilized for healing and preserving of our well-being till we accept grief. Thus the divided energy not only resists the grieving but it also impairs our well-being. On the other hand, after accepting the grief, not only grieving complete soon but our overall well-being is also improved due to ceasing the wastage of energy. Thus, when we accept grief; befriend with it; know its nature deeply and start to live with it face to face, suddenly we surprise to see that there is no pain anymore and we are feeling better. Thus we become able to remove the root of pain and open the door of our mental as well as physical health.

Actually, acceptance of loss is not only helpful in grieving but it is also helpful in the improvement of overall well-being. Even acceptance of your true feelings can be benefited related to your well-being. Therefore, accept your reality what you are feeling at this moment. Mean to say, if you are angry, accept your anger; if you are feeling sad, accept your sadness; if you are regretting about something, accept that regret frankly; if you are insecure, accept your insecurity etc. Thus acknowledge your true feelings and this acknowledgement of your true feelings may lead you towards your overall well-being.

Therefore, instead of pretending to be bold, accept the reality bluntly what you are feeling exact at this moment. However, if you have not such courage to acknowledge your reality, accept only one fact straightforwardly, "I cannot accept". Even acceptance of this fact may also soothe you. Thus it is not the matter that what you are accepting, only accepting the reality is the matter. Actually talking wholeheartedly can release your suffocated feelings and provides you relaxation. About acknowledgement of feelings a survey had been conducted which proved this hypotheses true.

The study, led by researchers at the University of Toronto, used a series of three experiments to look at the link between overall well-being and whether or not people accept negative emotions.

For first experiment thousand participants were instructed to fill out surveys rating their life satisfaction, depression symptoms, anxiety symptoms, mindfulness, number of stressful events, and more. They found that when people accepted negative feelings, they were healthier psychologically.

To further prove this point, researchers had one hundred and sixty life stressors within the past six months—either completes a neutral task or stressful task. The outcome was similar to the large experiment. The women who accepted feeling bad were healthier mentally.

Finally two hundred and twenty two participants were asked to keep diary entries every night for two weeks, and they were asked to make notes about stressful events they have experienced. They also rated the extent to which they felt twelve negative emotions like sadness, loneliness, helplessness, shame, guilt and more. Once again, the participants who willingly accepted their negative thoughts and feelings were happier overall.

Therefore, accept your true feelings whatever you feel at current moment irrespective to positive or negative. Thus acknowledging and expressing of your true feelings has a healing effect that can provide you mental health and happiness. In fact, our physical health and mental health both are interrelated. Thus to improve your overall well-being, accept your true feelings

Acceptance is the first step towards endurance.

Although endurance of the pain is related with acceptance, it is not necessary that every griever who has accepted the grief endure the pain also. Mean to say, the reality of any happening has to be accepted sooner or later because there is no other option while enduring the pain requires inner strength. Therefore, endurance is entirely depends on the tolerance power of the griever. So all grievers accept the pain how much the gap of time may be but many grievers escape from enduring the pain by one means or another. However, it is true that acceptance is very necessary in order to endure the pain.

Actually, acceptance occurs when you stop resisting with the circumstances. For example, now you feel no more irritation or anger on little things; you stop blaming or complaining; no more remorse or helplessness etc. Mean to say, you have compromised with the current situation. However, pain is still dwelt in your sub-conscious that may recur throughout your life. Actually, after completion of grieving, pain usually subsides. However, it cannot be eradicated without endurance.

Anyway, enduring the pain is a long and tough process that cannot be completed until you release your all painful emotions which have been suppressed knowingly or unknowingly during your initial stage of grieving. However, it seems that you have eradicated whole pain caused by the tragedy but bouts of intense pain are being recurred frequently. It means some painful emotions are still buried deep inside you. Thus enduring the pain is very necessary in order to resume the normal life otherwise pain will be punching from inside occasionally.

Endurance, in fact, cannot be started without acceptance. Therefore, first of all, we must accept the tragedy and its effects as well as those situations which cannot be changed. Thus, how much hardness we may face in acceptance, we should accept such things timely. Actually, acceptance of grief helps us to surrender our ego to the Divine's will and provides us peace of mind. In full tranquility, our understanding may reach to the point where we consider our each experience as part of cosmic plan. Then only we become ready for enduring the pain by synchronizing ourselves with the Nature.

The endurance should be welcomed just as we welcome the pain of injection in our body for the sake of our health. However, only after embracing the grief, we may complete this tough process of endurance. Mean to say, in order to endure the pain, only acceptance is not enough rather we have to feel the pain mindfully how much painful it may be. On the contrary, if we ignore the pain by pretending bold, it buries in our sub-conscious mind. Then it reoccurs again and again frequently till we endure it. Thus, those who do not endure the pain of grief, they have to face it in future. However, those who endure it, their whole anguish related to particular tragedy come to end.

Additionally, trying to reduce the grief by external sources such as consuming drugs, alcohol etc. only increase the suffering rather than decreasing it. Try as hard as you can, but it will not reduce. However, you feel relaxation for a while after their consumption but, in fact, later on you feel more pain. Thus intensity of pain increases along with the increasing of the consumption of intoxicated substances. Then the mind and body start demanding such substances again and again. Ultimately, individual becomes addicted for them and life becomes more complicated and burdensome.

Actually, the pain of any grief can be compared with a bank loan which has to be returned. Otherwise defaulters are being constantly chased by representatives of bank and are being harassed by them until they return the amount of loan. On the contrary, the persons who return the loan timely may sit comfortably in their houses with relaxation.

Likewise, if we endure the pain timely, we may live peacefully forever otherwise our mind remains disturbed due to suppressed pain. Anyhow, it is your own pain so only you have to bear it otherwise it will come to end only at your death.

Thus, instead of trying to avoid the pain through consumption of intoxicated substances, endure it otherwise you have to suffer it throughout your life. On the other hand, as soon as you will endure the pain, you will soon become free from negative thoughts and their chain reactions. Otherwise, due to law of attraction, more miseries are constantly being invited by negative thoughts. Thus instead of suppressing the pain, endure it.

Regarding enduring the pain, Old Testament says, "Gold is tried on fire and acceptance in the furnace of affliction". Therefore, endurance is neither a punishment nor a misfortune but a light that can be found only in the midst of grief. Thus only after endurance of your painful emotions which have been buried deep inside you, you can able to vacate your subconscious. Then a place for happiness and bliss will be created spontaneously inside you.

Endurance as means to happiness

Anyhow, grief spares no one else and every human being has to experience it. George Bernard Shaw said, "Everything happens to everybody sooner or later if there is time enough". Thus, you are not alone griever in the world. Therefore, each and every situation, how critical it may be, has to be faced boldly. However, those people who welcome the situation as it comes in their life can bear the pain in a natural way. On the contrary, those who are unable to face the adversity courageously, they only increase their suffering.

In addition, enduring the discomforts is essential to achieve comforts. For example, when we start climbing on mountain top, we face many difficulties on the way. Anyhow, after reaching there, we experience boundless joy. We found beautiful scenery of surroundings and enjoy the pleasant weather etc. In fact, after climbing, we forget the difficulties facing on the way of climbing. In other words, some difficulties and sufferings have to be endured for the sake of incoming happiness.

Swami Vivekananda illustrated the endurance with an example of rose flower. He said, "We have to endure the pain of thorn to pluck the flower. However, after plucking the flower, we forget the pain of thorn". Mean to say, nothing can be achieved without enduring pain. Likewise, we have to wet in rain to see the rainbow. It is impossible to accept only one side of the coin and reject another rather we have accept it with its both sides.

Even Jesus considered the grief as medium for happiness. He illustrated it with an example of a pregnant woman in labor pain. Actually, intensity of labor pain is almost unbearable but every pregnant woman endures it for the sake of her offspring. However, on seeing her offspring, the mother filled with happiness and realized much joy. For her, the happiness of becoming a mother is more than any other thing of the world. Thus she ignores the anguish gone through few moments ago. Even the pain was not only inevitable for her but necessary. Therefore, pain is an essential ingredient for achieving happiness.

In addition, Jesus compared the enduring with the grain of wheat. He said, "Without perishing in the earth, wheat cannot produce hundred more grains". Therefore, without enduring the pain, you cannot bring liberation and happiness to others. Moreover, this fact is proved true after examining the life history of Mahatma Gandhi and Nelson Mandela. However, Jesus himself had faced much grief in his life and endured its pain.

Thus enduring the pain is identical to a child who is being operated. On operating of a small surgery, a child starts crying because the child is unable to understand the relief that he/she is going to feel after operation. However, the mother does not mind the child's anguish even she herself help the doctor by griping the child tightly. Actually, mother knows well that pain of operation is very less cost to obtain the relief of the child going to feel soon after the operation. Thus the pain of the small surgery of the child is only medium for his or her well-being. Thus neither any happiness nor any type of relief can be obtained free. Means, we have to pay some price for each and everything let it be our lifestyle or our well-being.

In the same way, we are reluctant to endure the pain of tragedy which befell on us because we are unable to understand the mysterious way of God to lead us towards spiritual growth and bliss. Actually, God tests us thoroughly before giving the entry in state of bliss so He puts us in such a grievance state. Thus, the grief which befalls on us is only a part of Divine's plan however every Divine's plan is made only for our betterment as described earlier. Thus life always moves towards best.

Anyhow, neither we should lose our courage nor cease our activities on befalling the tragedy. Rather on facing the adversity, we should learn the lesson from the Nature which proceedings/activities never stop rather they remain continue forever, whatever may be happened. For example, days and nights occur routinely, seasons change as their schedules; grass grows spontaneously as soon as monsoon starts; plant flourishes constantly; flowers blossom in every spring. Thus everything in Nature remain continue without the concern of any happening such as disasters, calamities, pandemics etc. Mean to say, Nature is flourishing constantly, and cosmic system always remains going on without any delay and without fail.

Thus, there is enough with Nature to motivate us for carrying on our work throughout our life irrespective of adversities. Therefore, we should learn the lesson that the tragedy has to be faced boldly and duty has to be done without any excuse whatever may be the circumstances. Actually, every adversity makes us stronger to face future difficulties. In brief, each and every bitter experience pushes us one more step near to the state of happiness and bliss.

Chapter 4
Make adversity an opportunity

"Always seek out the seed of triumph in every adversity."—Og Mandino.

Every man in this world faces difficulties and adversities. Some face them in early stage while some in later stage. Those who face adversities in early age achieve experiences and become mature earlier than usual and live their rest of life wisely. On the other hand, those who face it in later stage, for them, it becomes very difficult to bear the pain of adversities due to lack of experiences. Mean to say, every adversity befalls on us makes us wiser and stronger than ever before. An American Author Zig Ziglar also said that sometimes adversity is what you need to face in order to become successful.

When we start our journey towards rightful living, on the way often we find rough road with some obstacles. Anyhow, when we reach at our destination, we only remember obstacles and pain given by them instead of beautiful scenery which we experienced on the way. Likewise, we remember the adversities, and regret them frequently but ignore their positive side. However, we cannot accomplish our feats without going through the adversities and enduring the pain caused by them. Thus adversities are also parts of life's journey like obstacles of road which are parts of travelling.

Actually, we should response just another way. Mean to say, we should ignore the tiredness caused by obstacles and should make celebration for approaching the destination. Thus, forget the adversity which has been already passed, and remember the joy which have been achieved after lot of suffering. Therefore, instead of regretting the events, we should reconcile with the past and should move further with enthusiasm and hope. Actually, every morning, when we wake up, wake up with fresh energy. Means today is not a continuation of yesterday. Anyhow, yesterday has been gone forever and today is front of us to live vigorously. Thus every new day may be proved mile-stone for us.

Events affect negatively as well as positively.

All events affect both ways. Mean to say, bad events not affected us negatively but they affected positively also. Optimists always seek positive aspect in all events while pessimists see negative. Two brothers have been given half glass of milk each by their mother. One sees half full glass while another sees half empty. Though the quantity of milk in both glasses was same, one's optimistic attitude makes it half full while another's pessimistic attitude makes it half empty.

Thus it is our attitude which makes any event worse or better. Likewise, in the calamity of flood pessimist sees the destroying of crops while optimist one sees the fertile soil brought by flood and has been deposited in the field which works as good manure for next crops. Thus the fields become more fertile than ever before. Therefore, it entirely depends on you whether you consider any event positively or negatively.

An event happened with prominent scientist Thomas Edition can motivate us in better way regarding positive attitude. In 1914 when Edition was 67 years old, his industries were destroyed by fire and total loss was about two million dollars. Though the loss was very huge, he showed a positive attitude instead of worrying and said, "There is a great value in disasters. All our mistakes are burned up. Thanks God, we can start new." Thus, it is entirely depends on our attitude whether adversities crush us or we crush the adversities.

Actually, we should always see silver lines in every cloud. In the words of Helen Keller, "When God closes one door, He opens another but either we see too distant to seek another door or we are unable to see the opened door due to tears shading in our eyes." Thus, instead of giving way to despair, we should keep hope and always try to find alternatives because we should not forget that in the deep of the despair even the slightest ray of hope is enough to show us right way.

In the words of Victor Hugo popular French poet and writer, "Emergency has been proved milestone in the progress of human beings". Mean to say, it was darkness which produced the lamp. It was fog that produced the compass. It was hunger that drove us to exploration. And it was depression which teaches us the real value of job. Even our health is being maintained only due to our illness. Without illness, our immune system would not be so strong and we will be unable to survive. Thus, abundance is always found hidden in scarcity which requires only our positive attitude to reveal.

That's why it is said that necessity is the mother of invention. If we get each and every thing without any difficulty at the time of our requirement, our research will come to end. Naturally, progress will be almost impossible without research. Mean to say, deficiency of anything leads us towards research of the substitute of deficient thing. Therefore, lack of things always becomes the cause of innovation and progress.

Thus, adversity often works as a catalyst to change grievers' life. You sometimes acquire the sharpest skills when you are going through tough times. Therefore, time of adversity is the perfect time to rediscover those little things that make life worth living. Actually, when any tragedy happens to us, an unexpected power emerges from within us to face it. If we meet the adversity with positive attitude, the adversity works as catalyst for creating something wonderful. Thus, the adversities have potential in disguise to change us radically.

This hypothesis can be better illustrated with a happening of Mahatma Gandhi. When Mohan Das Karamchand Gandhi had been thrown out from the first class compartment of train in South Africa in spite of having first class ticket, he converted this injustice into opportunity by raising the voice against injustice. Though it was big insult for him, he remained silent instead of doing violence on the railway station. However, he did not forget this insult rather he always remembered that insulted event. In fact, later on that painful happening catalyzed him to raise his voice against the oppressed behavior of British government.

Thus small happening of railway station in South Africa made him great and transformed into Mahatma. However, instead of respond violently on the spot, he controlled his angry emotions. Even he remembered the injustice and converted his painful emotions into non-violent movement against British government first in South Africa and latterly in India.

On the other hand, if he would not have been thrown from upper class compartment, he would not have become so great. In that case he may be remained unknown person throughout his whole life. However, due to his positive attitude and patience, he could become capable to convert the adversity into opportunity which transformed him and made a great personality. Therefore, it is not the event which has matter but it is the attitude of the individual which has more significance in one's life.

According to Oscar Wilde an Irish poet and playwright, what seems to us as bitter trials are often blessing in disguise. There is no doubt that death of loved one affects very seriously to those who experience it and generally grievers take time to recover thoroughly. However, research tells us that it can also be the catalyst for renewed sense of meaning that offers purpose and direction to life. That's why some tragedies become milestone in one's life. Flowering plants always flourish better in the garbage because garbage works as manure. Therefore, transform the garbage into flower rather than consider it dirty.

Anyhow, the greater is the adversity, the brighter is the opportunity. As and when clouds are very dark and their thundering is very much loud, the flash of lightning in the sky will also very bright. According to Josh Billing famous humor writer and lecturer in US, if we have no winter, the spring would not be so pleasant. Thus if we did not sometimes experience adversity, prosperity would not be so welcome. It can also be said that opportunity often comes disguised in the form of misfortune but it should be recognized timely.

Hardship of life is the main source of wisdom

Setbacks of life are very important ingredients for our maturity. Actually, maturity does not occur with the age but it requires experiences. However, experiences cannot be obtained without passing through hardship. Thus neither the experiences can learn from any book /school nor can they be transferred from any other source. Therefore, in order to attain the experiences, you have to go through all ups and downs; you have to embrace the grief; stay with it like a friend and feel it. Thus you have to endure the pain of grief. Mean to say, only after going through all type of life's hardship, you achieve experiences and can attain the state of maturity in your life.

Thus, it can be said that experiences are individual's own capital that is gained on the cost of your lots of comforts. Mean to say, discomforts are the best investment to gain this capital of experiences. Therefore, the duration of hardship is not a wasted time but it gains valuable experiences which cannot be obtained from any university of the world. Actually, an experience obtained by any happening of our life, creates new neural connections and strengthens the neuron network which ultimately leads us towards wisdom. This fact is described in details in chapter eleven.

Thus, lots of experiences have been accumulated in our sub-conscious mind throughout life. Our conscious mind forgets many experiences but they remain in our sob-conscious till we live. Or you can say that these experiences become our inner voice known as intuition. Whenever we face any problem in our life, they reoccur in the form of intuition and help us in solving problems. In other words, the accumulated experiences transfer into wisdom.

Therefore, success and wisdom are directly proportion to adversities and difficulties which we have faced throughout life. Mean to say, as much as hardship you face in life, so much experiences you gain in your life. Thus treasure of experiences becomes vast accordingly and as much as experiences you obtain in life so much wisdom you attain. Thus, way of wisdom goes through only problems, difficulties, adversities, hardship and grieves. Socrates and Chanakya are the best example of such wisdom. Once Swami Vivekananda said, "Tell me how much you suffered in your life, I shall tell you how great you are." Therefore, adversity is the main source of wisdom.

I am not trying to convince you that you should remain in grief and suffering conditions. On the contrary, your main purpose of life should be live happily. However, the grief does not spare anyone so it cannot be avoided. Therefore, instead of avoiding its pain by one means or another, it must be endured. Means, to reach the bright side of life, you have to cross the river of grief. Therefore, adversity should be considered as means to wisdom which ultimately leads us to the state of bliss.

On the contrary, when you afraid of facing the difficulties and avoid problems, you deprive yourselves from the valuable experiences. Additionally, the problems remain continue around you because they do not solve automatically. Therefore, you entangle in the web of problems in such a way that you feel only helplessness. Thus avoidance only increases the frustration. Only nature and pattern of problems change time to time otherwise problems remain occurring throughout your life. Therefore, there is only one way to tackle the problems and that is to face them boldly. Thus, as much as problems you face and solve them, you gain as much as experiences which are main sources of wisdom.

We ourselves create our destiny

Our future is unpredictable and depends on our free will rather predestined as we assumed. Instead we ourselves create our destiny every day. In other words our today is based on what we have done yesterday and our tomorrow will be based on what we are doing today. This is the law of action (*karma*) or law of cause and effect. Actually, every thought arises in our mind, every word we say and every activity we do create a cause. Thus, over a period of time all these *karmic* causes ripen to become effect.

Our past actions are, in fact, like a frog that has already taken a lap in one direction so it cannot change its direction until it touches the ground. However, it is another matter that frog can change its direction in next lap. In other words, we cannot change the effect of any previous cause. Whilst we can change only current cause in order to change future effect. Thus, we cannot change our today because our today has been already determined on the basis of our yesterday's action. However, we can definitely change our tomorrow by doing good actions on today.

Anyhow, along with our free will our current actions have such potential which can make our tomorrow's destiny. In fact, any action performed by us itself is cause' that creates 'effect', and that effect is nothing than our destiny. Thus we should not worry about our future rather we should focus only at our current actions. Therefore, this saying is true, "As you act so you become". The doer of good becomes good while doer of evil becomes evil. Mean to say, one becomes virtues by doing virtues acts while another one bad by bad actions. Thus what we sowed yesterday we are harvesting the same on today while what we are sowing today we will harvest the same on tomorrow.

Thus Buddhism considers attitude and actions more important than mind. Actually, the way we experience our mind is not as fixed entity but a constant flow of consciousness, awareness and clarity. Therefore, in this flow, our actions predispose use to experience future happenings in a particular ways whether virtuous or bad. Thus, a stream of consciousness is constantly flowing through our life and we are constantly shaping our destiny each moment. Actually, we are the sum total of the actions we have done so far.

In this context The Dalai Lama says, "Our present condition is not something causeless nor is it something caused by chance. It is the thing we ourselves have steadily constructed through series of past decisions and the actions of our body, speech and mind that arose from them".

Therefore, if we want to predict our destiny that how our life will be in future, we should analyses our today that how we think and act at this moment. Swami Vivekananda was also strong believer of the law of *karma*. He always emphasized on the cause and effect, and he said that man is maker of his own fate. According to him, we are responsible for what we are, and whatever we wish ourselves to be, we have the power to make ourselves. Therefore, what we are today, none else the blame, none has the praise.

Our yesterday's actions are, in fact, like a letter which has been already posted. So the posted letter cannot be taken back rather it will definitely reach its destination sooner or later. Therefore, everyone soon or late has to experience the effects of one's yesterday's actions irrespective to good or bad.

Thus, we are ourselves writer of our destiny and in order to write good destiny, we have to do something good at this moment. If we seek positive aspect in all our adversities, we may be able to do some virtuous deed and can make our good destiny.

Tragedy teaches us lesson.

Asti has been already described that nothing happens without reason, tragedy also happens for certain purpose. Thus tragedy happens only for teaching us lessons. Actually, we learn more in painful events than pleasurable. Iyanala Vanzant spiritual teacher and Author explained regarding painful events that everything that happens to us is only a lesson. We are expected to learn the lesson and move forward. However, when we don't learn lesson, the topic is repeated again. Even the topic is repeated again and again like a classroom teaching until we learn the lesson thoroughly. Thus we are only students of the cosmic school.

The life itself is a learning process but with different teaching methods. In school we learn first and then tested in order to get pass certificate while life take test first and then give lesson. This is the reason that similar events happen with us frequently till we become graduate on the particular subject. Actually, in the University of Life neither anyone can copy nor anyone can ask favor of examiner. Therefore, we ourselves have to go through the hardship of our life. Thus the learning process of the life is not only tough but fair also.

Actually when events happen with us frequently, we become habitual to face them and our inner strength increases manifold at the time of adversity. Moreover, we use that inner strength to face further adverse situation and this process is going on…….. Thus we can turn the effects of happenings towards our better developments. Additionally, in this process of personality development, Nature also helps those who are intended to do something beyond their capabilities.

Anyhow, tomorrow will another day—with fresh hopes and opportunities so we should look forward to experience happenings whatever they may be. Therefore, always be ready to face new challenges by considering them as teacher of your life. Thus hardships and adversities are the greatest teachers in life. Actually, you cannot understand all aspects of the life until and unless you will face the adversities.

Anyhow, people come closer to each other more in the time of hardship than in comfort. Thus they forgive each other and forget their differences. Even they help and support wholeheartedly one another. You would have noticed during disasters and calamities that people care much their neighbors, friends and relatives. It means, humanity increases manifold in calamity and adversity. In the words of Kier Keguard, "Adversity draws men together and produces beauty and harmony in life's relationships just as the cold of winter produces ice flowers on the window-panes, which vanish with the warmth".

However, adversity draws only those men together who happen to face together the same nature of adversity such as earthquake, flood, cyclone etc. Because all are sufferer of the same type of calamities. Otherwise, people usually go away from the man who suffers alone. It is also true equally that people join their hands at the time of adverse happening but very few remain with one another after few days.

Thus, the adversity is the time when you can know who is your real supporter and who is pretended to be helpful. Therefore, without adversity, we cannot recognize our friends and relatives, and this is the great lesson taught by adversity.

Anyhow, how much any one supports you and how much one intends to share your grief but the bitter truth is that **you and only you** have to bear your anguish of the tragedy. Moreover this is the ultimate lesson which tragedy teaches us.

Consider the adversity as challenge.

Generally, people become so tense in adversities that the anxiety disrupts their abilities to notice the optimistic situation and ultimately they miss the opportunities. However, we should not forget that options always remain open and choices remain in our hands. However, instead of choosing right option, we generally live our life according to our mindset. Actually, our mindset is nothing but opinion of some dominant people of the society and their opinion is generally based on false beliefs. Therefore, our mindset is also based on false belief thus we believe that adversities are part of fate and they occur to punish us. Instead we should consider the adversities as part of cosmic plan rather than our fate. And they occur in order to make us strong rather than punish us. Thus we should accept them as we accept challenges.

We may be more relax and open in this optimistic view. If we always ready to face unexpected events and open to new experiences then we can convert our adversities into opportunities. Actually, when we take any issue as challenge, we may be able to focus our complete attention on that issue. Thus the problem gets solution in unexpected and miraculous way.

Here, I want to share my own experience with the readers. I was diagnosed with diabetes at the age of 39 years. However, I was remained disturb for some period but I had collected information from various sources about diabetes. Moreover, I concluded that however diabetes is incurable but blood sugar level can be maintained by diet and right way of living. Then I prepared a chart of diets about what should eat; what should eat in moderate; what should avoid completely; schedule of meals and snacks etc.

In addition, I started aerobic exercise and morning walk regularly. Only with diet and exercise, I maintained my blood sugar level about fifteen years. Anyhow, when blood sugar level became somewhat higher than usual, I started taking medicine along with exercise and morning walk. Then I took it more seriously and sought some more information about diabetes and lifestyle. Moreover, I found really very amazing information and set my schedule accordingly. Then on the bases of blood sugar monitoring chart and diet taken time to time, I have fixed my medicine dose myself own.

Thus I have maintained my blood sugar level so far. Now, I am more than 67years old, good in health and do skipping, yoga, aerobic exercises, jogging and morning walk regularly and I am constantly monitoring my blood sugar level and body weight. Therefore, today my blood sugar level is so much in control that even my doctor surprises every time when he observes my blood sugar's monitoring chart. Mean to say, you are the best doctor of your body.

Thus, I took my diabetes as challenge and my whole schedule had been changed due to diabetes. If diabetes would not be diagnosed, perhaps I did not care so much of my body and till now I would start feeling old age. However, I feel much energetic thus diabetes proved boon for me.

We should consider every adversity as an invitation for us to challenge our ability, talent, wisdom etc. Then we find that every challenge surprises us to know our inner strength which has vast reservoirs of ability. Our ability is like a rubber band, it expands as and when we face new challenges. For example Helen Keller became deaf and blind in her childhood due to fever but she educated herself so highly that she became the inspiration of all such challenged individuals. Thus, facing the adversities successfully may become golden gift for us.

Adversities may be used as basic ingredient for self-improvement

Adversities may be used as basement on which the building of self-improvement can be constructed. If basement would strong, the building will also be strong. Thus, if we make adversity an opportunity, we can build a strong building in the form of our improvement on considering the opportunity as basement. Thus, adversities are like rain if we see towards its positive aspect, we can use the wet soil in sowing the seed.

Milton Berle American comedian and actor said, "If opportunity does not knock, build a door". Mean to say, we can seek opportunity in every situation however worse it may be. However, when we consider any difficulty as a problem, it becomes burden for us. On the other hand, if we handle any difficulty with patience and peace of mind, difficulty can become gift for us and soon we will become habitual for it. Generally, we are unable to recognize the gift due to our ignorance.

James Russell Miller popular Author illustrates this ignorance with the example of the birds. When wings start growing to wingless birds, they feel them a burden and it is very difficult for them to carry the wings on their bodies. However, as the birds grew, they learn to fold the wings. Soon they become habitual to lift this burden and discover the use of the wings.

Thus, the weights of wings which the birds consider burdens earlier due to their ignorance are, in fact, bliss for them. Thus wings make the birds capable to fly in the air freely. Now the birds become able to know that the wings which are considered by them as burden took them in the sky and make them secure from all the danger which they might be face on the ground.

Likewise, only due to our ignorance we generally consider difficulties and adversities as burden. However, when we start experiencing the adversities as we experience other normal happenings, we soon become habitual of them. Thus, when we start considering every difficult situation as a usual and start taking it with light hearted, every happening becomes gift for us. Actually, life always moves towards its best direction so have patience!

Thus adversities and problems also can be proved gift for us and may lead us towards bliss if we have to become habitual to face them. Actually, once we become habitual of anything, we generally switch-over our internal working system to the autopilot mode. Mean to say, we start doing all activates fast then all tasks become very easy for us. Even we start handling the difficulties like a routine work.

Anyhow, when we learn transforming the adversities into opportunities, these adversities become the source of fly high in the air where there is open sky free of all earthly miseries. Actually, it is such a high spot where there is no throat cut competition and worldly affairs which harsh us.

Instead, we are free to live there in peace. Moreover, that is the exact place where we realize bliss. Mean to say, after transformation, we reach at such height of spiritualty where no place is left for trivial things.

CHAPTER 5
Release your emotions

"Those who weep recover more quickly than those who smile."—Jean Giraudoux.

Releasing the painful emotions is very essential part of grieving. After releasing the painful emotions not only our minds become calm but our bodies also get relaxation. Therefore, grievers feel very light and they can return to the flow of life easily. Actually, greater empowerment, more inner strength, more freedom and greater ease are the result of releasing the painful emotions. Therefore, the more painful emotions you release, the more energetic and younger you feel.

Thus it is necessary to know about the details of emotions such as—what are the emotions? What are buried or suppressed emotions? How do the emotions affect human beings and how are they resist the process of grieving? Whether emotions can be controlled? If not, is there another way to manage them so that we may maintain our overall well-being. Anyway, in order to avoid harmful effects of our bodies, painful emotions should be managed properly and should be released because releasing of the painful emotions is very necessary in order to return to normal life.

What are emotions?

Actually, it is very difficult to explain the exact meaning of the term 'emotion' in words because emotions can be only felt and expressed. Emotions are biological innate, universal to all human beings and display through facial expression such as—a flushed face, muscle tensing, tone of voice, rapid heartbeat, sweating, breathing and other body languages. Many psychologists try to define the emotions according to their own views and knowledge but hardly anyone agreed with one another.

In this context professor of Neuroscience Joseph LeDoux said, "There are as many theories of emotions as there are emotions theorists". Some define the emotions as—they are mind's reaction to experience; sensitivity to events; individual specific reactions to experience; the description of intangible human feelings and the powerful internal sensation that color our every experience. It can be said that emotion is a strong feeling deriving from one's circumstances, mood, or relationships with others. Thus emotions are intense feelings that are directed to someone or something.

According to famous psychiatrist and founder of analytical psychology Carl Jung, objects draw and invoke emotions which are natural phenomenon. Thus emotions are specific and intense physical and psychological reactions to particulars events. Generally, emotions are considered as feelings so both are used interchangeably but psychologists consider emotions different from feelings. According to psychologists, feelings express our true identity while emotions reveal how we have been taught to respond to events in our life.

Thus psychologists believe that our deep feelings come from an unchanging belief about life that holds our identity together while our emotions are purely physically based, subject to change and are basically reactions to life events. Therefore, feelings are response part of emotions and that emotions include the situation or experience, the interpretation and the perception related to the experience of a particular situation.

Emotions are also different from mood. Although the emotions and mood are seemed to similar being intertwined with each other, both are different traits. For example, after discussing with colleagues on some particular topic, you might feel angry for a short period of time. On the other hand mood is a contextual stimulus which remains longer but tends to be less intense than emotions. Even in many cases, stimulus remains hidden. Mean to say, identification of the specific cause of a mood is very difficult. For example, you might find yourself gloomy for some days without any clear identifiable reason.

Actually, emotions are not only intertwined with mood but with temperament and personality also. Anyway, the words emotion was adapted from the French word emouvoir, in 1579 which means 'to stir up'. The term emotion was introduced in to academic discussion to replace passion. Therefore, on considering the emotion as passion, it can be concluded that emotions are naturally occurring response of a situation. Thus, emotions are either the result of a judgment of any current situation or a perception of changes facing place within our bodies. It can also be said that our emotional responses are the result from the way we appraise our experiences.

Actually, love and fear are basic emotions and all other emotions have been emerged from these two emotions. Emotions such as—sadness, hurt, guilt, anger, shame, disgust, confusion, lonely, anxiety, depression etc. are based on fear. On the other hand, the positive emotions such as—compassion, happiness, sympathy, contentment, joy, trust, satisfaction, caring etc. are based on the basic emotion—love. Thus thoughts and behavior come from either a place of love or a place of fear.

The effects of emotions on human beings

Emotions are complex and have both physical and mental components which exert a powerful influence on human being. Everyone experiences emotions but philosophers and psychologists do not agree on the point how the emotions should be measured or studied. According to some theories, emotions are a state of feeling that results in physical and psychological changes that influence our behavior. The physiology of emotion is closely linked to arousal of the nervous system with various states and strengths of arousal reality, apparently to particular emotions. Philosophers and psychologists have long debated the nature of emotions affect the quality of the work environment.

Emotions seem to value our daily lives. Emotions affect our physical bodies as much as our body affects our feelings and thinking. We make decisions based on whether we are happy, angry, sad, bored or frustrated and we choose activities and hobbies based on the emotions. We experience different levels or intensities of emotional energy during face to face interactions. Emotional energy is considered to be a feeling of confidence to take action and boldness that are experiences when they are charged up from enthusiasm and cheerfulness.

Thus emotions appear to serve several physical and psychological purposes. Some psychologists believe that emotions are one of the fundamental traits associated with human being. Emotions colored people's lives and give them depth and differentiation. For some scholars, strong emotions are linked to creativity and expression. Therefore, most artists, writers and poets are generally more emotional than common people. Actually, their emotions become the source of wonderful creation.

Thus, emotions serve as motivation to behave in specific way. Insensitive people usually remain passive in social affairs due to lack of motivation. On the other hand, sensitive people being emotional interfere in all social affairs. They jump suddenly whenever and wherever they notice social evils whether the affairs were concerned to them or not. They are so motivated to do something for the society that they ignore their personal interest even sometimes they suffer heavily. It is only their emotions which make them so bold. Anna Hazare prominent social activist is the best example of such sensitiveness.

During my service period as a teacher, whenever I felt some injustice with colleagues or students, generally, I interfered the matter then and there, and solved the matter on the spot. However, if the problem remained unsolved, I could not sleep comfortably in night until I decided to take any appropriate action against that injustice. That's why my most applications/letters have been written to the concerned higher authorities in night. It is another matter that they were posted on next morning. Even my most e-mails have been sent to higher authorities at 2 or 3 o'clock in morning. Only after sending the e-mail, I could sleep well because the action taken by me in the night released my emotions and soothed me.

Thus, only my emotions have motivated me throughout my life. Mean to say, my strong emotions encourage and strengthen me to fight against injustice. Moreover, whatever I have done in my life have been done due to my strong emotions and this trend of motivation is still continuing. Therefore, without passion and compassion, it is almost impossible to do something for others.

Although fear is a negative emotion, it also plays a great role in our day-to-day activities. Actually, fear is harmful for both body and mind but mild fearful emotions are good for our progress. We do hard work only due to the fear otherwise we may become overconfident and deprive from such progress. For example, mostly students study due to fear of failure in the examination. And candidate for any competitive exam for job also prepare well due to the fear of not getting the job. Actually, there is some hidden fear behind our all types of activities in our work places otherwise many of us do not work sincerely.

On the other hand, it is also true that too much fear is even worse so only mild degree of fear is enough to work hard. Therefore, our performance will be better if the level of fear remains low. If, however, the fear becomes too great which cause much anxiety then performance deteriorates. Therefore, emotions are linked to our activity in brain areas that direct our behavior and determine significance of what is going around us. It can also be said that all our day-to-day activities are directly based on our emotions. Actually, emotions establish our attitude towards reality, and create our drive for all life's pleasure. So emotions are essential for human survival.

Thus emotions help us to progress in our careers, increase our self-awareness, creativity, motivation, empathy and consciousness so that we can live here more happily. In other words it can be said that emotions take us to the height where we can able to touch highest goal of our life.

Meaning of suppress in the context of emotions

Actually, when we have to face painful circumstances which are very difficult to cope with the pain, we dismiss the emotions by one means or another. For example, either we get busy unnecessarily in eating and drinking a little bit or pretends to be bold and show others that nothing is serious. Even, we try to push away such painful memories by indulging in wine, sex or some other recreation but instead of going away, these painful emotions reach deep within ourselves. Mean to say, these painful emotions start accumulating in our unconscious mind which is, in fact, is a dumping ground for emotions.

Anyhow, by constant accumulation of painful emotions, our unconscious becomes just as garbage bin going on adding more and more pain without getting cleared and flushed out. Thus our unconscious is filled with layers negativity embodied with thick deep layers of sorrow. However, by sending emotions in unconscious, we become able to dismiss the painful emotion for the time being but not permanently. Thus unlike healing of physical wounds, the psychological wounds or hurt which have been pushed in unconscious reoccur with amplification.

These accumulated emotions in the unconscious mind are known as repressed, suppressed or buried emotions. These feelings stay in our muscles, ligaments, stomach, midriff, auras etc. Moreover, such suppressed emotions remain buried deep within us till we bring that emotions on surface, feel them and ultimately release them. Therefore, by one means or another, we have to bring the emotions up to our conscious level and release them otherwise they may be remain bury within our unconscious forever and they will be hurting us from inside.

In addition, our lot of energy consumes to keep stuffing the painful emotions back down so very less energy left over with us for other activities. Actually, by nature suppressed emotions want to come up so we can become aware of them, feel them and release them. Therefore, it is very difficult to keep the emotions down. The more we try to control our emotions the more we resist control.

Why do we suppress the emotions?

Actually, our fear is the main cause behind the suppression of emotions. We generally live our lives in the environment of fear. Whatever we do we do in fear, wherever we go, we go along with fear. We have no courage to feel our true feelings. Even we are afraid to confess our mistakes; to discuss the problems with friends and to tell our sorrow to our near and dear. Even we have no courage to accept any tragedy and to endure its pain. Thus fear affects our whole personality which resulting in decline the inner strength and tolerance. Thus we push our painful emotions inside.

Actually, we pretend to be great and prestigious. Therefore, male grievers pretend to be so bold that they avoid crying which is essential to release painful emotions. Even some of us fear to laugh so that they may not lose their seriousness and intellectuality. Many of us think that only serious people are intellectual and wise. Mean to say, in each and every step men manifest their masculinity so they pretend to be bold, intellectual and wise. Therefore, we generally wear mask of one type or another to hide our true identity. Therefore, our true feelings cannot be revealed until we remove the masks which have covered our true identity. Actually, due to this fear, we always hide our true feelings. Thus, our painful emotions remain burry.

In addition, we suppress emotions because they were too painful and difficult to deal with. However, life is about what we feel rather than what we think. Anyhow, we become accustomed to live a mundane life which is based on our thoughts rather than feelings. Whilst, being strongly connected to emotional life, it is essential for all of us to live a life with high energy, with contentment and happiness. Moreover, this state is possible only when we feel our emotions thoroughly and act accordingly.

Thus instead of releasing the emotions, we use one method or another to avoid feeling our emotions. People use the methods for suppressing or burying their emotions according to their comfort and resources. For example—excessive drinking, excessive sex, excessive reading, excessive recreation such as movie and TV etc., are some means to dismiss the painful emotions. Additionally, excessive use of recreational drug or prescribed drug such as tranquilizers; keeping superficial conversation; ignoring and acting as what happened is very insignificant, and burying the angry emotion under the mask of love and peace etc. are also some means of suppressing the emotions.

Human beings are generally different in nature by birth such as introvert and extrovert. Some people do not trust easily on others while some trust even on strangers. One may be kind and compassionate while other may be unkind and pitiless. Therefore, reasons of suppressing the emotions may also differ from person to person. Some people think that no one can understand them so they do not express their feelings to anyone and remain silence while some others remain silence due to their shyness.

On the other hand, some people have so much morality that they do not want to hurt anyone so they prefer suffering themselves rather than disturb others' feelings. Some are so timid that they afraid to open their mouth against those who oppress them even they do not tell others about such injustice so they are compelled to suppress their emotions. Some other people have no courage to break the society's norms which generally bind in old traditions. Although they do not feel comfortable in following traditional norms, they remain in suffocation due to social pressure. Thus they repress their emotions instead of open their mouth in front of dominant people of the society.

Some remain silent in order to maintain peace environment at home or work place. Thus, they suppress their painful emotions because they think that peace of mind is more important for them than anything else. Whilst, some others are such persons who are compel to keep mum due to insoluble of the problem. Mean to say, they think that problem will be not solved even after discussion so they prefer silence and suppress their painful emotions.

For example, most women are compelled to bear the bad habits of their husbands silently such as drinking, gambling, violence etc. However, their feelings hurt almost daily but they suppress their emotions. Anyhow, whatever may be the reason of suppressing the emotions; suppressed emotions deteriorate our overall well-being.

Effect of suppressed Emotions on our body and mind

The emotions are operated on many levels and affect our body as well as mind. According to Dr. Maurice, "Emotions work as a warning system for human being that tells us what is really going around us and how things are going on in our lives". Thus, emotions help us to keep on the right track by making sure that we are led by more than the intellectual faculties of thought, perception, reason and memory.

Therefore, next time if you experience—sweating palms, increasing in thinking, emerge of negative thoughts, racing heartbeat, rapid breathing or stomach lurch, concentrate on your buried emotions. It means that the time has come when only taking the medicines will not be sufficient but suppressed emotions also have to be released by one means or another otherwise buried emotions may push you towards serious physical or mental illness. Mean to say, diseases are directly related to the suppressed emotions.

Emotions that are buried for the long times create not only mental illness but physical illness also. Fear- based emotions stimulate the release of one set of chemicals while love- based emotions release a different set of chemicals. If the fear-based emotions are remained buried for long-term, they may damage the chemical system, the endocrine system, immune system or other system in our body. In other words these suppressed emotions are responsible for most type of disease. As we suppress, as they return back in the symptom of ulcer, appendix, headache, insomnia, arthritis, heart problem, diabetes or cancer because they cause chemical reactions in our body. Thus they affect our physical body as well as energetic system.

In addition, they not only affect our relationship but hamper our spiritual growth also by shifting our level of consciousness. The buried emotions cause holes in our auras, through which our energy leaks out create fatigue, a sense of vulnerability and low self- confidence. Buried emotions always reactions to past events rather than present. That's why our thinking process increases because we always think about past events. We cannot be fully present with those who love us until we have released our suppressed emotions and start living completely in present moment.

Thus, if we remain unable to release the painful suppressed emotions timely, they will suffocate us and the emotions which were already full of anguish will become so painful that they may push us towards depression. That's why some people take extreme step and decide to commit suicide when the pain inside them became unbearable. Generally, people around the sufferer remain unaware because they think that grieving process has been already completed as the individual acts by hiding the painful emotions. However, the hiding pain and suppressed emotions function as TNT which makes up the bomb and may explode any time.

Additionally, if we keep our painful emotions buried for a long period of time, we decrease our overall vibrations. Thus these lower vibrations not only push us towards illness but accelerate the ageing process also. On the contrary, releasing the suppressed emotions increase our vibrations resulting in improvement of our overall well-being and slower the ageing process.

Actually, the suppressed emotions are bundle of memories of those people who had hurt us in the past and let us down. Now they are either dead or have gone forever from our lives but hurting memories are still in our mind and we are continuously nourishing them. Thus such memories are only draining our energy. Therefore, we should release these suppressed painful emotions through one way or another.

What is regulation of emotions and how to regulate them?

Actually, we live in such a society which insists us to hide our emotions. Thus, people around us always busy in convincing us that we are born with emotions, must live with them and die with them. Therefore, people feel uncomfortable with those persons who express strong emotions. Even the people who express their emotions frankly make more enemies than friends. This is the reason that our society does not tolerate such honest and frank persons.

On the other hand, if you try to control the emotions, they will explode in the form of strong anger. Actually, instead of controlling your emotions, emotions control you. Means, your thoughts, behavior and actions are controlled by your emotions. However, if you cannot release suppressed emotions by some unavoidable cause, you can regulate them instead of controlling. Otherwise the emotions which you try to control may burst and your anger may release on your pet, domestic help, kids, relatives, friends or colleges. Rage, aggression and agitation, in fact, arise due to disturbed emotions so instead of controlling the emotions, regulate them properly.

Thus, first of all, it is necessary to know what actually emotion's regulation is. Regulation of emotion describes the mental and behavioral process by which people influence their own feelings and the feelings of other people. Emotion's regulation can also be described as the process in which people modify their emotional reactions— the coping process that increase or decrease the intensity of the moment. In other words, thinking about things from a different perspective is emotion's regulation.

Thus regulation of emotions enhances our well-being, our performance and our relationship. Actually, we always take our feelings with us wherever we go. Mean to say, a new job, new relationship, new place or new home cannot change how we feel. Thus nothing makes difference except our own feelings and attitude. Mean to say, only we can change ourselves what we feel and how do we feel but no one else. Therefore, you should handle the situations from different perspectives whichever suits you according to the situation.

Actually, emotions are vital part of our lives and our emotional responses result from the way we appraise our experiences. However, some emotional responses require no particular regulation. Thus, if the emotion is appropriate to the situation and helps us feel better, there is no need to change the way we handle the situations. On the other hand, if we feel uncomfortable in any situation, we should modify the situation so that we can regulate our emotions rather than suppressing them.

Anyway, there are many ways to regulate the emotions such as we can change our thoughts; we can shift our attention by changing the issue of conversation or we can avoid/ modify the situation. Here, I am going to explain with few examples how emotions can be regulated. We can handle most of the activities involved in regulating our emotions well before the provoking situation event occurs. By preparing ourselves ahead of time, we will find that the problematic emotion goes away before interfering with our life.

For example, if we knew our temperament that we lose our temper to reach late at any place. In other words, late going in office, any function or program may disturb us and spoil our mood then we should leave the home little early so that problematic situation may be avoided. Likewise, if you lose patience in traffic jam and become irritated in peak hours of traffic then you may avoid peak hours to escape from the rush of roads.

Secondly, a situation can be handled more politely and with assertiveness rather than aggressiveness. For example, suppose your son is being studied in school and the class teacher send a note regarding your child's notorious behavior and call you in school on next day. After getting the note, you become very upset and next day you reach the school in aggressive mood. After reaching the school, you immediately start talking loudly in favor of your son, says to teacher "you don't understand my son or your intention is only harsh my son and so and so....."

Even you threat the teacher on the pretext of reporting the matter to the principal or higher authorities. Then you not only provoke the emotions of teacher but your own emotions also. Even you spoil the mood of your son and whole class. Then your aggressiveness not only affects your own feelings and others 'feelings but it also spoils complete environment. Thus instead of handling the case in an appropriate way, you deteriorates the whole situation only due to your aggressiveness.

On the contrary, you can short out the matter with assertiveness and more polite way. After receiving the note you remain cool and next morning you reach the school with calm mind. After reaching the school, you meet the class teacher with politeness and listen her/him patiently. After listening thoroughly, you try to find out the reason of notoriousness of your son also. You talk to some other students in order to find out the reality.

Thus, after knowing all the facts, you settle the affair then and there. Thus, with assertive behavior, you convince the teacher without hurting yourself, your son and teacher. In addition, you can assure the teacher regarding better behavior of your son for future. This attitude is more appropriate, correct expression of feelings and correct regulation of emotions.

However, there is a third option also which pushes you towards suppressing of your emotions. For example, if after getting the note, you feel ashamed and helpless then next morning you meet the class teacher with apology. Actually, you know that your son is not so bad and he may be notorious due to any particular reason. However, you remain silent and apologies to the teacher because you are afraid that your son's academic progress is in teacher's hand so she/he may spoil his carrier. Anyhow, in that case you not only suppress your own emotions but you demoralize your son also. Anyhow, it entirely depends upon you how you manage your disturbed emotions.

Next way of emotion's regulation is to avoid the situations which provoke your emotions. For illustration, I would like to share my own experience. Approximately hundred meters from the main gate of our society lots of rubbish was dumped on both sides of the road. When I used to go for walking, I felt very disgust to see the rubbish dump even I irritated on concerned people who were responsible for dumping. Even after approaching to local authorities, administrative authorities and editor of a newspaper, the dumping could not be removed because the person who was involved in dumping was dominated person of the locality and has some political links also.

Then I changed my path of walking. After exit of the main gate, I started just taking right turn and join the same road after walking the distance about three hundred meters. Though, this path is some rough and elevated, anyhow I avoided the situation which provoked my emotions. However, my efforts regarding removing rubbish were continue and after many efforts, later I became success in removing existed dump. Thus this bad practice of throwing the rubbish comes to end even for future also.

Additionally, for regulation of your emotions, you may divert them towards the welfare of the society. For example, for fighting against injustice, corruption and other social evils, instead of violent means, you may minimize such evils by peaceful way. Such as- bring the issue in the notice of concerned higher authorities through applications and aware the mass through journals or social media. Along with these methods, some other legal means such as RTIs, PILs etc. may also be adapted. Thus doing so, you will not only transform your agitated emotions into assertiveness but also be able to do something for others who are incapable for doing such thing for themselves.

Therefore, in order to maintain your overall well-being, you must regulate the emotions through the means which may be most suitable for you according to the situation.

How to release the emotions

Dealing with emotions is very critical and it is almost impossible to control them. As we try to control them, they suppress and remain in our sub-conscious and reoccur in the form of disease. Generally, People ignore their emotions on the pretext of one excuse or another. They say that such and such thing doesn't really matter or very less important for them.

Actually, they pretend to be peaceful and agree to something that deep down they don't agree with. Mean to say, they do not follow their consciences and admit with others superficially. Thus they only talk about their feelings but not feel them in real.

Actually, doing so, they try to hide their painful emotions. They stuff down their feelings through excessive or artificial behavior. Therefore, they are pretended to be normal by one means or another.

We usually play games continuously with the people, friends and relatives even with ourselves by denying the reality. Generally, we do not accept our feelings and thus we deceive our mind that nothing has happened. We have worn a mask of boldness, happiness and peace walk around saying that what has been happened has not much significance and it makes no difference. Thus we are continuously doing acting while buried emotions are hurting us from inside.

However, we often go for weeks, months, even years acting in a manner that everything is normal for us. Thus, we have been continuously suppressing emotions since our childhood. So many painful emotions have been accumulated so far in our sub-conscious. Moreover, these buried emotions will not release automatically. Rather some concrete steps have be taken in order to release the buried emotions. Anyhow, there are many ways to release the emotions and you are free to choose the way which you found most suitable.

The most important factor in releasing the emotions is crying. Crying is a natural means of releasing the emotions. Human beings are born with this ability because through crying we release pain and stress. The Bible also says, "There is time to weep". Therefore, we should choose our time for weeping. Let it be in the movies, TV serials or somewhere else. If you have had very painful experience which is almost unbearable— scream, cry and cry.

Actually, anger is common phenomena in almost all bereaved in the initial stage of grieving. Anger is, in fact, nothing but your pain. Some feel strong angry feelings towards deceased person and even towards God. It is natural to feel deserted and abandoned so it is necessary to honor your anger by allowing yourself to be angry. Thus nothing is wrong in mock fighting with God or deceased rather this mock fighting along with crying will help in releasing the angry emotions. If you think that whatever has happened, God might avoid the happening. Then don't hesitate to blame Him even blame Him loudly and continue your crying also. Thus fight with God and do conversation with Him whatever you feel at that moment but nothing hold in your heart.

Thus, do not ignore the occasions of crying rather seek the occasions for crying and screaming because itis very important part of grieving. For this purpose, you may search any solitary place but let the angry feelings out at any cost. However, cry loudly and simultaneously allow yourself to feel the pain. Thus, repeat this crying, screaming and fighting process with God or deceased till you relieve some of the sensitive pain of the painful experience. Actually, in the grieving, releasing the emotions is more important than any other thing.

According to Psychiatrist Elisabeth Kubler- Ross, anger denotes that you are allowing all those feelings that were simply too much before come to the surface. However, by expressing them towards someone, you are releasing them. Thus it is good sign of progressing in the process of grieving. Therefore, it is important to feel anger without judging it; without attempting to find meaning in it during grieving. So seek ways to get it out without hurting yourself or someone else.

Secondly, share your emotions with others but choose someone whom you trust most. People often, listen you with tears in their eyes and disclose your feelings or secret to others with laughing so choose the person whom you think most trustworthy. The chosen person may be your friend, relative, counselor, therapist or priest. You need such person who love you and care you especially at the time of hurting. Tell the person whom you chose what hurts you, feel his/her comfort and tell frankly that only advice is not sufficient rather tell your feelings that you need a loving heart who can feel your agony.

I noticed many times that after releasing hurting feelings, people feel much relaxation. Even some unfamiliar persons shared secret feelings of their hurting to me in parkat the time of morning walk. Thus after sharing their painful feelings, they seemed more relax than before so it is not the matter that whom you share your painful feelings. However, it is sure that sharing your anguish with someone helps you in releasing your emotions.

In addition, you may also write diary on daily bases in which you may write your daily activities or write a letter to someone relative or friend. If you express your emotions in letter then also you may be success in releasing your emotions. Thus your emotions release then and there even before posting the letter in the post. However, after writing the letter, if you don't want to post the letter, you may drop the idea of posting it. It is no matter whether you post the letter or torn and throw away. The aim of writing the letter is only to release the emotions.

Next one is meditation which is the best method for bring back the painful emotions on surface so that they can be released. Thus by meditation you can also release the buried emotions. However, meditation is described in chapter twenty in details.

Therefore, don't afraid of your emotions.   Don't run away from them; don't block them and don't fight with them. Generally, people run away from anger and ignore it. Therefore, do not afraid of your anger rather welcome the anger and all other painful emotions, feel them and own them. The more you ignore the painful emotions, the bigger they grow.

Actually, emotions dissipate and disappear, if you feel them. Therefore, go deeply within yourself and feel the emotions and own them. Thus live with emotions just a snake charmer live with snakes. Concentrate on your emotion such as—"I am angry" or "I am hurt" and accept them. Once you find your emotion then describe it to yourself rather than pushing it back. Don't ignore or avoid it rather hold it and own it.

This concentration, acceptance and staying with the emotion, in fact, will allow you to feel the emotion. Actually, feeling the emotion means that you are enduring the pain. As you start enduring the pain, you begin to integrate this emotion into your conscious and this leads you towards releasing the emotion. Moreover, after releasing the buried emotions you feel very light, fresh and comfortable.

Thus, release all your hurt, guilt, anger and rage which are buried inside you due to being mistreated in the past. May be some emotions take couple of years for releasing but release them. Therefore, don't lose your patience and continue your process for releasing them. Thus use the means for releasing the emotions whatever suits to your personality but release them definitely. The buried emotions are invisible enemies which have to be overcome. Moreover, without releasing them, you cannot experience happiness and bliss.

Chapter 6
Absorb in the work

"For any sorrow there is only one medicine; better and more reliable than all the drugs in the world; work!"—Ferine Malnor.

Life is the series of events. Some events give us joy and happiness while some others give pain and grief. After facing of such event which provides grief, being emotional, the human being remains in gloomy mood for long periods. He loses interest in daily activities and job's work. He does not want to meet friends, relatives and all other people of surroundings so he prefers aloneness. Some people who does not cope with the grief, become depressive. Thus, the grief and depression affect the work in many ways.

Actually, we think that after improving our mental condition, we will start working. Thus we wait for long time so that we may regain our mental health. Days, weeks even months pass but our wait never ends. Therefore, it is better to start working rather than waiting. If we start working, our mental condition improves automatically. Actually, absorption in work helps you to stable your mind which breaks the cycle of negative thinking. After ceasing the negative thoughts, your anguish also starts to reduce. Then after some time your negative thoughts are replaced by positive thoughts that is, in fact, base of the improvement of overall well-being.

Therefore, the work is an antidote for grief and depression. In the words of George Bernard Shaw, "The secret of being miserable is to have the leisure to bother about whether you are happy or not. So don't bother to think about it. Get busy. It is the cheapest kind of medicine that is on the earth and one of the best. To break this worry habit there is the rule keeping busy the worried person must lose himself in action lest to wither to despair". Therefore, start doing from whatever you can do easily rather than sitting idle. Thus, doing something is enough to increase your mental stability.

How does the grief affect the work?

Actually, workplace is the site where we spend a considerable amount of time of our life. However, when some bad event happens suddenly which creates grief, we are disturbed completely. Our mental health and physical health also affected by this grief which further impact on our work performance. After passing the mourning period, we have to return to the work again. This is the time when not only we have to cope with our personal loss but we have to adjust also with the superiors, subordinates and colleagues at our work place. In addition, we must perform our duty for which we are paid.

However, the early days, weeks, or even months may be very difficult. The effects of grief on the work depend on the attitude and inner strength of the griever. Thus journey through grief is a highly individual experience. Grief can have a major impact on our work. Grief affects the person's thinking which disturb the concentration of the individual. However, concentration is the key factor of our life. Thus lack of concentration further affects the accuracy and quality of the work. Therefore, performance of griever diminishes.

Actually, in depression and grief, the mind is always remained in thinking process, perceiving something different which makes the individual confused. In confusion, the individual cannot take correct decisions and the difficulty with making of decisions makes it harder to deal with job tasks, and eventually decrease the productivity. Thus, working more slowly than usual, low work performance, low quality of work, feeling tired at work, laziness and inaccuracy in work make griever more irritated.

In addition, gloomy mood can make it hard to manage the work responsibilities. Thus sadness, irritability or emotional numbness makes it harder to do the job satisfactory. As griever becomes short-tempered as the colleagues either start avoiding him/her or a frequent conflicts start with the colleagues due to irritated mood of griever. Thus griever is derived from a good teamwork and thus, the workplace become less supportive. The inefficiency of workplace further impacts on griever's personal life, and his/her energy starts depleting, and therefore, a vicious circle starts. Thus work becomes burden for grievers and he/she deprive from enjoying the work.

Thus, reduced energy level and disrupted sleep make it difficult to keep up with the job demands, and physical symptoms may further undermine workplace performance. Due to the unending vicious circle, depression stretches for long duration and becomes more sever. However, if a person experiences the depression intensely for a long period, it labels clinical depression.

On the contrary, some people throw themselves into work as a distraction to their grief. They work as longer hours without any break or very fewer breaks. Thus, they become compulsive workaholic which is a potential dangerous coping strategy. However, by doing this, they want to forget their grief but this workaholic habit pushes them towards another type of problems. Thus instead of getting well, they spoil their health.

Additionally, work addicts or workaholics have been shown to experience higher levels of family conflicts because workaholics usually, avoid the family responsibilities. Thus the actions which do not felt by heart but done superficially only for passing the time leads towards more problems. Thus it is necessary to cultivate interest in work so that grieving can be completed in natural way without interruption of work performance.

How to cultivate interest in work

When an unexpected grief befalls on you or you are hurt very much, you lose your hope and enthusiasm. Even you start to hate your life; you don't want to live more. You consider yourself such a worthless fellow who has no purpose in life to live further. Even some of grievers try to commit suicide. You start to avoid the day-to-day activities, domestic activities and other activities which related to your workplace. Your shrinking from work makes you lazy. Thus due to the habit of laziness, procrastination and being too depressed, you cannot concentrate to particular activities which push you towards more problems mentioned above.

Therefore, in order to avoid these problems, you have to cultivate interest in work and have to create the desire to live. However, there is no meaning in living without hope and enthusiasm, and no meaning to do the work without passion and dedication. So, get up and kick the self-motivation. Instead of suffering and feeling uncomfortable due to laziness; weak desires; lack of self-confidence and inner strength, it would be much better to fill your mind with positive stuff. Then positive thoughts enable you to produce sufficient inner strength and motivation to take action and do things.

Actually, motivation and enthusiasm function as divinely force that pushes you to take action. This will make you feel much better and satisfied. Laziness and passivity cause sorrow, weakness and lack of satisfaction while enthusiasm and activeness bring a sense of joy and inner strength. By getting motivated, you start doing activities which take your mind away from problems and difficulties, and increase your attention in certain activity. In addition, when your enthusiasm grows, you will able to push yourself to greater things.

Thus, start from small or unimportant activities which you usually avoid doing so far. Thus, first of all, leave your bed or switch off the TV and move somewhere else. Go for walking or play with kids or pets. Start from light activities such as gardening or cleaning; dusting the shelves or racks and other gadgets in the house etc. You may rearrange your wardrobe, book shelves, drawers or you may do some other activities according to your hobby. Doing such activities may help you to increase your faith, ability, confidence and inner strength.

Actually, when this happens, you will possess the ability to focus on what you want to do and awaken the energy you need. In the situation of grief and depression, the only will power is not enough. Therefore, in order to engage in further activities, you have to seek any purpose or goal in life. Therefore, search any goal oriented activity and obsess yourself with productively obsessions. Generally, obsession is used in negative form, and your mind is already filled with lot of such unproductively obsessions.

Unwanted obsessions arise because human beings are anxious creatures. Our negative thoughts keep cycling repeating to the beat of anxiety and produce obsessions. We obsess about some trivial matter in the work, home or elsewhere. We remain anxious for such future happenings out of them ninety five percent events never happen. Thus we remain worry without any reason and filled our mind with lot of anxieties.

Actually, our mind which ought to be ours, but it has been stolen by a great thief—anxiety. Thus, we have to take our mind back from anxiety. The iron itself use for cutting another piece of iron. The obsession is double edge sword so we have to use the obsession for taking back our mind. Mind cannot remain vacant and it always requires some stuff for generating and nurturing thoughts. So replace the stuff of negative thoughts with the stuff of positive thoughts.

Thus obsession can do a work miraculously in another way also for recovering our mental health. Actually, we obsess our mind about things which we want to happen or which we don't want to happen. For example, if we want to a new job or promotion, we can fill these thoughts in our mind. On other hand, if we don't want to be ill, we can fill our mind with healthy thoughts, and the obsession will work in both ways. This type of obsession is called productively obsession.

Thus, consciously creating and actively nurturing productive obsession amount to the very best solution for the problems that so many people are experiencing today such as—easily distracted, starting things and then losing interest etc. Turning mere interest into obsessions is a process that by its nature ignite your passion, is amongst the most important keys to self-motivation. So fill your mind with productively obsession which is an antidote of anxiety and grief.

Actually, we are creature of habit; the brain organizes life into pattern and behaving in order to process life more efficiently. When you change your context and activate different parts of your brain, you tap different part of thinking and you see yourself things from new angles and you get fresh insight. Therefore, change your thinking; change your routine; add any new hobby in your schedule; accept something challenging task; do something new and seek new experiences and compel yourself to pay more attention in particular activities.

Thus you may able to eliminate your weakness which drain your energy, and make feel you depleted; cheerless and hopeless. After eliminating your weakness, you may focus on developing and growing your inner strength. Inner strength is a fuel for your work. Anyhow, once your schedule returns back on its previous track, you may achieve your lost reputation and lead towards dedication.

Dedication to Selfless work brings happiness:

Actually, action leads us towards happiness and peace while inaction leads towards depression. It is also said in *Bhagwad Gita* that we can achieve peace and happiness if we devoted to selfless work. On the contrary, some people renounce the work and go in lonely places or in jungles to attain the peace. They think that work brings stress while truth is just opposite because the work eliminate the stress. Actually, they themselves invite stress because they wish the fruition of their work instantly. They resist things going against their wishes, and they forget that result of any activity is beyond their control. Thus when they cannot get expected result of any activity, they invite stress.

Anyhow, when you expect the fruition of your action, it will impact negatively on the results. Thus, in duration of work if your focus remains on result, then your concentration on work may shift and you remain unable to perform the work whole heartedly. Thus, due to lack of concentration, the result will be affected. Therefore, instead of focusing on the result of an action, concentrate only on activity rather than on fruition.

The Cosmic Forces work to the supplement of our effort so no needs to worry about result rather concentrate on the action. In the words of Ramakrishna Pramahansa, "Perform your duties in an unselfish spirit. Always try to perform your duties without desiring any result and without any expectation. So do your work and surrender the result to God because work is in your hands, not the result".

It is true that sometimes we do not get the result of our efforts according to our will. It does not mean that our efforts have been wasted. No, efforts never waste. It will definitely work one way or another so need not to be frustrated. It means either time has not yet come for fruition or God has some better plan for us beyond our understanding. So do your work and leave rest upon God. This is also the theme of *Bhagwad Gita* that human being should only perform the duty and forgets about its fruition.

Thus such selfless work leads us toward peace of mind and happiness while who works with selfish motive, being attached to the fruit of actions through desire, get frustration. Therefore, devote yourself in the selfless work without any expectation.

In addition, we cannot predict what is going to happen in the future. Who knows that consequences of any effort which seem bad now may prove good for us in future? Our destiny is the result of our previous thoughts, deeds and their chain reactions known as the theory of cause and effect' or law of *karma*. The theory of cause and effect is so subtle that slightest invisible variation in the cause can shift the effect which again can change the consequences in long term.

Therefore, it is impossible to predict whether the result is good or bad because we do not know all variables of cause and effect' which make the system too complicated to understand. Thus, instead of trying to understand this complex system of cause and effect', it is the better to accept the result of an action with calm mind whatever the result may be. In other words, live each day as it comes without analyzing the events because law of *karma* never fails rather it will manifest definitely sooner or later.

Thus forget about fruition, and perform your duty with dedication. Actually it is true that devoted to one's work leads individual towards happiness and joy. Here, I would like to mention the result of a study conducted in Kansas State University. The researchers found that the employees who are invigorated and dedicated have a happier life. The researchers studied how positive work experiences extend into family life and facilitate family interactions. They found that the employees who are engaged in their work, which includes higher levels of vigor more dedication and absorption in daily activities, have better mood and satisfaction.

The research team involved Clive Fullagar ,professor of psychology; Satoris Culbertson, assistant professor of psychology and Maura Mills, graduate student in psychology, Manhattan concluded the following results. "Our research indicated that individuals who were engaged in positive experiences at work and who shared those experiences with significant others perceived themselves as better able to deal with issues at home, become better companions and become more effective overall in the home environment," Said Culbertson.

The researchers tracked 67 extension agents for two-week period to determine the relationship between daily work engagement and work-to-family facilitation. The participants responded to two daily surveys, one at the end of their workday and the other immediately before going to bed for the night. They also completed a separate survey prior to the start of two-week period and another after daily data collection had ended.

Culbertson said stress at work and stress at home interact in ways that affect outcomes in both domains. The study suggested that engagement is significantly related to daily mood, and mood also is positively correlated with work-family facilitation. The researchers found that both work engagement and work to family facilitation vary considerably day- to- day.

"One's work can facilitate things at home to a different extant depending on that particular day," Culbertson said.

The researchers also found that daily work engagement had a positive effect on family life. Heavy or light work hours were not a factor. Culbertson stressed that engagement refers to positive work involvement rather than more negative forms of job involvement like work holism and work addiction, which differ in their efforts on home lives.

Work addicts or workaholics have been shown to experience higher levels of work-family conflict. On the contrary, the study of research team showed that higher levels of engagement were related to higher levels of work-family facilitation rather than conflict.

It is evident from above research that devoted to work leads us toward happiness and peace. Elbert Hubbard also said, "Get happiness out of your work or you may never know what happiness is". Thus we should enjoy the work rather than its fruit. Thus, devotion to work makes your each and every moment worth, and you may enjoy your life fully. So enjoy the process rather than keeping your eyes on goal. Love your work; absorb in your work; enjoy it and make it celebration. If your work becomes your hobby then not a single day in your life you feel tired doing the work because working with dedication gives you energy rather than sucking.

On the contrary, if you focus only to the fruit of the action, then whatever the outcome may be your happiness will be for short period. After few days you again feel emptiness in your life, and your life becomes mundane again. Then you again desire to achieve something new, and again focus on the new goal rather than work..........and so on. This process will carry on throughout life over and over again but you cannot get long-lasting happiness and peace. Thus you remain unsatisfied because you always miss to enjoy the work or process

This process is termed 'destination addiction' by Dr. Robert Holden, Founder of the United Kingdom's Happiness Project—a Research and Training Institute. He defines it succinctly as "Living in the not now" but a preoccupation with finding satisfaction "tomorrow".

Thus, long-lasting happiness and peace can be attained only through selfless work. The Dalai Lama also says," Happiness is not something ready-made. It comes from your own actions". Moreover, any ordinary person can experience this happiness and peace if he/she is devoted to his/her work. In addition, if you focus on your work rather than its fruit; enjoy the work and absorbed in it, perfection will come spontaneously.

What is Karmyoga and How to be a *Karmyogi?*

A person who performs one's duty without expecting the fruition of action is known *Karmyogi*. *Bhagwad Gita* says, "To action alone have you a right and never at all to its fruits; let not the fruition of action be your motive, neither let there be in you any attachment to inaction". In other words *Karmyogi* involved fully in actions when performing them without being attached to the fruition of actions.

Generally, it is said that *karmyoga* is the most effective way to progress in spiritual life while it is equally true that spirituality is the necessary ingredient to become a *Karmyogi*. Both are complementary to each other. Though the *Karmyogi* does not seek any personal benefit in his/her actions, selfless motives bring happiness and peace in his/her life spontaneously.

In the words of Vinoba Bhave, "A Karmyogi by giving up fruition of his actions does not lose it but paradoxically enough gets it". On the other hand, selfish motive brings unhappiness. *Bhagwad Gita* says, "Work done with selfish motives is very inferior to selfless service or *karmyoga*. Therefore be *Karmyogi*, O Arjuna. Those who seek to enjoy the fruitions of their work are verily unhappy because one has no control over the results".

Mahatma Gandhi said in the context of action and its fruit that it is the action, not the fruit of the actions that's important. You have to do the right things. It may not be in your power, may not be in your time, that there will be any fruit. In other words, he emphasized on actions and the right means to perform them rather than results.

The *Bhagwad Gita* further says, "Offering the fruits of actions to God, the *Karmyogi* attains everlasting peace in the form of God realization. Thus, those who realize the God through their work are true *Karmyogi*.

Therefore, absorb in your work whole heartedly and learn to enjoy in actions rather than expecting the fruits. If we start to enjoy the work then each and every moment of the work become celebration. This celebration will be long-lasting because it is the celebration of actions rather than fruits.

Here, I want to illustrate it with my own experience. During the writing of the book, I absorb in writing. This absorption of writing brings me in such blissful state which is beyond explanation. Thus I feel writing as *Samadhi (last* stage of *Patanjli yoga sutra* is described in chapter 21). The bliss feel in writing emanates from action which I feel deep dawn within me.

Thus, writing is the source of happiness and infinite joy for me rather than earning the money, fame etc. Actually, the main purpose of yoga is to attain peace and bliss. Here, the same purpose is being done by absorbing in writing or it can be said that in dedication to work. Thus the peace and bliss attain by work is known as *Karmyoga* and those who dedicated in their work and worship it, are *Karmyogi.* Thus when you do your work with dedication, naturally the outcome of the work will be very nice.

However, my belief about *Karmyogi* is beyond the theoretical definition. I believe that when a person acts with selfless motive and involved in his/her actions with whole-heartedly, spontaneously he/she attains such high stage of spirituality that the actions convert his/her misfortune into fortune. Mean to say, when you perform your work dedicatedly, Divine power remains present with you and contribution of Divine is more in the performance of your work, and you get miraculous results. Such spiritual person is known as *Karmyogi*. It means to become a *Karmyogi;* you have to be dedicated in your actions selflessly.

Actually, throughout my life, I remained absorb in my work in such a way that the experiences I experienced are unbelievable. However, one thing is sure that if you take the work in your hand with whole heartedly how much it may be difficult; it will be completed in a miraculous way. Thus the proverb is true that "put cotton wool on spinning wheel and spin first yarn then God will complete your whole spinning". Actually, any work done with determination, efforts, inner strength and persistence, definitely accomplish in miraculous way because it always supported by Invisible Power known as 'Devin's roll'.

Moreover, in all our accomplishments, the Divine's roll is always more than we think. So need not to be worry about result. Only do your work and leave rest upon God. God is invisible guide and companion to help us in completing our actions. God bless only those people who effort. In this context, Aeschylus says, "When one is willing and eager, the gods join in". Therefore, we should devote to work. The devotion to work leads towards bliss spontaneously.

It is not the matter what is the nature of work, whether it is interested or mundane. According to Mihaly Cishszentmihalyi, "It does not seem to be true that work necessarily needs to be unpleasant. It may always have to be hard, or at least harden than doing nothing at but there is ample evidence that work can be enjoyable, and that indeed, it is often the most enjoyable part of life".

Therefore, mundane work also may become interested if we feel enjoy doing it. For example, at the time of washing the dishes, you may play with the bubbles and you will never notice the time when the washing has been completed. Therefore, if you involve in the work; absorb in it and devoted in it, the work will become hobby for you which you never feel doing.

When we absorb in any activity wholeheartedly, we forget the time, even we forget ourselves. Moreover, forgetting the time and self is the state of 'being' which is not less than bliss. So seek bliss via *Karmyoga* means through dedication in work. Thus, absorb in your work and be a *Karmyogi*.

I would like to close the chapter with the following lines of Buddha, "Your work is to discover your work and these with all your heart to give yourself to it. Meditate. Live purely. Be quiet. Do your work with mastery; like the moon come out from behind the clouds. Shine!"

Chapter 7
Transform the grief into spirituality

"The soul that is without suffering does not feel the need of knowing the ultimate cause of Universe. Sickness, grief and hardship—are all indispensable elements in the spiritual ascent"—Anandymoyi.

Grief is a necessary ingredient for spiritual growth. In the words of William Penn, "There is no pain, no balm; no thorns, no throne; no gall, no glory; no cross, no crown". As diamond polished with friction and gold purify by heated in furnace, Man become real human beings when they go through trails. After facing such experiences their life become better, not bitter. According to Buddhist Monk Mathieu Richard, happiness is a way of being and experiencing the world—a profound fulfillment that suffers every moment and endures despite inevitable setbacks.

Thus after experiencing of grief and enduring its pain, we become like pebbles which turned beautiful only after they were caught in the arms of pitiless waves of river, tossed and rolled, rubbed together on the way of the river. Thus friction turned the piece of simple stone in to a beautiful pebble. Therefore, you can say that suffering is the medium for transforming us into bliss. So without experiencing the grief and enduring its pain, it is almost impossible to elevate ourselves to the higher stages of spirituality.

Actually, the moments of suffering we experience in our life mound us the most. There is no doubt that during the suffering period we feel vulnerable. However, after enduring the pain, we realized that it was the time before the dawn of the day. Actually, just before the daybreak, the darkness of night increases. Thus, intensity of darkness is the ray of hope which reminds us that dawn of the day is not very far. Therefore, we should remain optimist at the time of grief in our life. However, this optimistic attitude helps us in enduring the pain and eventually leads us towards spirituality. Thus, only after experiencing the grief, we may able to know the value of happiness.

In the words of Anne Bradstreet, "If we have no winter, the spring would not be so pleasant; if we did not sometimes taste the adversity, prosperity won't be so welcome." So without experiencing the darkness, brightness cannot be recognized. Thus these ups and downs are indistinguishable parts of our life. In this context, Robert Byrne said that winter is Nature's way of saying, "Up yours". Thus, transformation in human beings emerges from grief.

Grief changes the temperament of human beings

Grief spares no one else but how to deal with it is the choice of the individual. After happening of big event such as bereavement of spouse or kid, griever becomes a changed person. In spite of accepting the event; coping with the grief; resuming the routine activities and office work, we are something different person than we were the person before the event happened. Mean to say, our personality becomes something different after experiencing the grief.

Thus, how much we try to be same, we can never the same. Though we meet the friends and relatives; attend the programs or celebrate the festivals, functions etc., we are something different. It is no matter that how much we visited at tourist places or religious places in order to resuming our normal behavior or attitude but we are never the same person. Even changing the residences and jobs over and over again cannot help us to become same person. However, we still survive and live the life but with a changed temperament.

Actually, after some days or weeks, the people who were accompanied you or consoled you at the time of suffering get back to their own lives. How much you try to normalize latterly but you feel that you have been abandoned. Then you start feeling lonely and you realize that no one is around you to support emotionally. These lonely moments are such critical moments when you start introspecting. Then you truly realize that you have lost something very precious that cannot be reclaimed.

In other words, your support system has been withdrawn when you need emotional support the most. However, till then most of your supporter have been gone and those who are still present with you, they advise you to 'overcome the grief' and get on usual life. Actually, they don't want to listen your same story over and over again. Thus, your network of friends and relatives start avoids calling and meeting you, and you have been almost deserted. Then you become compel to live alone.

Actually, bereavement never really ends because there is no 'certain' length of time for it. It is not a simple process which you complete after crossing all the way and able to come other bright side and get back on with life. Loss remains stay in your unconscious mind and continuous to permeate long after it first happened. You may forget the grief for a particular time—when you surrounded the people when they make you feel happy.

However, the sadness triggered again by certain occasions such as—on seeing the photo album; on visiting to particular place; at particular time or date; on watching particular movie or TV program, listening particular song; hearing particular dialogue or word etc. Even familiar smell related to deceased can trigger you sadness. Mean to say, you never stop missing the person you lost. However, fortunately, if you get enough emotional support, you may come back to your life's track and regain happiness again. Otherwise, you may trap in the associated effects of grief such as sadness and depression.

Thus, if you are not able to get right support to come back on life's track, grief which has been considered overcome can shake everything up—your belief, your personality and even your reality. It is a turning point in your life because it is such a critical situation when any griever can shatter. Anyway, there are two paths emerge from this point. One goes towards clinical depression which further leads to many other problems which are by-product of clinical depression while second path goes towards spirituality.

Unresolved grief may become clinical depression which is more severe than grief.

Moreover, choice of the path is entirely depend on the inner strength and nature of the individual. Thus, the journey of the suffering is experienced differently by each one according to his or her personality. Generally, people believe that grief is more severe than clinical depression. They think that depressed person will come back on the track spontaneously after few days. However, the reality is just opposite because depression demands strong will power and inner strength for its recovery otherwise depression may push the griever towards dead end.

Whilst, grief is not a disease or mental disorder; it is a normal emotional response to a significant loss and there is no any loss of self-esteem. Numbness in initial stage and afterwards sadness is natural so clinical treatment is not required in grieving. It must go on its own course if grievers have some patience and tolerance. However, instead of having patience, if you try to take shortcut to complete grieving, the process will be interrupted and you may entangle in various problems.

On the other hand, depression is clinical disorder, a physiological chemical imbalance in the brain. The mind filled with obsession of low sense of self, and the depressed person think about committing the suicide. It is often treated with medication, and sometimes psychotherapy is also required. Thus, if your thoughts are changing rapidly; you don't feeling able to get up from bed; you spend too much time unnecessary in the bathroom and other lonely places, you have reached at the stage of depression. Means, you became depressed because these all symptoms are generally notice in depressed person. In addition, if you don't want to get to the work; do not eat properly; sleeping schedule is being disturbed completely and neglects yourself especially in dressing and appearances, these all are also sign of depression.

In depression, you want to live alone and avoid meeting to friends and relatives and shrinking to face even small problems. Thus do not ignore these symptoms because you are moving towards clinical depression. Thus you need help of professional psychotherapist so don't hesitate to consult the professional. Actually, depression is hidden disease in which you seem well but actually you are not well. Your whole temperament has been changed silently. Thus in depression neither your mind nor your body is well.

Whatever we think and feel, in fact, has direct effect on our biological system. So accept the reality that you are suffering from a clinical depression and don't shy to seek help. In the words of Sigmund Freud, "In grief, the world looks poor and empty while in depression, the person feels poor and empty".

Grief as means to spirituality

Unfortunately the grief is deeply painful but it leads towards bright side also which is, in fact, spiritual aspect. Actually, it is the only a ray of hope which brings out you from the darkness of grief. It can also be said that suffering is the entry gate to the spirituality. Therefore, you should look to the bright side of suffering and choose the second path which goes towards spirituality and ends nowhere. Mean to say, this path goes up to the infinity so you can enjoy this blissful state throughout your life.

Thus the grief enables you to let go and embrace new beginnings and opportunities. It can also discover strengths you did not realize you possess them. The grief can also enable you to spend time focusing on things that really matter to you rather than unnecessary things. Above all, after facing the grief, you may found yourself more sympathetic, compassionate and kind to others which are actually foundation of the spirituality.

Anyhow, first of all, it is very necessary to know about the spirituality. Spirituality is a sense of connection to Bigger Power than us and it involves a search for meaning in life. Spiritual experience may be described sacred or deep sense of aliveness and interconnectedness. According to Ruth Beckmann Murray and Judith Procter Zenter, "The spiritual dimension tries to be in harmony with the Universe, and strives for answers about the infinite, and comes to focus when the person faces emotional stress, physical illness or death". It means spirituality is a search for meaning, purpose and direction in life.

Actually, grief is milestone in human's life. After facing the big grief, we try to cope with its pain by all means, and most of them are external. Though we success to some extent, the external means prove unreliable and impermanent. How much we try to fill up our dissatisfaction by consuming the materialistic things, we remain dissatisfied even we feel more discontent and emptiness. The happiness which we get by external means has been rightly coined as "stock market happiness". However, the sufferer ultimately turns towards spirituality.

Thus, crushing the grief may well force you into spirituality. You may challenge or question your faith or religion beliefs. You may angry at God even you may deny the existence of God. Thus you reach at such unprecedented stage where you feel that life has no meaning and you feel emptiness. Then some questions related to your grief arise—such as why did this particular event happen to me? Was the event a coincidence or was it part of my destiny? Is my destiny predetermined? Could the event be prevented? Thus, so many unanswerable questions arise in your mind.

Therefore, you try to seek the answers of the above questions. Sometimes you are in mood of denying any Supreme Power while sometimes you include the prayer in your process as you feel the need and desire for it. Actually, due to lack of your mind stability, your thoughts change frequently. Anyway, when you start introspecting yourself then not only you gain your mental stability but you realize peace also. In fact, this is the beginning of spirituality. Anyway, after experiencing the feelings of contentment in above process as you go more within yourself, you turn completely towards spirituality. Actually, suffering is a mental phenomenon while spiritual practice is a means to transform your mind which involves a holistic appreciation of Cosmos in which everyone and everything is connected seamlessly with everyone and everything.

Thus, spiritual practice is the wise way to regain mental health and it provides an emotional support for survival when everything else seems to have failed. Therefore, when one realizes that external world is ephemeral, temporary, and ever changing then individual seeks permanent happiness and peace internally. So the sufferer dives within deep inside and found an inner realm which is still, timeless and indestructible termed as 'Soul or self'. Therefore, spirituality is the one and only one way to diminish the suffering what you have been experiencing for a long period.

Actually, spirituality helps you gain mental stability, and freedom from external sources. It realizes you that there is something beyond mere outer appearances of the five senses. Thus, sufferer meet with 'Self' and able to attain peace within himself or herself. Actually, it was the grief which leads you towards deep inside yourself. So without suffering, we would not turn towards spirituality. Moreover, once we start living the life spiritually, everything of the material worlds seems superficial.

What is Spiritual Awakening?

Actually, your mind is racing very fast and you are thinking incessantly without awareness. Mean to say, you are thinking continuously but you are not aware about your thoughts. You are not aware whether your thoughts are positive or negative; whether they are necessary or waste. You are not aware of their effects on your body and mind. You are not aware how much your energy is being wasted in your thinking. Actually, continuous streams of thoughts generally have repetitive nature. Thus you are identified with your thoughts.

Anyhow, you have had a sudden first time glimpse of awareness or presence of your thinking and you become conscious about your thinking—known as awakening. Mean to say; now you are fully conscious and aware moment to moment what is happening around you and within you. Moreover, the moment when you get that awareness at first time that is exactly awakening. It is also known as spiritual awaking. Before spiritual awakening, your identity was only your intellectual faculty such as reasoning, cognition, consciousness, memory, thinking, judgment, etc. In other words, you have been identified yourself with your mind so far.

However, you have just dived within yourself where there is no mind rather there is vacuum. Thus, now you are fully aware of your thoughts, and you have realized that now you are not identified with your mind. However, you have experienced a realm of your being which is deep within you, and that realm is much still, vibrant alive and more significant than thoughts. It means, now the incessant voice ornoisein your mind has been ceased because you have entered in eternal vacuum. Actually, this vacuum is your Soul which is itself a center of bliss and its circumference is nowhere.

Actually, spiritual awakening is sometimes a single event that miraculously changes one's life in an instant. In general terms, a spiritual awakening is an altered state which is beyond intellect. Moreover, it is the moment when your soul awakens to new awareness, a new perception and a real world. As you have just awakened from the sleep of ignorance, thus from today onwards you will be known as awaken person or *budh*. Thus, spiritual awakening is the spark that ignites your long buried ancient spirit within you.

According to Steve Gunn, a metaphysical practitioner, "A spiritual awakening is a process of considerable inner change that some people will go through where there entire being, consciousness and intuitive abilities ascend to another—higher level of energy and awareness. As an experience it can, and most often will be profound and disturbing with little or no feeling of control and most often no idea what's actually happening".

Thus, the awakening is the moment when the confused and frightened self-transcendence to a higher consciousness an awareness full of love and peace. Though awakening and enlightenment both seem the same, they are not same. An enlightened person may grasp the idea spiritually. Mean to say, ones require spiritual practice in order to attain enlightenment. Whilst, spiritual awakening is allowing oneself to be open and inviting the living spirit of god and the love of god to enter ones heart and its realization arises suddenly from nowhere.

In other words, it is the moment when the very deep layer of your unconscious opens to your consciousness and brings about the depth and breadth of the glory of God within you .Thus, the arousal of the spirit within begins with the deep realization that God does indeed live within your own Soul. It can also be said that your true Self is not different from God because the kingdom of God is within you. Therefore, single moment of awakening is so powerful, so magnificent that removes your confusion, and enables you to enter in a 'state of certainty' which transforms you in the state of peace, joy and bliss.

Grief may be the catalyst for spiritual awakening

Unfortunately grief, any emotional trauma or near death experience are very painful but all these experiences can become catalyst for awakening.

Thus severe suffering or any other critical situation that pushes a person to the limit of his or her endurance may also become the means by which an awakening can begin. Our emotions originate from our mind which is, in fact, software of our brain. Actually, during suffering our emotions are at the peak which affects the chemical and electric charges that flow through our body including brain.

Thus, the right combination of those charges activates the certain part of the brain which leads towards awakening. That's why most of the great personalities are awaken during their suffering period or hard time. Thus intensity of grief is directly proportion to spiritual awakening. In addition, turning to God is common whenever a person goes through an ordeal, feels helpless, or shaken. Thus tragedy or agony of grief can be channel that increases awareness which help in occurrence of awakening. It is not necessary that every grieved awakens but the chances of awakening are increased during suffering period.

Anyhow, grief cannot be avoided but after occurrence of the tragedy, fortunately if you get the spark of true awakening, your inner world transforms completely. Peace and love replace the old stuff such as—limiting beliefs, fears and other emotional toxins. However, all five senses of hearing, sight, touch smell and taste can be increased with awakening.

In addition, new creative talents, telepathy and precognition ability are also increased. Fears are also reduced and our entire being is infused with the beauty of the Nature. Negative emotions are replaced by positive emotions. Thus not only our mind becomes fresh but we start to feel more energetic than ever. Wastage of energy ceases thus energy can be restored. In addition, Psychic healing takes place and a feeling of tranquility affects many areas of your behavior.

How does spiritual practice bring bliss?

Spirituality is not the end but it is the means to reach the end. It can also be said that it is the means to achieve the bliss. When you start living spiritually, your positive aspects also go upwards. As your spiritual practice increases so the positive traits increase. In spirituality, you feel more content, more peaceful and more open-hearted and compassionate. You experience more guidance and support of Devine; feeling more joy and grace; receiving new insights and going deeper in self-understanding.

Thus in spirituality, you experience more cosmic co-incidences even it seems that whole universe is being governed for you. Moreover, you feel deeper connectedness with spirit and with all life. The spiritual life is just differs from materialism world. Love and affection take over the sexual desire, and faith take over the doubts. In spirituality, your personal problems and difficulties are reduced to minimum level so you can spare more time related to your duty and social work. Due to ceasing of vague thoughts, your much energy is being saved and you feel more energetic.

Therefore, in spiritual life, being more confident and courageous, you don't accept injustice. Being a spiritual person, you face each and every tragedy with calm mind. Thus you always choose the right path even accept the difficulties and challenges happily whatever comes in your path. Now you are beyond the state of fear, violence and struggle. Additionally, you are growing into a more enlightened state of being which is characterized by unity, peace, co-operation, compassion and harmony. Thus your insight enhances and your all prejudices come to end.

As you practice more, as your clarity increases more and your true nature emerges. Actually, true nature is the real Self which is the beyond duality such as— good and bad; loss and profit; honor and dishonor; etc. It is the state of beyond sorrow. In such state of tranquility, you become able to maintain the equilibrium in day-to-day difficulties of your life and during any other adversity. Now you are moving in this world without developing any attachment to the objects and persons. Now you are a spiritually evolved personality. Such state of perfection can be attained after facing all ups and downs of the life.

Therefore, suffering leads us to the peak of spirituality. In the words of Albert Camus, "In the depth of winter I finally learned that within me there lay an invincible summer". As you ahead more on spiritual journey, you get more miraculous experiences. Whilst you are on the path, you can encounter ever expanding pools of bliss as you learn what constitutes a life of joy and contentment, free from worry and suffering.

Thus, now you are connected to a healthy energy and live your life effortlessly in the flow without any resistance. Now you live your life in the present without fear for the future, and you are feeling of gratitude for yourself and those around you. Thus, much energy is being saved that can be used for other higher purposes. Naturally, these all factors help you connect the whole Universe; in fact, this state of being is not less than bliss.

I would like to close the chapter with the extract of the letter of Tibetan Buddhist Lama Zopa Rinpoche which he wrote to a depressed student who was contemplating suicide.

Assailed by afflictions, we discover *dharma*.

And find the way to liberation. Thank you, evil forces!

When sorrow invades the mind, we discover *Dharma*.

And find the unchanging way. Thank you, adversity.

Through being impelled to by others, we discover *Dharma*.

And find the essential meaning. Thank you who drive us on.

Thus, grief is not always brings destruction but it leads us towards bright side of life also which brings bliss for us via spirituality.

PART II

After recovering from the grief, a person starts living the life normally. Thus, in second part of the book, emphasis is given on happy living process such as how to live simple and optimist life. Man's own conceit is the main obstacle in attaining happiness so how to control the ego is also written in this part. Role of self- trust and faith in God in one's life are also theme of this part.

When we become comfortable in one place or one situation, we prefer to remain there. Actually, we don't want to leave this comfort zone due to fear of unknown. Anyhow, if we leave the comfort zone, unknown is ready to welcome us whole-heartedly. So it is also described in this part that how to leave comfort zone and embrace the unknown.

Usually, negative attitude is the main problem in day-to-day activities so it is necessary to develop positive attitude to live happily in this world. So how to develop positive attitude is also described in this part. Generally, we do not observe things we are grateful in everyday life. However, if we notice them mindfully, we will see that these small things make us happy. But we consider them guaranteed therefore, we generally ignore them. Instead of ignoring, if we express our gratitude wherever it requires, our happiness increases manifolds. So, gratitude and appreciation are the key factors for better life which are also described in this part of the book.

Without forgiveness of those who have hurt us is very difficult to attain peace of mind. So how to forgive someone and move further is also theme of this part. Thus, the second part of the book is about how to live in peace and harmony in the modern world.

Chapter 8
Forgive and move on

"Forgiveness is pure happiness."—Martin Luther king

Forgiveness is the most powerful aid for achieving happiness. Generally, we develop ill feelings in our mind for the person who harms us which, in fact, spoil our own health. The insulator injustice which was done once, we remember it again and again. By remembering constantly, we nourish the grievance, thus our suffering is remaining forever. However, instead of mulling over and over again, we should try to forget the bitter experiences and move further. There is a Supreme Power which governs this Universe, and we should have faith in the justice of that invisible power.

According to the philosophy of Epictetus "Forgive others for their misdeeds over and over again, this gesture faster inner peace." Life is an interdependent web therefore tolerance, patience, compassion and sympathy are necessary for our happiness as well as for others' happiness. When we love people, they also attain happiness and joy. Actually, the happiness is also one type of infection which spreads from one man to another and the circumference of the web of happiness becomes wider and wider.

However, this phenomenon of happiness cannot be achieved until we use the principal of forgiveness. According to Buddhism, all sentient beings including our enemies desire happiness and liberation from sorrow so we should forgive our enemies and forget about revenge.

Cherie Carter- Scott New York Times Best Selling author also says "Forgiveness is the act of erasing of emotional debt. As you move towards forgiveness, your heart is already open, and you engage in a conscious and deliberate release of resentment. Then happiness will not be far from your reach".

Thus, instead of looking the shortcomings of anybody, we should see other side of the coin and that is certainly forgiveness. Nobody is perfect in this world and if we seek perfection, we find only one thing and that is unhappiness.

Forgiving, in fact, opens the door of joy and happiness for us. Otherwise if we think regarding revenge, we have to dig two graves one for enemy and another for ourselves. In addition, due to chemical reaction revengeful thoughts poisoned our stream of blood. It can also be said that you cannot burn another house until you burn your own hand.

What is forgiveness?

Some people confuse forgiveness with weakness and condoning hurtful behavior. Experts who study about forgiveness make clear that when you forgive, you don't deny the seriousness of an offence against you. Thus forgiveness doesn't mean condoning excusing offenses.

Forgiveness does not demand you to welcome people back into your life. Though forgiveness can help repair damaged relationship, it doesn't obligate you to reconcile with the person who harmed you. Actually, reconcile requires the reestablishing the trust. Thus when you reconcile, you make an agreement for the future. Therefore, reconcile requires two people while forgiveness requires only one person—you. Thus you can forgive someone without even conversation with the person, and it makes no difference whether you tell that person regarding forgiveness or not.

Generally, forgiveness is mistakenly considered forgetting. Therefore, we are afraid that if we forgive, we will forget the incident and the harm may happen again. On the contrary, to avoid the hurting with hitting against same stone over and over again, you may remember the incident of hurting so that you may remain aware about future happenings. But for the sake of your own health forgiveness is necessary. Thus forgiveness should not be considered forgetting. However, instead of mulling again and again on the same issue, forgive the person who has hurt you, and move further. Now question arises, if forgiveness is neither reconciliation nor forgetting then what is the forgiveness?

Actually, forgiveness is conscious and deliberate decision to release feelings of resentment or vengeance toward a person or group who has harmed you regardless of whether they actually deserve your forgiveness. In other words forgiveness at a minimum is decision to let go of the desire for revenge and ill will towards the person who had hurt you.

In the Bible, the Greek word *aphiemi* translated in English as 'forgive' and literal meaning of forgiveness is 'to let go' because forgiver doesn't demand payment for a debt. We forgive others when we let go of resentment and give up any claim to be compensated for the hurt or loss we have suffered. The Bible teaches that unselfish love is the basis for the forgiveness, since love does not keep account of injury. Thus, forgiveness means letting go of your right to punish another, and choosing through the power of God's love to hold on to the other person rather than his or her offense.

Thus forgiveness is a natural resolution which completes the grieving process. Therefore, forgiveness is the necessary acknowledgement of pain or loss. Psychologist Sonja Lyubomirsky calls forgiveness 'a shift in thinking' toward someone who has wronged you, "Such that your desire to harm that person has decreased and your desire to do him good has increased".

Therefore, the process of forgiving involves acknowledging yourself the wrong that was done to you, reflecting on it, and deciding how you want to think about it. Thus forgiveness is something that depends entirely up to you. Actually, it is your inner response to another's perceived injustice. Moreover, it is also your personal decision about whether to reconcile with the person who is forgiven or whether to maintain a distance.

According to the American Psychological Association, forgiveness is the mental and spiritual process of ceasing to feel resentment and anger against another person for a perceived offense or mistake, and ceasing to demand punishment. In other words, when someone deeply hurt you, he or she owes you a debt; he/she has taken from you your sense of happiness and wholeness. Thus, forgiveness erases that debt and allows the forgiven person the freedom of your generosity.

Thus, it can be concluded from all above definitions that forgiveness is more in favor of forgiver than the person who is forgiven because forgiveness is a decision to let go of resentment and thoughts of revenge. These feelings harm the person who nourishes them. Therefore, it is better to release them in order to maintain your well-being. Otherwise they will destroy your health and peace of mind completely. In other words, forgiveness is self-forgiveness. You are hurting only yourself until you release your vengeful feelings. On the other hand, if you will carry them with you rest of your life, you will never be free from the burden.

Therefore, forgiveness is a sacrifice in the sense that you choose the more difficult path but definitely a positive way which leads you towards joy and happiness. Thus, forgiveness is a beneficial practice for letting go of your own pain. So forgiveness is a valuable gift that you can give to yourself.

Though it is very difficult to forgive, in order to achieve peace of mind it is necessary to forgive. Therefore, don't wait. Don't wait until you find yourself on deathbed. So it isn't too late to forgive someone whether individual is dead or alive makes no difference.

Why is forgiveness so Difficult?

True forgiveness doesn't happen instantly and easily rather it takes time, patience and energy. Actually, letting go is very difficult challenge. It is very easy to say than do. Even I have waited some months to start this chapter because I could not forgive the persons who have hurt me. However, after doing lot of meditation practices, I became able to forgive those persons. Actually, without adapting the practice of forgiveness by myself, I could not write the content freely and impressively. Anyway, I myself realized that forgiveness is really very difficult.

Forgiveness is a process which takes some time to work through our emotional problems before we truly forgive. So forgiving cannot be occurred without completion of this process. Actually, resentment, hate anger etc. are such emotional factor which should be come to end before occurrence of forgiveness. As it has been already written in chapter five that emotions neither can be controlled nor can be they suppressed. Thus for completion of this process, the hurt feeling should be sublimated through proper way and painful suppressed emotions should be released from our unconscious.

Therefore, In the process of forgiving, the first barrier you have to remove is your deep seated avenge, even you yourself are not aware about such revengeful emotions. You have not only to take the decision to let go of the offense but you have to let go the desire to punish the offender also. The bigger the offence, the more challenging it can be let go. But the less you ruminate on the offense and feed your anger, the easier it becomes. The main reason of not forgiving the offender is that most of us assume what if we forgive our offenders, they let of the hook-scot free-and get to go about their merry ways while we unfairly suffer from their actions.

Actually, we wish to harm as we have been harmed. An eye for an eye often feels viscerally satisfying. When we feel satisfaction to punish the offender ourselves or see the offender as helpless and miserable condition, we release our anger in such type of self-satisfaction. Thus, if we lack the power to actual harm, harboring anger may feel like a second-best option. Holding a grudge does in a certain sense feel good. Actually, when someone commits an injustice, we often cease to believe that they are capable to do any good. Thus, we tend to consider them only 'our offenders' rather than human beings.

To be an excessively sensitive is also a reason of not forgiving the offenders. A longitudinal study showed that people who were generally more neurotic, angry and hostile in life were less likely to forgive another person even after a long time had passed. If we still feel harmed at the present—even years after we actually were—we frequently continue to feel angry and it is inherently difficult, if not impossible to forgive someone whom we are still angry.

Generally, it becomes more difficult to forgive the offender when we give more importance of past rather than present. When we do not live in present and ruminate over past, we waste a portion of our energy in lamenting the past. Sometimes we ruminant over our bad days of past while sometimes we are busy in remembering good old days that have been gone forever. That is the reason why we can't be happy and satisfied in the present. However, in order to live happily, we have to forget about past irrespective to its good or bad. What had been happened had happened forever? Even God cannot reverse it.

Thus release your hurtful emotions, forgive those who have hurt you and move on. Actually, you can attain peace only after forgiving. A peaceful person attracts peaceful energy. No doubt that forgiveness is very difficult but living with a grudge is even harder. Keeping grudges can be very dangerous, and can hurt people in ways you might not have imagined. Though forgiveness is very hard, it is sweeter when we reconcile with whom we deeply love. It is hard because it makes us look at our selfishness, our judgment, our expectations and ourselves.

Additionally, the forgiveness is very difficult because we often think more highly of ourselves than we ought to, and it is easy to judge others and be critical of their weaknesses and shortcomings. However self-righteous attitude is a sin that we can be blinded to because we are so focused on what the other person did wrong. The reality in this attitude is worse than the wrong behavior we are judging. The people who do not forget find excuses to talk about what people have done to us.

Thus, if you are holding on to the offence, then you haven't forgiven the person who has hurt you. Actually, the refusal to forgive is a way you resist life. Or you can say that you hold on to your suffering and cling tightly to your past. However, you should not forget that you hold on to not just memories but tensions also. Thus resisting forgiveness is like grasping a hot coal and saying, "I am not going to let go until you apologize and pay for what you have done to me". Thus in our effort to punish, we are the ones who get burned. Therefore, in order to obtain your own happiness, forgive the offenders irrespective to its easiness or hardness.

In the words of Robin Caesarian, "Sometimes forgiving was easy for me; sometimes it was very bold choice. Whatever it was, it always left me happier and free to move on to create healthier relationship with others."

Therefore, how much hard may be the forgiving, bear the hardness and forgive ones who hurt you. Say good-bye to old wounds because by forgiving, you can release yourself from sufferings which have been confining you ever since the event took place.

How does forgiveness improve our well-being?

Actually, forgiveness frees the forgiver from anger and provides peace of mind. Thus the benefits of forgiveness ensue primarily to the person who forgives others. However, boosted mood and reduced resentment help in depression reduction. Therefore, when we forgive, our stress level decreases and people who are more forgiving are protected from negative health effects and stress.

A study at the University of Michigan showed that who do the forgiving, unconditionally linked to well-being even more strongly than did forgiving others who offered apology and express contrition. Thus forgiveness improves our health in many ways.

According to Mayo Clinic, forgiveness brings plenty of health benefits including improved relationships, decrease anxiety and stress, lower blood pressure, a lower risk of depression and stronger immune system and heart health. In addition, the act that hurt or offended you might always remain a part of your life, but forgiveness can lessen its grip on you and help you focus on other more positive parts of your life.

Dr. Robert Enright from the University of Wisconsin-Madison who founded the international Forgive Institute found in his studies that people who forgive others are happier and healthier than those who hold resentments. The first study to look at how forgiveness improves physical health discovered that when people think about forgiving an offender, it leads to improving functioning in their cardiovascular and nervous system.

Another study of the University Wisconsin found, the more forgiving people were the less they suffered from a wild range of illnesses.

The research of Dr. Fred Luskin of Stanford University, and Author of the book *"Learning to Forgive"* presented evidence that forgiveness can be learned based on research projects into the effect of forgiveness, giving empirical validity to the concept that forgiveness is not only powerful, but also excellent for your health.

Whilst when we dwell on our grudges, our blood pressure and heart rate increase which is clear sign of stress which may further damage our body. Holding grudges decrease our immune system, making us less resilient to illness. In other words, the less forgiving people are suffering a greater number of health problems.

Forgiveness enhances compassion and kindness

Researches also suggest that forgiveness not only feel positive towards someone who hurt them but they are also more likely to help others and donate more money to charity, and they feel more connected to other people. Therefore, forgiving others is the only way to break the cycle of violence. And it can be a gift that we give to ourselves in the form of peace that help us going on with life. Even forgiving others is more beneficial to forgivers in another way also that they themselves receiving God's forgiveness for one's own sins.

In three separate studies, including one with Catholics and Protestants from Northern Ireland whose family members were murdered in the political violence, Dr. Luskin found that people who are taught how to forgive become less angry, feel less hurt, are more optimistic, become more forgiving in a variety of situations and become more compassionate and self-confident. Thus his studies show a reduction in experience in stress, physical manifestations of stress and increase in vitality.

Additionally, experts found after research that not only happy people are more likely to forgive but forgiving others can make people happy, especially when they forgive someone to whom they feel close. Thus, letting go of anger and resentment can help us to keep calm and increase our happiness.

Forgiveness allows us to let go pain not by sugarcoating it with positive thoughts, but by allowing our experience to come forward so that we can touch our pain with mercy. Thus in forgiving, we get to know our pain more intimately. Forgiveness asks us to move closer to our suffering, and in doing so, discover a larger, more compassionate part of ourselves that can touch our wounds with kindness and understanding. Thus, forgiveness can lead to feelings of understanding, empathy and compassion for the one who hurt you.

Gradually, we shift away from being someone who is only afraid of pain to become one who is capable of embracing it. As such forgiveness opens the mind to the natural compassion of the heart. In the process, we not only liberate ourselves from that particular moment in time when we suffered our wounds, but we also begin to recognize ourselves as something more than our pain.

From all above studies, it is concluded that the only thing which can release us from the insane grip of a painful past, is forgiveness. Thus, by embracing forgiveness we can also embrace hope, peace of mind, gratitude, joy and happiness.

How to forgive?

In order to forgive, first of all, we must release our suppressed painful and angry emotions. Otherwise suppressed emotions are not only continuously hurting us from inside but they may evolve as time bomb and explode someday. Even they may be burst out to those who have committed no crime against us. Therefore, in order to avoid the innocence people from our irritated attitude, we have to release our suppressed anger with one way or another.

Secondly, we should resist our current angry emotions from suppressing. Thus instead of suppressing the anger, it can be transformed it into compassion and empathy. When you are kind to the people surrounding you and help them selflessly, you feel calm within you. This calmness spontaneously reduces your anger. So expand your compassion and empathy by listening and talking the people even outside your social circle.

In addition, instead of complaining, express gratitude. Expressing gratitude can change your attitude towards the situation and people around you. So be grateful for each and every thing including Nature. Actually, the feelings of resentment decrease in the proportion of higher amounts of gratitude.

If you are still having difficulties for releasing your resentment and forgiving someone, you may seek professional help. Otherwise negative thoughts patterns may affect your health and other aspect of your life. You may consult to any clinical psychologist, or psychotherapist who may help to overcome past hurts and help you in dispelling the negative thoughts pattern which you developed unconsciously. Even you may also take help from spiritual counselors to achieve peace and resolution. However, remember that no one is perfect in his/her profession, so do not hesitate to change the professional. Anyway, find someone with whom you feel comfortable.

Actually, forgiveness is not an occasional act but a long process which comes in stages. We may be able to forgive partially because the roots of anger are deep in our unconscious mind. Though resentment has been taken the form of passion, it is essential to forgive someone for the peace of our mind. How may be the painful of hurting, let it given by someone who is very close to you, it is now only a thought and feeling that you carry around.

In order to forgive, next necessary act is to forget the past event in which you were hurt. For doing this, you have to live in present. When you start living in present moment, most of your sorrows and worries spontaneously cease. Moreover, the best way to live in present is meditation. As you practice meditation, living in present follows. And as much time as you live in present, you become able to go very deep in your unconscious during meditation practice. Both are interrelated and directly proportion to one other or it can be said that living moment to moment in the present is itself meditation.

Therefore, instead of mulling over and over again on the negative thoughts, make some goals which may keep you engage in life and simultaneously help in breaking the negative thoughts pattern. Thus, as you forget the past hurting, and start to live in present moment, the forgiveness will become very easy.

In addition, when you start living in present moment, you feel calmness inside you which is essential for forgiving. Otherwise how much you pretend, you cannot forgive anyone until you attain peace of mind. Moreover, this tranquility comes from within you. Thus, meditation leads you to such calmness within you which is essential for forgiveness. It can also be said that Divine's grace is required for forgiving someone who have hurt you knowingly or unknowingly. It is also written in *Adi Granth,* "Where there is forgiveness, there is God Himself."

Finally, I would like to close this chapter by mentioning the quotation of Cherie-Carter-Scott. She once said, "Everyone I know has been morally wrong or severely hurt by another person at some time in his or her life to such a degree that forgiveness seems impossible. However, harboring resentment and revenge fantasies only keep you trapped in victimhood. It is only through forgiveness that you can erase wrongdoing and clean the slate."

Thus, life is very short and there are lots of works to do so don't waste the time. Every work can be done only with tranquil mind which cannot be attained without forgiveness. So forgive and move on.

Chapter 9
Express gratitude

"If the only prayer you ever say in your entire life is 'thank you', it will be enough"—Meister Eckhart.

Human being is simply part of Whole rather than any isolate entity. Thus being part of this complex cosmic system, we should understand that millions of things come together, mesh together and breathe in order to take even one more breathe for us in air. Thus we are miraculously interconnected with each and every thing of the Universe. Actually, Cosmic Forces bring together these millions of things and arrange in such order that we may survive on the earth.

Thus, without this complex system of the Universe, we would have neither come in existence nor can we survive even a fraction of second. Buddha also told about interdependence of all things and explained that all things depend on one another for their arising, development and decline. Thus, nothing can exist independently.

The food which reach at our dining table; the clothes which we wear; the house in which we live; The TV which we are watching, the melodious songs which we are listening whole day; the skills which we have learnt; the education formal as well as informal which we have got throughout our life and many other things which we utilize are the product of the endeavor of millions of living or dead people. Therefore, nothing can be created without the help of social circle. Mean to say, whatever we consume, are provided by the contribution of Nature and efforts of the whole society. Therefore, we all are owed of the Nature as well as society and our ancestors.

However, we give thanks only to that person who provides the thing or service to us at the end place whom we meet personally while we forget the people who have helped us indirectly being part of the production chain. Even hardly any one of us express gratitude to Mother Nature and Cosmic Forces which generate all things and make us able to survive. Thus we should express gratitude to those persons also who play their role in whole production system. Additionally, it is our moral responsibility to pay our gratitude to Mother Nature and God too.

What is gratitude?

Generally, gratitude can be defined to give thanks and expressing an appreciation for the blessing and gift of life. Actually, it is a feeling that spontaneously emerges from within. However, it is not simply an emotional response; it is also a choice we make. We choose to be grateful if we feel owing for the blessing and gift or we choose to be ungrateful if we consider our gift and blessing for granted. Thus, gratitude is the matter of individual's decision.

However, it may be the choice of individual but being a part of society, we all should express thanks in one way or another for whatever we receive from the others. We can express thanks in words—spoken or written; in deeds by expending time; resources or gift to support people in unexpected ways or to help those in needs. Even we can express our thankfulness in gestures; after all it is an inner feeling of our hearts. Moreover, expressing of inner feeling in gestures is more effective than expression in the words.

Thus, gratitude is both feeling and attitude in acknowledgement or benefits which one has received or will receive, and thankfulness, gratefulness and appreciation are the demonstrative expressions of it, whether it extended to us or others.

Dr. Robert A Emmons, a Professor of psychology at the University of California, Davis, a world's leading scientific expert on gratitude explains that gratitude has two key components.

First one is an affirmation of goodness. We affirm that there are good things in the world, gifts and benefits we receive. Secondly, we recognize that the sources of this goodness are outside of ourselves. We acknowledge that other people or Mother Nature give these gifts—to help us achieve the goodness in our lives. Being supported by other people, the social dimension is very important to gratitude. Thus, gratitude encourages us not only to appreciate gifts but also repay them or pay them forward.

Buddhist teacher Jack Cornfield relates gratitude with mindfulness. To be mindful, he said, is to see the world as it is without judgment. It is responding to the world rather than reacting to it. So gratitude helps us to be fully present and attentive to our surroundings. Thus, if we remain in the state of mindfulness, we will not wrap up in our own everyday dramas which cause of forgetting the Nature and beauty which are surrounding us and provide lots to us. Moreover, if we ever remember that each and every thing is provided us by Nature, then we will not forget expressing the gratitude to the Nature.

Therefore, it can be said that the gratitude is state of mind which arises when you affirm a good thing in your life that comes from outside of your life. In other words, counting your blessings, noticing small pleasures, experiencing joys, and acknowledging everything that you receive in your life are part of gratitude. Actually, gratitude shifts you from the focus what your life lacks to the abundance that is already present.

From all above statements, it can be concluded that gratitude is a personality trait, a mood, an attitude and an emotion. As an emotion, gratitude is a feeling of happiness that comes from appreciation. More grateful personalities are more likely to experience grateful moods and emotion. It is a virtuous circle of positive emotions.

Role of religion in promoting gratitude

It has been found after studies of scriptures that religions had paid great role in promoting gratitude. Thus gratitude has very important place in all religions and all civilizations since ancient times even this trend is still continue in all the religions. It is observed that those who regularly attend religious service or engage in religious activities are more likely to have a greater sense of gratitude in all areas of life. Most of religious festivals and rituals are deliberately associated with thank giving so that worshipers can express gratitude to God ultimate giver of everything.

The gratitude has remained a bond between giver (God) and receiver (human) throughout history. Thus, the expressing of gratitude has historically been a focus of several religions of the world and has been considered extensively by moral philosophers such as Cicero, Dr. Radhakrishnan and Le Clement. According to Cicero, Gratitude is not only the greatest of virtues but the parent of all others." Therefore, worship with gratitude to God is a common theme of all religions.

In Judaism, gratitude is an essential part of the act of worshiper's life. According to the Hebrew Scripture, all things come from God and because of this, gratitude is extremely important to the followers of Judaism. The Hebrew Scriptures are filled with the idea of gratitude such as—"O Lord my God, I will give thanks to you forever" and "I will give thanks to the Lord with my whole heart."(Ps. 30:12; Ps. 9:1).

Thus the Jewish prayers often incorporate gratitude beginning with the Shema, where the worshiper states that out of gratitude, " You shall love the Eternal, your God, with all your heart, with all your soul and with all you might (Deut.6:5).

Christians are strongly encouraged to praise and give gratitude to their Creator because each Christian believes they were created by a personal God. Martin Luther referred to gratitude as "The basic Christian attitude" and today it is still referred to as "The heart of the gospel". Jonathan Edwards has described in his book 'The *Religious Affections* 'that gratitude and thankfulness toward God are among the sings of true religion.

In Christian gratitude, God is seen as the selfless giver of all good things. Thus gratitude in Christianity is an acknowledgement of God's generosity that inspires Christians to shape their own thoughts and actions around such ideals.

The Islamic sacred text, The Quran, is also filled with the idea of gratitude. Islam encourages its followers to be grateful and express thanks to God in all circumstances. Islamic teaching emphasizes the idea that those who are grateful will be rewarded with more. The prophet Muhammad said, Gratitude for the abundance you have received is the best insurance that the abundance will be continue. Many practices of Islamic faith also encourage gratitude. In the Quran it is also stated in *Sura* 14 that those who are grateful will be given more by God.

Gratitude is the base of Buddhism. Buddha said, "The greatest of all gifts of the Dharma is the gift of gratitude". The greater the gift, the greater the gratitude we should feel. He taught that every human birth is precious and worth of gratitude. He used to express the gratitude himself throughout the life. We think of the all-wise Buddha, the compassionate Buddha but we don't usually think of the grateful Buddha.

One of the very first expressions the Buddha expressed after his attainment of Enlightenment was to show his gratitude to those who had helped him in the process of attaining nirvana. He was even grateful to tree. The Buddha knew that the Bodhi tree had sheltered him, and he knew that Sujata, Svasti and his five companions had been helpful to him so he felt gratitude towards all of them. Thus, gratitude found a place in the ethical and spiritual teaching of Buddha.

Thirteenth century Buddhist priest Nichiren has described gratitude in his letters 'as an essential component of humanity'. He himself felt the deepest gratitude even toward Hei no Saemon-no-Jo the government official who prosecuted him and attempted to have him killed. Nichiren letters to his followers almost always open with a detailed and heartfelt expression of thanks for their offerings and support. Daisaku Ikeda has also described gratitude as the very essence of Buddhism.

In Hindu Scripture Mahabharata the character of Karana is best example of thankfulness. Though he knew well that Dharyodhana has not as much moral values as *Pandvas*have, he continuously accompanied with Dharyodhana throughout his life. As Karana was made king by Dharyodhana of a small part of land known as *Ang*, the Karana considered himself in debt of the Dharyodhana. Eventually, Karana died in the battle of Mahabharata fighting from the side of Dharyodhana. Thus, he might able to free himself from the debt whatever had been given to him by Dharyodhana in the form of *Angraj*.

The Aryan considered Nature and other natural objects such as Sun, Air, Earth etc. as gods and goddesses so they worshiped Nature. Many rituals of Hinduism are revolved around gratefulness. For example—the worshipers offer flowers and fruit in temple in front of the deity in order to return back to God whatever they have received from the Nature—is gesture of expressing gratitude to Nature. That's why in the rituals of Hindu religion—grass, flowers, fruits, leaves of plants or crops and other natural objects are main ingredients of the worship. And before eating the food, there is a ritual of the sprinkling water around the dish in which the food has been served is also a symbol of thanksgiving to Nature that provides us food.

Here I would like to quote some paragraphs from Hindu's scripture *"Satapatha Brahmana"*so that it may be clarified that how much importance has been given to gratitude in Hindu's scripture:-

"When a man is born whoever may be, there is born simultaneously a debt to the gods, to the sages, and to the ancestors".

Therefore, when he performs sacrifice, it is the debt to the gods which is concerned. It is on their behalf; therefore that he is taking action when he sacrifices or makes an oblation.

And when he recites the *Vedas*, it is the debt to the sages which is concerned. It is on their behalf; therefore, that he is taking action, for it is said of one who has recited the *Vedas* that he is guardian of the treasure store of the sages.

And when he desires offspring, it is the debt to the ancestors which is concerned. It is on their behalf; therefore, that he is taking action, so their offspring may continue without interruption.

Thus, in all religions the practice of thanksgiving is common in one way or another. Sometimes or somewhere it has been realized every one of us that Higher Support generally called Divine's role is very essential for us in order to survive on this planet. This is the reason that paying gratitude became the gestures of rituals in all religions. Thus thanksgiving is inseparable part of religion.

Spiritual aspect of gratitude

When people do something good for us, we express our gratitude to them. However, only few of us, express gratitude to Cosmic Forces which have great roll in the formation, evolution and sustaining of life on the earth. Even we do not express gratitude to other such factors which help us to survive, for example--atmosphere, water bodies, wind, etc. The cyclic movement of earth is such a cosmic phenomenon which helps in sustaining the human's life on this planet. If the earth were to stop spinning on its axis, day and night would not occur and if it were to stop revolving around the Sun, the seasons would not change.

In addition, the atmosphere contains in such a proportion of gases that life could be possible on the earth. If only fraction of in the composition of atmosphere changes, the life cannot sustain on the earth. The correct distance between Sun and Earth; tilting of earth on its axis; the gravitational force of earth etc. are such factors which make the earth possible to sustain the life on it.

The scientist Newton also said, "When I look at the solar system, I see the Earth at the right distance from the Sun to receive the proper amounts of heat and light. This did not happen by chance".

Even the rate at which nuclear fusion releases the energy in stars, such as the Sun by squashing hydrogen atoms into helium and then other elements is in exact proportion which require for evolution of life. Astronomers have found that exactly 0.7 percent of the mass of hydrogen is converted into starlight and that, if this figure were to be just a fraction off, carbon and other elements essential to life could never have formed.

Sir Martin Rees an astronomer of the Royal Society says, "It could be that the laws that govern our Universe are unchangeable, but it is a remarkable coincidence that these laws are also exactly that same as what is needed to produce life."

Thus, Universe evolves and exists only due to fine balance between several crucial factors. Moreover, Nature organizes these factors in such a way that all living beings may survive on this earth in perfect harmony. Thus existence of human race on the earth is only due to this system of Cosmic Forces.

Mean to say, we have lots of reason to express our gratitude to Cosmic System as well Mother Nature. However, hardly anyone of us express gratitude to Nature and Cosmic Forces which created the life and such other conditions which help to sustain the life. Actually, we do not feel the need to express gratitude to these natural forces and Mother Nature. This is mainly because we think that the creation and sustaining our existence is automatic and spontaneously. Therefore, we consider everything granted on the earth and we do not express gratitude.

However, without the Cosmic Forces, the existence on the earth could not be possible. This Cosmic system, in fact, is beyond human comprehension so we call it 'God'. Thus God is not any living entity but a harmonious combination of Cosmic Forces which governs the whole Universe.

Thus expressing gratefulness to Cosmic Forces is very essential ingredient of spiritual practice. The ability to live in this feeling of gratitude is an important and intrinsic part of seeker's spiritual journey. So only accepting that we are created by God is not enough, we should also feel gratitude to Him with whole heartedly. Then only we will be able to live happily on this planet and that happiness will be long-lasting.

Actually, in my view, God is not noun but a verb. Mean to say, the activities of God do not cease after creation of life. Human being is a part of whole Universe so role of God remains continuous throughout human's whole life. Therefore, God is an activity which is going on continuously to sustain the life. It is another matter that we cannot understand the role of God in our lives until we evolve spiritually. As we evolve spiritually, we begin to feel God's presence in our lives. As we realize God's presence in our lives, we experience Divine's grace and start realizing that whatever happens in our lives is happened as per cosmic plan.

Only after experiencing Divine's grace, we realize that cosmic plans are better than ours. Actually, cosmic plans are always in favor of human beings. However, we are not as wiser as we think so our plan may be imperfect. At the time of making plans, we know only beginning while God knows beginning as well as end. Thus, as and when we experience this reality, then not only we drop our plan but also start to adjust ourselves with the cosmic plan. Then we begin to really appreciate and expressing gratitude to God. As we immerse ourselves more and more into spiritual practice, we become able to understand that each event that is considered miracle, in fact, is such happening which is part of cosmic plan and well synchronized with the other elements of the Nature. Thus as and when we understand that these miracles are part of Divine's plan, we start expressing gratitude to God.

The spiritual experiences which we realize are, in fact, the way of God talking to us. When we feel gratitude and express thankfulness repeated throughout the day, we gradually develop the spiritual emotion of gratitude. Thus, in spirituality, there is continuous realization before, during and after the action that everything happens as per God's wish, He does everything. God knows better than anyone else about us; our good and bad; every secret; every grief and bliss. Mean to say, Even He knows us better than we know ourselves.

Thus, as and when we start to understand reality of Cosmic Forces, our appreciation and expressing of gratitude to the God and Nature also increases. Hence one's gratitude is continuous and is automatically expressed in heartfelt thoughts. Thus in this higher state of spirituality, gratitude is present and reflected in every action, movement and thought of spiritual person. When this higher stage of evolvement is activated, the ego starts reducing, and we express more gratitude to each and every thing including Nature. Thus this positive feedback is going on.

Expressing gratitude enhances our happiness level and overall well-being.

The expressing gratitude is beneficial for us in many ways. For example, it improves mental health; enhances compassion; develops patience; enhance happiness; provides life satisfaction; increase positive emotions and decrease negative emotions. Thus the expression of gratitude creates an opening that invites many other positive states and experiences in our lives. The people who express more gratitude are moved to offer themselves to others without expecting anything in return. Thus it is, in fact, gratitude that inspires people toward act of kindness which strengthen our bond with other people.

Neuroscientist Alex Korb described in his book, *'In the upward Spirit How you can be Happier'*, "Benefit of gratitude starts with the dopamine system because feeling grateful activates the brain stem region that produces dopamine. Gratitude towards others increases activity in social dopamine circuits, which makes social interactions more enjoyable. Gratitude can also boost the neurotransmitter serotonin, which does the work as antidepressants do".

A study conducted by Mc McCullough, Emmons and Tsang (2002) found that gratitude is correlated with generosity, empathy and helpfulness.

Another study conducted by David Desteno and Monica Bartlett (2010) found similar correlation between gratitude and economic generosity. In this study, using an economic game, increased gratitude was shown to directly mediate increased monetary giving. From these results, this study shows that grateful people are more likely to sacrifice individual gain for communal profit.

Gratitude has not only showed to improve a person's altruistic but also it is strongly linked to mental health and life satisfaction. Grateful people experience more joy, love and enthusiasm even they enjoy protection from destructive emotions like envy, greed and bitterness. Gratitude also reduces the risk of depression, frustration and anxiety. Thus people who express gratitude cope better with stress and recover more quickly from physical illness.

John Henry Jowett Author and British Protestant preacher said, "Gratitude is a vaccine, an antitoxin and an antiseptic". Thus, in order to enhance your overall well-being, spare some time daily for reflecting on what you are thankful for.

Through research of happiness, Psychologist Sonja Lyubomirsky has proved that expressing gratitude is one of the most reliable methods of increasing happiness and life satisfaction. It also boosts feeling of optimism, joy, pleasure and other positive emotions and reduces negative emotions.

Dr. Emmons who has been studying gratitude for almost 10 years and is considered by many to be the world's leading authority on gratitude—is Author of the book, *'Thanks! Howthe New Science of Gratitude can make you Happier* is also correlates the gratitude with happiness and joy. The information in this book is based on research involving thousands of people conducted a number of different researchers around the world.

One of the things these studies showed is that practicing gratitude can increase happiness level by around 25 percent. Thus, it has been concluded from the above research that continuous practice of gratitude raises your "happiness set-point". So you can remain at your higher level of happiness regardless of outside circumstances.

In addition, Dr. Emmons' research shows that those who practice gratitude tend to be more creative, bounce back more quickly from adversity, have stronger immune system and have stronger social relationships than those who don't practice gratitude. He further points out that "To say we feel grateful is not to say that everything in our lives is necessary great. It just means we are aware of our blessings".

In another study conducted by Emmons and his colleagues Michael Mc McCullough suggested similar suggestions. Such as gratitude strengthen the immune system, lower blood pressure and reduce symptom of illness and make us less bothered about aches and pain, promote forgiveness and strengthen the relationship. In addition, it is also proved from study that the people who express gratitude regularly, sleep more hours and enjoyed sound sleep because they spend less time awake before falling sleep. Even they feel more refresh upon awakening.

In addition, psychologists have corroborated the gratitude-patience link. Thus, gratitude helps develop patience. The researches proved that people with a strong sense of gratitude are more likely to be able to delay gratification, passing on a small reward now in favor of a greater reward later. In other words, it can be said that gratitude is an antidote to greed. Greed often comes from a sense of not having enough or at least not having as much as everyone else has. On the other hand, gratitude assures that what we have is enough; it seems that greed and gratitude cannot peacefully co-exist. The same apply for other negative emotions such as jealousy, anger, regret, resentment etc.

Reasons for ingratitude

The expression of gratitude works as glue that consistently holds society and relationship together while ingratitude contributes to societal dissolution and separation. About gratitude and ingratitude Buddhism explained, (Nikaya 1.61), "The worthy person is grateful and mindful to benefits done to him: This gratitude, this mindfulness is congenial to the best people. On the contrary, the unworthy man is ungrateful, forgetful of benefits done to him: This ingratitude, this forgetfulness is congenial to mean people".

Zoketsu Norman Fischer, a Zen Teacher said, "Lack of gratitude means we are not paying attention; we take our life and existence for granted; we take it as a given, and then we complain that it isn't working as we wanted it to". "But why should we be here in the first place? Why should we exist at all"? He further questioned.

According to Buddhism, benefit has to be recognized as benefit. If we do not feel that someone or something actually has benefited us, we won't feel gratitude them. This suggests that we have to understand what is truly beneficial, what has really helped us to grow and develop as human beings. We also have to know who or what has benefited us, and remember that they have done so—otherwise no feeling of gratitude is possible. On the contrary, ingratitude means not knowing or recognizing what has been done for one's benefit. So many people do not recognize any benefit is the main reason of not feel gratitude.

Secondly, we may recognize benefit as benefit and even recognize that they have been given to us by other people, but we make those benefits for granted. No realizing that they are free gift; we may think that they are owed to us that we have a right to them, and that therefore in a sense they belong to us already so that we have no need to be grateful for them. Thus people tend to think that everything is done to him, that they have a right to everything.

Third reason for ingratitude is egoism. Egoism takes many forms and has many aspects. Such as attitude of individualism: The belief that one is separate from others and independent in any way and being not dependent on others, one therefore does not owe anything to others. One feel that one is not obliged to them because one can do everything oneself. The person who is egoistical in this sense is incapable of feeling gratitude, and cannot admit that he has been benefited by others.

Finally, forgetfulness is also a cause of ingratitude. We forget the benefits because the benefits are given to us a long time ago, even so long ago that we have no distinct recollecting of them, and no longer feel grateful to whoever bestowed them upon us.

In brief, the four reasons for ingratitude are— failure to recognize a benefit; taking benefits for granted; egotism and forgetfulness.

How to cultivate a mind of gratitude

Dozens of studies have shown that gratitude is like a skill which can be increased with practice and the right perspective; there will be always many things to be grateful for. Thus, for cultivating a mind of gratitude, the most important element is doing daily practice and remembers to be grateful for the practice. Moment to moment mindfulness and gratitude are both go hand-in-hand. It is suggested in Buddhist Naikan Therapy, "Review your life and begin to remember all the things you have gratitude towards, even the things that were difficult and taught you lesson, and the people that were difficult".

However, who have criticized you; were unfair with you; commented something immoral to you; challenge you etc. were also play an important part in changing your life. Actually, when I look back at my younger age and remember such persons who challenged me one way or another, I found myself fortunate for their sarcastic comments and hurdles put by them to resist me. In the words of Winston Churchill, "Kites rise highest against the wind, not with it". Therefore, such persons also deserve your expression of thankfulness because they also help you indirectly for making your career and developing your personality. The reason is that that criticizes and sarcastic comments always work as motivation for you in achieving the goals. Buddhist teacher Jack Cornfield advices us to be grateful for difficulties because it is really the difficult times that teaches us the most.

There are some more practices which can also be practiced such as—you may tune into the positive events in yourself; you may keep gratitude journal and may write a gratitude letter. You may also regularly reflect on being grateful. For practicing more gratitude, you should remain in joyous mood and your focus should be on good intentions. Moreover, positive emotions such as kindness, compassion and generosity should be part of your daily activities.

In addition, Share your grateful feelings; express thanks daily to those who cooperate or help you; give complements and appreciations wherever and whenever you feel nice and pleasurable. When you receive a gift or when something happen nice in general, considers how someone tried on purpose to bring that goodness into your life. So write unexpected 'thank you' note or give some surprising gifts in return. Moreover, accept the gratitude politely such as—it is my pleasure; you are welcome; no matter, it is very miner thing etc. Mean to say, do not miss any occasion without expressing thankfulness.

A Research suggested that thinking hard about our own morality makes us more grateful for life. The morality and grateful are directly proportion of one another. Mean to say, how much we are moral, we express gratitude in same proportion. Another study found that praying more often increase gratitude. Our character and virtue also cultivate the attitude of expressing gratitude. The more you become virtuous, the more you become thankful person.

Anyway, the gratitude won't happen overnight. However, with consistent practice, it will grow. Thus gratitude is like all other skills in which you can be trained only by doing practice and more practice. Therefore, start your day with thanksgiving to God that you have got one more day to live, Thanks to earth on which you are going to put your feet after awaking. Then at the end of the day, thank yourself and your surrounding atmosphere for things have gone well. In other words, thanks to whole Nature every morning for supporting you by one means or another. So make gratitude a habit and include it in your daily routine.

However, when we develop habit for any work or procedure, we are shifted to auto pilot mode. In this mode—every thought, sensory experience, action, emotion and behavior in which we engage is reflected in a corresponding activation of cell in the brain. Thus every time we think in specific way or perform a certain action, a pattern of neurons lights up in the brain. When this pattern is activated, changes occur within the cells and in the connections between them, gradually making it easier for that pattern to be activated in future. When a certain pattern of cells is activated many times, it becomes very easy for it to be activated in future. Thus repeatedly expressing gratitude makes it easier for expression of thankfulness spontaneously when anyone does something for you.

According to Buddhist Lions Roar Magazine, "The enlightened nature is not just with in you. It is everywhere. You can see it and appreciate it. That's the main cause of happiness—gratitude and appreciation."

Therefore, don't be miser in thanksgiving. Express your gratitude each and every living and non-living thing surrounding you because everything gives its contribution to help you directly or indirectly.

Moreover, I would like to close this chapter with an email of Robert Emmons:-

"We all begin life dependent on others, and most of us end life dependent on others. If we are lucky, in between we have roughly 60 years or so of unacknowledged dependency. The human condition is such that throughout life, not just at the beginning and end, we are profoundly dependent on each other people. Gratitude is the trust approach to life we did not create or fashion ourselves. We did not birth ourselves. Life is about giving, receiving and repaying. We are receptive beings, dependent on the help of others, on their gifts and their kindness".

After reading this email, it can be concluded that if we acknowledge timely whatever we receive from other people, we will be able to repay the debt of this life. However, after repaying debt of the life, one feels internal peace. Thus dying with tranquil mind without any regret is the greatest achievement in human's life.

Chapter 10

Keep your ego under control

"Once the game of chess is over, the king and the pawn go back in the same box"—Italian Proverb.

Actually, vulnerability is direct proportional to the egocentric. Thus the more egocentric we are, the more vulnerable we become. Small things can hurt us and we brood over again and again on such hurting. Every dialogue of others which we do not like can shatter our happiness. Attitude of other person which does not suit with our thoughts can spoil our mood. Egocentric person become jealous even on the progress of the neighbors and colleagues which resulting in unhappiness. Therefore, egotism is the main cause of suffering. However, to achieve happiness, it is necessary to keep our ego under control.

What is Ego?

Actually, the ego is ambiguous word so it is difficult to bind the ego in any particular definition. Some psychologists refer the ego as self-esteem, self-respect, self-confidence, self-worth, self-image etc. which are, in fact, positive and important traits of human being. Some others refer it as self-centered, self-interested, vanity, proud, self-obsessed, conceit, etc. which are opposite to humility. On the other hand, some sages, saints and Buddhist monks consider the ego with the self, soul or spirit which is the core of personality.

Thus, ego is not a specific thing rather it is made up of many such different beliefs which have been acquired by human beings throughout their whole lives. These beliefs are different in each person and even can be diverse and contradict in same person. Sometimes, it seems that many persons live within one person .Sri Aurobindo said about this state of contradiction "We find that we are composed of not of one but many personalities and each has its own demands and differing nature". Thus the ego is a combination of different beliefs which have been developed throughout in our life. Thus ego is indistinguishable part of our personality. That's why it is very difficult to define and explain the ego.

The definition of European psychologists such as Freud and Jung is quite different from the definition of Eastern philosophers and Buddhist monks. Even some Tibetan Buddhists have some separate views from all others. Anyhow, I have tried much to define and explain the ego with the all perspective along with my personal knowledge and experience.

According to Freud, ego is the most central part of the mind which mediates with one's surroundings. The ego is meant to be our window to the world around us—a neutral and extremely useful source of information about what's happening. In the Freudian sense, the ego is organized part of the personality structure that includes defensive, perceptual, intellectual-cognitive and executive functions. Conscious awareness resides in the ego although not all of the operations of the ego are conscious.

According to Buddhist concept, ego is the absence of true knowledge of who we really are. Ego can also be defined as incessant movement of grasping at a delusory notion of "I" and "mine" self or other, and all the concepts, idea, desires and activity that will sustain that false construction. Thus ego is not entity but a unified field of identity—it is not fixated on a point, but operates within spatial consciousness.

According to Buddhist master Sheng-Ven, the idea of ego revolves around the idea of attachment or clinging. The ego originally does not exist. It is created as a result of attachment to one's ideas or one's own view point. However, body and mind are impermanent and constantly changing over time so our attachments to them are also remains changing constantly. Thus, as the attachments change, the ego also changes. Therefore ego does not exist in the sense of being a permanent entity.

Whilst according to Tibetan Buddhist Ven Thubten Chodron, the meaning of ego refers to a part of the mind that mediates between animalistic instincts of the id, the values of super ego, and the demands of the environment. Subsequently, within general society, ego came to refer to the self, and later to a conceited and inflated sense of self.

In the negative sense, the ego is refers to the self-grasping ignorance which is root of self-centered attitude which prevent us from developing impartial love, compassion and altruism. Actually self-centeredness enhances our gross disturbing attitudes. It is the attitude that thinks our own happiness is more important than that of everyone else because we experience the happiness only on our egoistic state. Thus ego's belief is to be owner of everything which "I" belong such as—my qualification, my property, my post and portfolio, my family, my occupation etc. Means, egoistic persons are always associated with first person singular rather than plural first person or second or third person. For example, Instead of saying it is 'our village' or 'our house', egoistic persons say, 'It is my village' or 'my house'. Thus they always want to possess everything and maintain their separate identity. Thus they believe in individualistic characteristic rather than feeling interconnected with the whole.

Actually egocentric thoughts do not have any concerned with reality. It can also be said that ego is the part of us that clings to things outsides of ourselves, making them a part of our identity. Ego and feeling of ownership are intertwined which are unable to differentiate between conscious thought and reality because thoughts are stimulated by emotional undercurrents. Means, ego generates powerful emotional reactions.

After attaining Nirvana, Buddha found that what we call ego is merely conventional terms that do not refer to any real independent entity. According to him, there is no difference between ego and self. Even all other related terms such as soul, spirit, personality etc. are also same. That's why he always emphasized on non-self.

Author of several philosophical books, Dr. Deepak Chopra refers the ego as self-image. According to him, the ego is our self-image rather than our true self. It is characterized by labels, masks, images and judgments while the true self is the field of possibilities creativity, intention and power.

Osho a spiritual teacher related the ego with past. It is the continuity all that you have done; all that you have accumulated; all the *karmas*; all the conditionings; all the desires and all the dreams of the past. Mean to say, the whole past is ego. Further he said that ego is time—the more time, the much ego. Thus he connected ego with time.

From all above concepts and definitions, it is concluded that ego is the part of the mind containing consciousness and memory, and ego is the beliefs about ourselves which are made up throughout our life's experiences. In addition, ego is accumulation of emotions, traumas, thoughts, feelings, hopes and activities which separate us from everything else. Actually, the word 'ego' is derived from a Greek word 'I', refers to the *core sense of self*, a distinct and unique expression of personhood, albeit one part paradoxically exists in connection or in relation to life and others.

Actually, the difference between 'what we really are' and 'what we pretend to be' is—ego. It can also be said that all the masks which we wear to hide our true self are forms of ego such as power, property, position, post, rank, name, fame, qualification, etc. Such identities, in fact, are false identities because they work as a veil to hide our true self. Even we do not hesitate to utilize some noble traits such as love, humility, generosity, altruism, sympathy, empathy etc. for making our mask. Mean to say, we pretend to be religious, altruistic, sympathetic, generous etc. but in realty we are very far away from these traits. Actually, we require a mask whatever they may be in order to hide our true identity. Means, we always try hide what 'actual we are' through showing off. Thus all such type of masks which are used to hide our true self is—ego.

Thus by wearing these masks, we have made a false self-image about ourselves. In addition, we always increase the thickness of these masks by twisting the fact about ourselves and by continuously boasting. We always want to impress others. We try to become someone else by changing our true self. Even we do not care about our originality and uniqueness, and ready to lose them in this rat race and competitive world. Thus, this blind competition is—ego.

Thus the desire to become someone else is ego; the desire to remain in limelight is ego and boasting is ego. We try to show others that we are knower of the entire Universe and we always right than someone else. So such beliefs of being rightness is ego, and belief about ourselves that we know more than others is also ego. Means, our showing-off is ego.

Actually, we are not satisfied with 'what we are' so in the desire of becoming better, we seek appreciation from society instead of improving our positive traits. Thus seek admiration is our weak point and we want to cling with it at any cost. That's why we always seek identity in the forms of masks one type or another so that people may admire us. When we use these masks as our identities, these identifications become permanent for us and we assume them true. Though these identifications seem true, they are only illusions which mislead others. However, we have become habitual of these identifications and feel pleasure in living in such type of illusion.

Thus the false self-image which we have made for ourselves is ego. The desire to gain appreciation and seek approval is ego. The desire to be pivot of the society is ego. The desire to listen complement from society is ego. Giving always unwanted advices and suggestions to others is ego. Shifting the blame of our mistakes to other's ego. Mean to say, the role we play in order to hide our true self's ego.

What are healthy ego and ego-strength, and their importance in human's life?

Actually, everyone has ego. Though it is a selfish part of human being, it plays an important role in our life. According to Arnold Bennett, "If egotism means a terrific interest in one's self, egotism is absolutely essential to efficient living". Therefore, due to following reasons, it is necessary to maintain the reasonable ego. First of all, it can be useful in dealing with certain difficult situations or people. Actually, it is the ego that pulls the alarm for fight or flight when you are in physical danger. So it is the ego's role to get out of harm's way. Thus the ego is antidote for vulnerable and works as shield to protect us. Therefore, such ego which acts as bodyguard of our self is termed 'healthy ego'.

Dr. Athena Staik Author and family therapist not only differentiate between healthy ego and unhealthy ego but she describes the characteristics of ego-strength also. According to her, ego may take different meaning depending on where it falls on a continuum between a healthy ego on the one end of the spectrum, and unhealthy one on the other. According to her, a healthy ego is foremost an ability to regulate painful emotions rooted in anger and fear. Thus healthy ego increases self-esteem and lead towards such maturity in which ideas from other sources may also be accepted.

In addition, a healthy ego gives us the required ego-strength to navigate challenging moments, and emotions of vulnerability rooted in fear and anxiety with ease and resilience. A healthy ego-strength is connected to a healthy self-concept, one that is resilient, that can look at a situation and see beyond it, understand difference between wants and needs. The healthy ego gives understanding between 'what can be changed' and 'what cannot be changed'. Then healthy ego practice acceptance 'what cannot be changed' and gives courage to act according to the situation 'what can be changed'.

However, according to Dr. Athena Staik, ego-strength refers to a cultivated resiliency or strength of our core sense of self, the extent to which we learn to face and grow from challenging events or persons in our lives in ways that strengthen our relationships with our self and others and enrich our lives with meaning. Thus, our ego- strength is an integral part of our psycho-social-emotional and cultural development and forms our sense of self, or self-concept, in relation to self and others around you.

When Mohan Das Karamchand Gandhi was thrown away from 1st class railway compartment, he never forget this humiliating incident which hurt him very most. Actually, it was his healthy ego which always kept him motivated to remember this pain of insult. Moreover, later on, due to his ego-strength, this pain of humiliation raised him so high that ultimately he became very great.

Paul Arden author of the book 'Whatever you Think, Think the Opposite' also expressed similar views about healthy ego and its strength. He said, "Great people have great egos; may that are what makes them great". That's why when you say that someone has a big ego then you are saying he is too full of himself.

High ego-strength helps to adapt idiocentric viewpoint. People who are idiocentric orientation tend to emphasize their own goals and follow their own ways rather than the ways of others. Generally, they deviate from norm and thus make their own path.

Therefore, a person with well-developed ego-strength is resilient, optimistic, and has a strong sense of self as capable in challenges. They take learning approach to life that increasingly grows their strength and confidence in handling triggering situation.

In addition, the healthy ego is also necessary for our healthy existence because the healthy ego is tied to self-esteem and self-worth. Actually, the ego wants to control, manipulate, look better and perceive smarter than others. That's why it is better tool to deal with ourselves. Being related with self-respect, self-importance and self-confidence, the healthy ego increases the self-determination and strengthens the character. The healthy ego has an ability to tolerate discomfort, enough to regulate their emotions as opposed to feeling overwhelmed by them.

On the contrary, the persons who have the weak ego-strength cannot easily face, take in and cope with the situation 'as it is'. Instead they fight with the reality, hate it and wish it otherwise. Thus, their expectations are unrealistic and based on inadequate understanding. Reality seems a big, too frightening, and too overwhelming for them. So they avoid encounter and feel un-resourceful, weak, fragile and unable to cope with the situation.

Thus, the stronger the ego- strength, the more comfortable one feels in taking ownership of their problems and giving ownership to others for theirs. Whilst, weaker the ego-strength, the less one engages in reality and more ones flees to superstition rather than taking action.

Which type of ego should be controlled and why?

If ego is referred to self-esteem; self-importance; self-worth; self-respect and self-confidence, the ego need not be controlled because these are positive traits of life. In addition, if the meaning of ego is referred to self, soul or spirit then also there is no need to control it due to its spiritual aspect. In other words, these both types of ego can be categorized in healthy type of ego.

Actually, how we perceive the world around us depends a great deal on our ego. Mean to say, our ego directs how we interpret everything that goes on in our daily experience and thus our perception of any event determine. So our ego exercises a very strong influence in our perception even without our awareness.

Ego, in fact, sees us as separate from everything else and tries to shape our perception accordingly. Thus ego acts as a filter so we get everything after filtration through our ego. Our version of reality is slanted by our ego's agendas. It is our ego which can either tremendously enhance our personal development or create an insurmountable obstacle to personal development. A healthy ego can open the door to a rewarding and fulfill life while an unhealthy ego can slam the door of personal development and confines us in self-imposed limits. Thus before controlling the ego, we have to recognize the type of ego whether it is healthy ego or unhealthy ego.

However, the healthy ego is beneficial while the unhealthy ego affect our life negatively. Actually, often times others can clearly see such type of ego that tends to operate behind a curtain even when we can't notice. Therefore, such unhealthy ego should be controlled for happy and peaceful living. For example, all types of veils which we use to hide our true identity; our showing off attitude; our desire to seek appreciation and approvals are categorized in unhealthy ego. Conceit, pride and vanity are also included in this category. Thus, such type of ego which revolves around your self-interest should be controlled.

In addition, negative ego is associated with such person who boasts; is arrogant; treats others with scorn; easily offended by opposing views; considers others inferior and lacks empathy. Intolerable of criticism; unacceptance of others' ideas; and always require special attention than someone else are some other signs of negative and unhealthy ego. Even the reflection of negative ego can be noticed in our behavior i.e. How do we speak, listen, walk, stand, sit, and can be noticed through our body languages also. Thus, if the ego lies in this negative mode, then this unhealthy ego should be controlled.

Unhealthy ego creates a sense of separations between us and others that labels the peoples and things as 'better than and worse than'. It is the part of us cling to things outsides of us making them a part of our identity. Actually, this clinging is the source of all suffering. For example our pride, looks, our job, our house, qualification, our post and rank, even personality traits such as generosity, humility, altruism etc. we identify with are all such clinginess. Thus when we begin to define ourselves through things and concepts, it becomes painful not only for others but for ourselves also.

Actually, ego wants to differentiate between 'self' and everything else. No doubt that everyone is important in different ways, and each one of us feels worthy in one way or another. However, problem arises when this sense of self-worth becomes exaggerated to the extent of the sense of such self-centered that it pushes the person to a life full of suffering and pain. Meantime, individual remains unsatisfied, and when one does not succeed in satisfying one's ego, one leads to frustration. Thus, if our achievements were not much enough to satisfy our ego's demand, then we will certainly end up with depression and other mental disorders.

Our main cause of suffering is that we are not touch with the reality. We are touch only with the version of reality. Therefore, due to our ego, we cannot see the reality. We are connected with the others only superficially that's why we do not feel the suffering of human beings. Thus neither we can remove the suffering of other people nor can we escape ourselves from suffering until we break the chain of the unhealthy ego. Anyhow, when we realize that we and others are one, the negative ego will have no power over us.

As the ego is a mask over all loving higher self, it blocks out lot of inner love and kindness when it is relied upon heavily. While goes to serve an important service to us, an out of control ego can cause us to take actions that are unloving and unkind. Moreover, if you have a high unhealthy ego, you always expect that world should govern according to your point of view. You become habitual to complain about all the wrong that is in it. In unhealthy ego, the blame is always on someone or something else; your advice is extremely valuable and others should take your word seriously. In other words, due to your unhealthy ego, you think that everything should revolve around you.

In addition, if you have big unhealthy ego, you may get angry when people try to give you suggestions about things because you think that you already knew. Even you may refuse help when people offer viable ideas that outshine your own; you dismiss them so that your own ideas may not dismiss. If someone disagree with your viewpoint or criticize it, you feel offended by opposing views even you may have trouble noticing the sign of being easily offended. Many times you started fight just to satisfy your ego because you feel that people do not treat you the way you think they should.

As the ego believes it is separate from everything else, it often feels the need to justify its importance to itself and others. The ego separates us from our surroundings rather than connecting us to the oneness between humans and natural world. Whatever you do best again and again but the ego never satisfied. It always craving for more and more, and you will always be in search of some unknown thing to fill this vacuum. Even you yourself do not know about that 'unknown thing' which you are seeking in order to satisfy your ego.

According to the Buddhist teacher Susan Piver, "If we didn't have such a big ego, our feelings wouldn't be hurt by rejection and wouldn't crumble with despair when our plans don't work". She further says that we wouldn't wish to be treated thoughtfully, as important beings that matter, in fact, whether or not we mattered to anyone wouldn't matter at all if we didn't have ego. Thus negative ego can lead to bring out of harmony and pushes us towards distress.

Therefore, if we want to enjoy the life, we can't let the ego distract us. Thus, the big unhealthy or negative ego should be kept under control so that we may live peacefully and happily. Otherwise we will spend our valuable whole life fighting for the sake of satisfying our inflated ego.

How to control the ego?

As our ego is the accumulation of whole life's experiences and other multiple aspects of life, it is very difficult to let go, and sudden control is even more difficult. Actually, attitude and habits are skills which require time and patience. Thus, ego cannot be control in short time because our ego is associated with our attitude and habits. Therefore, controlling the ego, and changing the attitude or habits will be going on simultaneously. No one can learn swimming and driving in one or two days because skills cannot be developed in few days. However, with suitable methods, proper procedure and right practice, we not only become able to change our attitude and habits but we become able to control our ego also. So, no need to be hurry. Have patience!

Anyway, recognizing that we have a big ego is the first step towards controlling it, and for recognition, the awareness is the best way. Thus awareness can help not only in recognition but it also helpful in letting go of ego. Moreover, awareness is possible only in meditation because meditation is the only way to notice the emotions and feelings which are integral part of the ego. During meditation, practitioners start to observe their thoughts then superficial thoughts which are not more than false ego are started to sideline, and practitioners connect deeply with true self. When practitioners practice more meditation, it becomes easier to see the ego as a mask over true self.

Thus, we can go beyond ego through self-awareness. Living in present or live mindfully is another option for self -awareness. Actually mindfully living is itself another form of meditation. When you start to live mindfully, you remain aware of your environment including your thought patterns. Then you realize that your thoughts are nothing but past memories contain with only feelings and emotions. Thus, observing the feelings and emotions is itself recognition of the ego. After recognizing, the controlling and letting go of the ego become easy.

Buddhism also recommends meditation and mindfulness to control the ego. According Buddhist concept, ego can be pushed into a corner by practicing sitting meditation and practice mindfully living. Spiritual growth is based on growing and expending awareness. When our identity expands to everything else in the Universe, we will connect personally with all the creation. The line of demarcation which wants to see us exclusive from everything else will also obliterate automatically. Moreover, this expansion is possible only in meditation and through living mindfully.

No doubt that living mindfully and practicing meditation require lots of patience. So along with the practice of meditation, some other ways also can be used to control the ego. First of all, it is necessary to introspect about your attitude. No one is perfect including you, and anyone can be neither hundred percent right nor hundred percent wrong. Therefore, change your attitude whenever and wherever it requires so. Thus, our lives can be changed by altering our attitudes.

When someone disagrees with you at particular discussion, listen carefully. Instead of interrupting, reply patiently and ask some more questions related to the topic. Even only your smile can make the difference. It will help you to convince the other person to end the argument. Additionally, not only you may learn something new that you do not know before but you will also have a better understanding of what the other person's opinion is based on. To meet others in the middle is not defeat but it is the art of compromising. Thus, searching a middle ground may be mutually beneficial for everyone and the ego of both sides will also satisfy instead of hurting.

Listen someone patiently leads you towards better understanding and turns your energy outwards rather than focusing on yourself. Moreover, knowing the viewpoint different from your own can push you to look at the world in a brand new way. Thus, practicing compassion, kindness and convincing with love and affection always bring sweet fruits in comparison trying to force others to be interested in you. Then people will appreciate you due to your true personality rather than your masks which you have used as your identity so far.

In addition, if you are too much adamant and habitual to win in every situation then you should think again about your stubbornness and always win-win attitude. Along with the success, embrace the failure and criticism also. It is quite natural to fail so accept it. Failure provides you with an opportunity to refine your knowledge and skill. Therefore, accept the failure and criticism calmly. Actually, learning to embrace failure and criticism will bring you one step closer to success. Thus, if you change your view about success, your ego starts to fall under control spontaneously.

Actually, pride comes from lack of appreciation of the society because you expect too much and get it very less. Your mind is preoccupied and your ego does not allow you to accept less. Thus, high expectations for yourself only increase your ego problem and suffering. Expectations shape the way we view ourselves and our environment. Therefore, set your expectation- level somewhere low than it has been so far in your life so that you may escape from this trap of ego. When your expectation will reduce, naturally you will appreciate everything and blame no one else which is the clear sign of letting go of the ego.

Finally, change your belief that you are the knower of entire Universe. Actually, no one can know each and everything except God. Thus believing that we know everything about a certain situation can cause us not see the full aspect of the situation. Many times our previous experiences are not sufficient to face the particular situation. If we deal every situation as if we are dealing it first time and doing accordingly, then new ideas and new point of view will remain unfold for us.

However, many of us assume that we are the master of particular subject while the reality is just opposite. Actually, we cannot be even master of pencilas Psychologist and Author Ken S Keyes has written in his book *How to Develop Your Thinking Ability*. He illustrated with an example of a pencil, he wrote, "Even you cannot be master of the pencil because after studying its outer surface when you enter in the study of its lead, you entangle in the theory of electron, proton and neutron contained in the lead. You became mad but you cannot become master of the Pencil".

Anyhow, the more you know, more is left to be known. When you find out the answers of some questions which were mystery for you, some other more questions become mystery. Moreover, after unfolding these questions, you face some more such type of questions which are still unknown to you. Thus, the procedure will going on because Nature never reveals all its mysteries at a time. Albert Einstein also said in this context that "Nature shows us only the tail of lion. But I do not doubt the lion belongs to it even though he cannot at once reveal himself because of his enormous size".

I myself realized above truth when I had completed my M. Sc.post-graduation degree in Disaster Mitigation in 2003. Actually, one of my colleagues in army labeled me 'jack of all trades, master on none'. Actually, when I started studying, there were not many questions which I wanted to know. However, after completion of the degree, I found that there are more questions than previous which are still unknown to me. Mean to say, during study of my post-graduation degree I found the answer of that questions which I wanted to know but many more new questions emerge from the answers of that questions. In other words, as I understand more and more about the Nature as I noticed that more and more is left to know. Thus Nature is very vast and no one can know about it completely. Actually, my aim of doing post-graduation was to know about Nature deeply rather than departmental promotion or any other purpose.

Even after completion of my post-graduation degree, I studied about Nature through informal way also such as by Discovery and National Geography Channels about three years. Then I started to write a book on environment, and again studied nearly three years about Nature so that I could write the book properly. Anyhow, I noticed that there are still more left to understand for me, even after writing the book on environment *'Man Towards its Own End'*. Then a time came when I raised my hands and accepted that I know only a fraction about the Nature. However, I am still learning something daily but I am still 'master of none'.

Actually, Nature is beyond human's comprehension and as we go deep in it, we find more surprising fact. Thus, it is better to study for enjoying the Nature rather than explore it because Nature cannot be explored completely. Moreover, as and when human being will understand this fact, the masks or false self or false ego whatever it may be will be sidelined automatically and true 'Self' will reveal which will lead you towards peace and happiness.

Actually, when we were born, we were naked (pure) means without ego. However, as we start growing, we start to cover ourselves with many types of coverings such as Educational degrees, properties, social status etc. These coverings are, in fact, nothing than masks (ego). Thus our pure self has been hidden somewhere very deep under these masks. Though our true self feels suffocation under the heavy burden of these masks, we don't want to leave this pleasurable delusion. Thus, in order to satisfying our ego, we want to remain in this pleasurable illusion. Actually, we cannot return in our pure state until we throw away these masks (layers of ego).

Thus, only after removing this unnecessary burden, you can feel light, and only such type of living is real living in this materialistic world. Therefore, in order to achieve peace and bliss, it is very essential to remove all masks which you have worn to hide your true self. Thus throw all these impurities so that you may become pure again like infant as you entered in this world.

Chapter 11

Leave your comfort zone

"Everything you want in life is waiting for you outside of your comfort zone."—Anthony Fernando.

Actually, it is our tendency to live in such a state which is most favorable for us and gives us comfort. We feel much secure in this comfortable situation that's why we always try to retain this status quo position at any cost. However, the truth is just opposite because generally the unknown is found more favorable than we imagine. In this context, Christine Kloser said, "Your greatest dream, your greatest goals, your greatest accomplishments, your greatest satisfaction, your greatest authentic expression is outside of your comfort zone". I myself experienced that unknown is always more enjoyable and thrilling than certainty.

Thus, break the boundary of your familiar situation in which you have been confined yourself so far. The role you have played in the past is not means that you are wedded to that role. Therefore, in order to evolve, quit that role and choose something different for you. Actually, for generating worthy goals, we always require new environment which forces us to become more than we currently are. If we have been in the same role too long, we have lost touch with who really we are.

Actually, our original nature demands from us to strive continuously. Therefore, if we categorize ourselves in a particular role, we get stuck in a rut and our evolution will cease. Generally, wisdom does not attain with the proportion of the age. Mean to say, it is not necessary to be wise as we age. Actually, wisdom requires experiences that cannot be acquired without facing new challenges. Thus, wisdom is directly proportion to experiences rather than age. So in order to attain wisdom, it is necessary to get as much experience as you can get.

However, if we remain stay in comfortable position, we may miss the opportunity to learn something new or to acquire new experiences. Anyway, after missing the opportunity, our growth may be stopped. Actually, a beautiful butterfly can come into existence only after breaking of its ugly pupa. So come out from your safe cocoon and dive into unknown. Thus, by doing so, the result may be bigger than the risk.

Meaning of comfort zone

According to Cambridge English Dictionary, comfort zone is such a situation in which you feel comfortable and in which your determination and ability are not being tested.

The Wikipedia describes about the comfort zone, "It is a psychological state in which a person feels familiar, at ease, in control and experiences low anxiety and stress so steady level of performance is going on".

Belle Beth Cooper a co-founder of Melbourne startup Hello Code also describes the comfort zone something similar to Wikipedia. She says that your comfort zone is any type of behavior that keeps you at a steadily low anxiety level. Thursday-to-day activities that you are used to won't make you feel anxious and uneasy are, in fact, part of your comfort zone because these activities function in auto pilot mode. Thus, the activities which are included in our general routine function because they are unable to stimulate our mind are come under comfort zone.

Dr. Judith Bardwick Author of psychological books defined the term as a 'behavioral state where a person operates in an anxiety-neutral position'. Mean to say, a status free from anxiety is termed' comfort zone'.

Brene Brown a research professor at the University of Houston emphasizes on two words 'uncertainty' and 'vulnerability'. According to him, where our uncertainty, scarcity and vulnerability are minimized is known as comfort zone. He elaborates it—where we believe we will have access to enough love, food, talent, time, admiration.

Actually, the idea of comfort zone goes back to classic experiment in psychology by psychologist Robert M Yerkes and John D Dodson in 1908. They found in their experiment that state of relative comfort created only steady level of performance. However, higher performance requires some challenges, difficulties, somewhat stress or anxiety which can be faced only outside of your comfort zone.

Thus from the all above definitions, it can be concluded that comfort zone is such a psychological and behavioral state where your day-to-day activities follow a certain routine and pattern. In your comfort zone you feel a sense of ease, familiarity, security and certainty where stress, anxiety and risk are minimized. In other words, comfort zone is a behavioral space where your activities and behaviors fit in a routine and pattern that minimize stress and risk. Thus comfort zone is such a closed house where everything is comfortable so everyone tends to live in the house.

On the other hand, when we step outside of our comfort zone, we enter in the field of uncertainty where we may face more stress and anxiety. Actually, it is such risk where no one is quite sure what will happen and how we will react. Thus after leaving the comfort zone, uncertainty can have positive as well as negative results. However, we have to push the boundary of comfort zone to enjoy more experiences.

How does brain evolve out of comfort zone?

Actually, many of us want to live comfortably even without doing any hard work because we want to conserve our energy. Our brain's tendency of conserving the energy is also like human beings. Thus our brain functions in such a manner that it can conserve the energy and in order to conserve the energy, brain performs all routine activities habitually in less energy than usual. However, in this process, slowly and slowly it becomes drowsy and lazy. Thus due to inactiveness, brain starts reducing its potential for evolution.

In this context, Neuroscientist Charles Duhigg Author of the book *'The Power of Habits'* described, "The neuroscience of habit formation and change tells us that habit arises because the brain needs to conserve the energy. When we first learn any of the endless habitual routines that get us through each day, the brain pays a lot of attention and exerts a lot of energy". Naturally, when these routines are repeated the less energy and attention is required so the brain conserve lots of energy. Thus after practicing over and over again these routine works become habit and habits require even lesser energy.

Therefore, these routine works generally have been performed without any awareness in a lethargy manner. Anyway, the positive aspect of habits is that we do not have to think twice for routine activities which finish spontaneously so the advantages of habits cannot be ignored. However, simultaneously our mind ceases to evolve in habitual work because mind constantly requires some stimuli to evolve. Naturally, there is no any stimulus in routine work so evolution of mind comes to end.

Regarding the drawbacks of habits Tara Bennett Goleman Author of the book *'Mind Whispering'* warns how the emotional habits that may be harmful for us in long-terms so she describes in her book, "We don't realize that how habitual routines lull us in complacency into going through the same motions over and over mindlessly while it is great to do the same activity without a second thought. But every time we act on these habits, we strengthen the brain's circuiting for them".

Mean to say, the neurons which function in a circuit for particular habit get strength from such routine activities while other neurons remain inactive. Thus in such condition the inactive neurons start erasing so brain's evolution also stopped. In other words, in habitual activity the brain's potentiality cannot be utilized completely so ultimately it starts reducing .Thus the question arises that what can be done in order to utilize full potential of the brain. There is a popular saying regarding body, 'either use it or lose it'. This saying is correct for brain also because our brain is also a part of our body. Therefore, we should use the brain properly to its optimal extant to avoid its losing.

Moreover, for utilizing the brain in its full potential, our intellect is not enough. Mean to say, for utilizing the brain in its full potential, we require something more than intelligence, knowledge, study, engage in activities etc. and that 'something' is such a hard and challenging task in which neurons of our brain may stimulate fully. Mean to say, in order to utilize the brain in full potential, maximum neurons should be remained active and their strengthening process may be continued.

Therefore, for activeness of maximum neurons' circuit, we require to achieve as much experiences as much we can achieve. In other words, instead of going on a trodden path, we have to seek alternate paths to learn new things and to get new experiences. However, these all things cannot be accomplished in status quo position. Rather we have to leave our comfort zone and have to face the unknown.

Anyhow, before knowing how our brain evolves out of comfort zone, it is very important to know about the human's brain, its structure and its function. Therefore, I am going to describe about the brain whatever I had experienced and learnt throughout my life and knew during writing of the book. However, some readers may feel difficulties to understand it due to complexity of brain's structure and function. Therefore, I have simplified the description as much as possible so that description may become easy to some extent.

The, human's brains a physical organ shaped by evolution, composed of cells called neurons. More than one hundred billions of interconnected neurons stuffed in the brain and each of average neuron has about ten thousands connections. In the skull portion of nervous system alone there are hundreds of trillions of connection linking the various neural grouping into this complicated network.

Though neurons are not linked directly with each other, the communication between them is occurred by transmitting the message in the form of electrical impulses. Thus for this purpose, neurons are extended in both sides called dendrites and axons. Axon is a long thread-like segment that acts like fiber optic cable which transmits the electric signal while dendrite receives the electric signals. After receiving the input through its dendrites, the neuron stimulates and becomes active.

In other words, the neuron works as a radio-set consisting with two antennas, first one is axon which transmits the electric signals and second one is dendrite which receives the signals of another neuron and stimulates the neuron in order to activate it. However, the signals transmitted by axons of one neuron move across synapses (a junction between two neurons consisting of a minute gap) and then reach to the dendrites of another neuron for receiving.

The communication between neurons is called neurotransmission that operates through electro chemical process. In the neurotransmission process a chemical substance is released at the end of fiber by the arrival of a nerve impulse and, by diffusing across the synapse, affects the transfer of the impulse to another nerve fiber, muscle fiber or some other structure known as neurotransmitter.

The brain's possible 'on-off' firing patterns in synaptic connections can be understand with the help of the description of Daniel J. Siegel neuroscientist executive Director of the Mindsight Institute Author of book *'Mindsight'*. He describes, "Brain's on-off firing potential for various states of activation has been calculated ten to millionth power. Thus the brain's complexity gives us virtually infinite choices for how our mind will use these firing patterns to create itself. If we get stuck only in few patterns, we are limiting our potential".

Mean to say, if we will do the work on routine bases, we will strengthen only few those circuits of neurons which will be utilized in that particular patterns of habitual work while rest of the neurons will remain inactive, and after some period inactive neurons will perish. Naturally, in such situation, evolution of mind comes to end.

Actually, at birth only ten percent of our brain's synapses are present while the remaining ninety percent are formed later. However, for further continuous evolvement of the brain, neurons require stimulation so that they can be activated and set up their networks to manage the major functions such as—sensory, motor, cognitive etc.

Anyhow, our neurons can be stimulated by many ways but best one is breaking the habitual routines. Mean to say, search new ways of doing the same things rather than repeat what you already know. Don't do things in the usual way? Rather do them in unusual way to achieve new experiences. In brief, change your habits, hobbies, schedules and interests frequently rather going round and round on the same path like bullocks of Persian wheel.

However, exchanging the ideas with others; learning new skills; choosing different paths; changing the setup of your office or home; changing the menu of your diets etc. can also stimulate your neurons. Actually nothing is fixed and everything is flexible so you can bring change anywhere you want to do so. Thus our brain is also flexible which can be changed any time irrespective of our age. However, our brain has ability to adapt a new condition whatever grim it may be, and for this adaption, brain form and organizes new synaptic connection. Thus in response to learning or to get experiences, our brain has the ability to change throughout our life.

This brain's amazing ability of physiological changes and adaption is termed 'neuroplasticity'. However, we can now observe how the brain changes with different learning experiences with the help of Magnetic Resonance Imagery (MRI.) Thus this process of brain's changing and adapting in new environment remains continue throughout life time making it possible for learning new things; changing the habits; choosing different path in life etc. Mean to say, the process of evolution of our brain from birth to death remains continue. However, the speed of evolution is differ from person to person depends on varieties of activities and experiences of varies fields.

Our neurons contribute to neuroplasticity in a number of ways. The best known of these processes is the way that the connections between the neurons or synapses strengthen with use. The more often we put these to work, the more neurotransmitters they produce, and the stronger the electrical signal conducted by dendrites. However, the neurons which are never used gradually wither and eventually disappeared. Thus, in order to save our neurons, we have to stimulate them frequently so that they may remain active and in use.

Thus as we learn something new, the end of axons spurt new branches, which then come into contact with the dendrites of the next neuron. New networks are formed and remain for as long as they are used. The more the neurons are stimulated, the greater the number of new connections formed. Thus new networks of neurons can be formed, organized and reorganized irrespective of age. However, brain's stimulation not only brings changes in neuron networks but it increases the size of hippocampal (part of brain mainly associated with memory, in particular long-term memory), gray matter also.

Neuroscientist Eleanor Maguire of University College London (UCL) got an idea in 1990s to study London cab drivers 'hippocampus when she had noticed that they have high navigation skill. However, to earn their licenses, cab drivers in training spend three to four years driving around the city on mopeds, memorizing a labyrinth of twenty five thousand streets within a ten kilometer radius of Charing Cross train station, as well as thousands of tourist attractions and hotspots.

Maguire found that London taxi drivers had more gray matter in their posterior hippocampi than people who were similar in age, education and intelligence, but who did not drive taxis. Mean to say, taxi drivers had plumper memory centers than their peers. The MRI also revealed that the longer someone had been driving a taxi, the larger his hippocampus, as though the brain expanded to accommodate the cognitive demands of navigating London's streets. However, the hippocampi of the taxi drivers were much larger than that of bus drivers, whose driving routes are well established and unchanging.

However, in starting, the research of Maguire was not accepted by some neuroscientists. Neurobiologist Howard Eichenbaum of Boston University comments the study for answering the "chicken-and-egg question" posed by Maguire earlier research. "The initial findings could have been explained by a correlation, that people with big hippocampi become taxi drivers," he says. However, Maguire and her associates carry on the study and after more than four years of their hard work, they have proved that it really was the training process that caused the growth of the brain.

Moreover, in 2003 Maguire won Ig Nobel Prize for medicine, awarded for 'presenting evidence that the brains of London taxi drivers are more highly developed than those of their fellow citizens'.

Thus, the London Taxi Cab Study provides a compelling example of the brain's neuroplasticity, or ability to reorganize and transform itself as it is exposed to learning and new experiences. Having to constantly learn new routes in the city forced the taxi cab drivers' brains to create new neural pathways 'in response to the need to store an increasingly detailed spatial representation.' These pathways permanently changed the structure and size of the brain, an amazing example of the living brain at work.

Therefore, don't be miser in using your brain because it will never terminate in your life time rather it will evolve more as you use it more. However, you have to cross the boundary of your comfort zone frequently. Moreover, your brain will be evolving till you will be challenging yourself and this process can be continued throughout your life.

How do knowledge, understanding and wisdom enhance out of comfort zone?

Actually, main positive character traits of our all careers are—knowledge, understanding and wisdom. However, those who always stay in their comfort zone are unable to achieve these qualities. Thus, lacks of these qualities affect their careers. It is a blunder to stay in the comfort zone because when you stay in your comfort zone, you limit your understanding to know the new things. Actually, comfort is like circumference of a well where not only your knowledge resists but your understanding and wisdom also ceases.

Researcher Denise Park of the University of Texas at Dallas says, "When you are inside your comfort zone you may be outside of the enhancement zone". Thus, by limiting yourself to what you already know, you are likely missing out of whole knowledge which may be achieved only out of comfort zone. Therefore, if you will close yourself in safe cocoon, you will lose so much in your life which can be only attained out of your comfort zone.

In this context, I would like to mention the description of Fritz Lieb who was professor of Theology in the University of Basel Switzerland. Lieb said that spiritual enquiry involves alternating questions and answers with silence and listening. In silence we enter the space of ayin, of not knowing. Our surroundings of thoughts and thinking invite new levels of wisdom, understanding and knowledge to reach us Ein Sof (The Endless One or Eternal).

Lieb described how spiritual enquiry takes us beyond the limits of our current level of understanding. Our questions open up previously locked doors, revealing new levels of understanding with which to make sense of the world and ourselves. As we continue evolve over time, these new levels of understanding may again feel limiting. At these moments we must return to silence and listen deeply until our silence becomes what Lieb named 'pregnant silence'—one that gives rise to a whole new level of understanding.

Thus, in order to reach Almighty, we have to enter the next level or state of spirituality where a brand new paradigm gives us more knowledge, understanding and wisdom for further proceeding. Moreover, this progression goes on infinitely. However, when a seeker reaches the outermost limits of his/her knowledge, he/she arrives at the point where knowledge originates. Naturally this process of knowing more and more cannot be completed without leaving the comfort zone. Mean to say, if we always remain in comfort zone, we cannot step up to the next level of spiritual level.

A.H. Almaas, Author and founder of the Diamond Heart School also described this silence stage and the various levels of understanding. He says, "On the journey of spiritual enquiry, first we find out that we don't know. Then we begin to know. We come to know more and more until we pass through all the knowledge and beyond it. When we stay with our enquiry until everything—all the details—have been revealed, then we arrive at the source from which all the knowledge springs—the pure awareness, the pure light of our Being where the mind is dissolved in wonder."

According to him, when everything that one can know about that particular level has been understood and even then some questions find no answers from existing pool of knowledge. Then a silence stage occurs and a new level of 'knowing' is born that is connected to an entirely higher level of understanding. It utilizes all of one's previous knowledge and questions as a means of attaining this level of knowledge. Thus these levels of 'knowing' can be climb like a ladder which is comprised with many rungs. However, there is no fix gaps between these rungs rather each has its own boundary. Thus this ladder reaches higher and higher up to infinite.

Every level creates its own silence that open recently and entirely new level of awareness for us. Thus our ability to know and understand things at different levels evolves throughout our whole life. Actually, by allowing ourselves to not know, we create a space within which we can learn something brand new. As we evolve spiritually, we must be willing to let go of all our prior knowledge, assumptions and understanding. Thus this silence stage is our guide holding as we grow in wisdom, understanding and knowledge.

Thus knowledge, understanding and wisdom cannot be enhanced without letting go. Moreover, letting go is only possible when we leave our comfort zone. Mean to say, Knowledge, understanding and wisdom can be attained only out of comfort zone because that is only area where we can know about various fields. Thus instead of confining yourself within limited levels of knowing, go through maximum levels of knowing, Moreover, for achieving this goal you have to leave your comfort zone.

How does our personality improve out of comfort zone?

Actually, to achieve maximum performance, we need a state of anxiety—a space where our stress levels are slightly higher than normal, and where our mental productivity and performance reach their peak. This space is called 'Optimal Anxiety' and it is just outside the comfort zone. Some research conducted on this topic show that when you really challenge yourself, you can turn up amazing results. For the reason, stepping out of comfort zone raises anxiety and generates a stress response which enhances the level of focus and concentration.

Thus, challenges are the essential requirement for our growth. On the contrary, if we are not growing, we are decaying and dying. Thus at elevated risk, we feel more alive. Actually, it is a state of flow which is an optimal state of consciousness where we can achieve highest performance. When we encounter with challenges, our focus and complete attention fix on the target and we completely absorbed in action.

Actions are, in fact, energy in motion, thus actions attract the things we want. Anyhow, miracles happen the moment we take the leap into the uncomfortable, thus risk and uncertainties compel us to stay in action until we achieve the goal we set out to accomplish. This is, in fact, law of attraction. On the contrary, if we are not willing to be uncomfortable, the law of attraction will not function. Thus the comfort zone which we do not want to leave will limit our professional opportunities, life experiences and personal growth.

Alan Henry an astrophysicist says —it is important to push the boundaries of your comfort zone, and when you do, it is kind of big deal. Cortisol the stress hormone helps the mind to develop new reactions to fear triggers. Thus a little anxiety can help us perform at our peak so anxiety leads to personal growth when it mixes with the feeling of success. Adventures induce anxiety and unease but when completed, they give us a huge feeling of accomplishment and increase our base level of confidence.

Pushing the boundary of your comfort zone can help you hit your stride sooner, get more done and find smarter ways to work. Once you acclimatize to work in the uncomfortable zone to that new level of anxiety, you have successfully expanded your comfort zone. Thus, once you start out of your comfort zone, it gets easier over time. Moreover, the more time you spend outside your comfort zones, the more you achieve. When you achieve, it spurs you onto push your comfort zones further and achieve more. Thus this process of expanding the comfort zone may be carried on forever.

Brene Brwn a research professor in the University of Houston also supports the above fact in her researches. She describes in her article *"You'll have an easiertime dealing with new and unexpected changes"* published in 'New York Times', "Learning to live outside of your comfort zone can prepare you for life changes that force you out of it. Thus as you step out of your comfort zone, you will become accustomed to that state of optimal anxiety (productive discomfort) becomes easier and push you further before your performance falloff".

Actually, this state of optimal anxiety termed as 'Productive discomfort' by psychologists because at this state, the production is maximum in spite of feeling uncomfortable. Therefore, from the research of Bren Brwn, it can be concluded that as you challenge yourself, your comfort zone adjusts accordingly. Thus the state which produces anxiety and seemed very difficult before leaving the comfort zone becomes more normal after entering in unknown and uncertain field; even it becomes easier as you repeat it.

Additionally, you learn some new skills when you work in any new field. Thus, there is an overall self-improvement you get through the skills you are learning. However, it is necessary to recognize your comfort zone minutely because everyone's comfort zone is different. Moreover, what may expand your horizons may paralyze someone else. Thus remember that 'optimal anxiety' can bring out your best while too much is bad thing and you have to remain aware so that you may not cross the limit of optimal anxiety.

In this context, psychologist Robert M Yerkes reported that anxiety improves performance until a certain optimum level arousal has been reached. Beyond that point, performance deteriorates as higher levels of anxieties are attended.

Dr. Elizabeth Lombardo, therapist and Author of 'Better than Perfect' describes, "Breaking your own mold can only make you stronger and more confident to reach higher levels in your profession. In order to more creative, you have to try new things, see things in new way and put pieces together in a new manner".

Thus, it can be said that in order to become more creative and emotionally resilient you should regularly seek out fresh experiences instead of remaining stuck in routine.

Actually, novelty tends to increase levels of dopamine in the brain which is part of the brain's 'reward center'. Moreover, Dopamine's roll, novelty and creativity altogether increase the urge. Novelty has also been shown to improve the memory, and increase the possibilities for learning by making our brains more malleable.

William J Hall, M D, Director of Centre for Health aging at University of Rochester Medical Centre says, "When you start something new, particularly in the creative area, it is just like a whack on the side of the head to your brain so always do something new which boost creativity, and zest to life and amp up your brain power".

Hall further says, "Find a new hobby associated with physical movement, painting, dancing, learning musical instrument etc. because Neurons that fire together grow together; there seems to be some kind of connection between thinking great thoughts and doing something with your feet, mouth or body". Thus, these types of things have a real blunting effect on more serious disorders such as Alzheimer's disease.

Dr. Denis C Park an orthopedic surgeon in San Mateo found in a study that learning new and demanding like skills while also maintain a strong social network, can help us stay mentally sharp as we get older. Further he says, "It seems it is not enough just to get out and do something—it is important to get out and do something that is unfamiliar and mentally challenging, and that provides broad stimulation mentally and socially. The new findings provide much-needed insight into the components of everyday activities that contribute to cognitive vitality as we age".

"We need as society, to learn how to maintain a healthy mind, just like we know how to maintain vascular health with diet and exercise." Says Park

Actually, we cannot expect to evolve in our lives and career until we leave our old habits and routine. Reaching new heights, in fact, involves the risk of attempting something we might not succeed at. Thus we have to take risk in order to improve our personality, and risk cannot be taken until and unless we leave our comfort zone.

Margie Warrell Author also wrote in Forbes magazine that in an increasingly competitive cautious and accelerated world, those who are willing to take risks step out of their comfort zone and into the discomfort of uncertainty will be those who will reap the biggest rewards.

Thus it is concluded from all above facts that stress is not a negative word but a little bit of healthy stress can actually act as a catalyst for personal growth and provides powerful motivation to do something seems impossible. Now it can be said that staying in comfort zone can result in consistent, steady performance while stepping out of comfort zone into a new and challenging task can create the conditions for the optimal performance.

Why is it so hard to leave the comfort zone?

Generally, it is a tendency of human being to cling with such object or remain in such situation which provides comfort. Thus we hold on our position, relationship and other such things which give us comfort. We do not want to leave our comfort zone because we have become habitual to live in this zone. We have become much dependent on comfortable state. We feel uneasy when we have to move at new place because we fear from unknown and uncertainty. Therefore, we are afraid to leave our comfort zone.

Actually, we have no courage to face new situation and challenges. We feel so secure in comfort zone that we always maintain status quo at any cost. Thus it is much easier to remain within the boundaries where we feel comfortable than it is to face the fear of venturing beyond them. Comfort zone associated with certainty so we know what to expect. As we leave the comfort zone, we have to face unexpected situations due to uncertainty. That's why we generally choose certainty.

Photographer and speaker Gary Arndt who has travelled almost all over the world said in this context that inertia is the most powerful force. Thus due to the tendency of inactivity, most people do what they do because changing what they do would require work and effort. That's why people get stuck in bad jobs and relationships. Everywhere around the world, generally, people get trapped into a typical lifestyle. However, to improve your personality and situation, you have to be able to do something which makes you uncomfortable. This usually goes away as soon as you adjust to having a new norm; ultimately this uncomforted zone will make you prosperous.

Fear of failure is also a reason for not leaving the comfort zone. We do not want to enter in unknown zone because we fear of failure. According to Dr. Elizabeth Lombardo, fear of failure is the main factor that holds most of us back from stepping out of our comfort zone. Any new skill always feels awkward and stressful at first, but the more you do it, the more comfortable with being uncomfortable. Generally, children are natural risk takers but as we grow older, we fear to fail. We stop learning due to fear of failure. Thus, we start holding ourselves back and attempting fewer new things.

The Author John Gardener also wrote about this fear of failure in '*Self Renewal*', "We pay a heavy price for our fear of failure". Thus, it is a powerful obstacle to growth which narrows personality of human being and prevents exploration and experimentation. Therefore, fear of failure pays a high cost to our tremendous potential for lifelong growth and transformation.

Denis Waitley who advised Olympic Athletes on 'How to gain mental edge' says, "We are ruled by habits. We do things the same old way because it is comfortable. However, the risk is in staying firmly inside our comfort zones is that it creates psychological barriers that can lead to dimensions". "As we haven't done anything dynamic in a long time, we begin to think we can't". He further explains.

Fear of uncertainty is also a big reason to remain in comfort zone. Actually, we afraid of uncertainty but the thrilling and excitement can be experienced only in uncertainty. In comfort zone we always know what will happen next. Therefore we are compelled to live a life which revolves around dull routine. Thus due to fear of facing the uncertainty, we live mundane life. However, we prefer to live in certainty which can be found only in comfort zone.

Let the fear of failure or fear of uncertainty, whatever may be the fear, fear has the potential to paralyze the people. Actually, we live in the world of phobia which is being increased day by day by social media and inexperienced and very selfish people. Actually, those people who have never left their comfort zone in their lives do not want that other people leave this zone, and able to get something which they themselves could not get. They are, in fact, live their lives in frustration. Thus, such frustrated people busy in spreading rumors to increase the phobia. Sothis negative environment and so-called fear hold you back and compel you remain in the comfort zone.

Generally, people believe on the rumors and myth instead of believing their own understanding. Thus, they remain in the same situation where they feel comfortable. I have noticed that many employees approach for cancelation of their transfer order to avoid new place of working. Even some refuse to take promotion so that they may escape from more responsibilities. Thus they remain stay in comfort zone even they use unfair means to avoid the forthcoming unknown situation. Mean to say, people want to remain in comfortable position on one pretext or another.

Anyhow, if such cowards have to leave the comfort zone due to some unavoidable circumstances, they feel queasy in their stomach; their mouths go dry; their knees feel weak; their hearts start beating rapidly. Even some of them are hospitalized. That's why most people remain in doing what they are doing for a long period. Actually, they are so accustomed in the habitual pattern that the pattern has become part of their life. For them, to leave the comfort zone is as difficult as cut their own limbs.

How to leave the comfort zone?

Actually, happiness is hidden in the unknown. Pearls cannot be found by sitting on the coast of the sea. They lies deep in the sea and only those who take risk of their lives and get inside can find them. Therefore, you have to push the boundaries of comfort zone to get something valuable. How far you push your boundaries is depend entirely on you. What methods you adapt is secondary thing, first you have to take first step towards breaking the boundary of comfort zone. How much the first step hard may be but you should remember that the longest journey starts with that single step.

Moreover, the first step is to face the fear and overcome it by doing what you afraid to do. Thus transform your feeling of fear into feeling of excitement and opportunity. For this, probably you have to bear the sarcastic comments of the relatives and society. However, ignore such things and go head. Instead of taking long jumps regarding overcoming of fears, take small steps towards the fear you are trying to overcome. Stay longer where you feel uncomfortable. After some period in staying the uncomfortable situation, you will realize that you are in comfortable situation. Means, every uncomfortable situation becomes comfortable when you become accustomed to live in it.

Actually, it is natural tendency that after some duration new things which impress us too much become ordinary. Interesting things, if you do them continuously, become common. Even hobbies become boring if you do not innovate something new in them. This phenomenon is known as hedonistic adaption. That's why, to live a vigorous and zestful life; we have to always do something new and challenging.

Actually, as we take on something challenging, we experience an endorphin rush and often feel recharge afterward. Mean to say, challenging work acts positively and keep us fresh and cheerful. On the other hand, fear pushes us towards gloomy side.

Actually, fear is only illusion, a ghost which exists only in our mind. When we overcome of this ghost, the journey of our future will become very easy.

After overcoming of fear, you can start with little things such as take different route for work or walking; change your diet pattern; change the setup of your workplace or room; open the door lock with blindfolded; makeup or shave yourself in dark; try new restaurant; observe fast in any day of the week; observe a silence day weekly or monthly etc. Mean to say, do something you wouldn't normally do for fear of looking idiot. Be that idiot. Then with a little practice and adjustment you can break your routine.

After breaking the routine, you will find that it wasn't as scary as you imagined. These things can help you to get comfortable with the discomfort that comes from trying something new. Then start to change something big and great situations such as take transfer in new office or new place if you are employees; change the modus operandi of your business; shift the house if you are living in rented house; even sale your own house and buy new in another locality; change the job if you are not satisfied with your current job etc.

I was transferred sixteen times in my career of two central government's jobs and where I am now residing is my twenty seventh residence of my life.

In addition, I had done my own business and remained succeeded. In other words, I always preferred new situations and different nature of work in order to achieve more experiences. Therefore, I always chose the activities involved more risk; successfully handled the situations full of problems and difficulties and faced four court cases and all verdicts of courts had gone in my favor. I always performed courageous feats and accepted the challenges, even this trend is still continuing.

Mean to say, in spite of leaving many comfort zones throughout my whole life, I am living happily with peace of mind in the lap of Nature at a beautiful hill station and enjoying the pension of two services. Mean to say; by leaving the comfort zone, nothing will happen wrong rather you will live your life at its full stretch with more cheerfully as I am living today. It is another matter that in spite of living very comfortable life here, I am planning to leave this comfort zone also so that I may live a challenging life once more. Thus don't confine yourself in any boundary rather break it and step out where a wondrous world is waiting for your welcome. Anyhow, take risk by changing the status quo because only taking risk push you towards growth.

If you always use same path you already know, no doubt that you will find your destination easily but you will lose yourself. Mean to say, you will be not more than the pigeon that carried the post in olden days from one place to another. Anyhow, if you always do same things in the same old way, you will get same results. You have noticed that in work places it is easy to fall into the trap of doing the same old things in the same old ways and ending up the same result. However, changes are painful, but nothing is more painful than staying in the wrong places and accepting wrong decisions. Thus be courageous and change the status quo.

Actually, when you change a single area of your life, other fields of your life also move towards transforming. Thus allow yourself to become new. Consider this world a dynamic place where ups and downs are parts of life rather than considering it a safe and predictable place. I experienced that those who remain in comfort zone invite frustration and disappointment for themselves. Thus, breaking up the comfort zone and taking risk is better than frustration.

Additionally, start gardening; learning new skills; new languages; musical instruments; some challenging games; such sports which you never played in your life and visit frequently new places even new countries. Watching movie of other languages and trying to understand with gestures of actors is also an interesting experience. Mean to say, change over the switch what you are doing to something else which is challenging and more interested, and broaden your horizons in different way and different direction.

The aim of stepping out of your comfort zone is to embrace new experiences and to get that state of optimal anxiety which stimulate your brain. Thus, novelty in activities is required in order to change your routine. The more often you do somethings in the same way, the more difficult it is consider doing it differently. Therefore, don't waste your time rather bring changes now. However, if you cannot bring changes now, you cannot bring them throughout in life time. If you ignore this basic desire for change and remain unable to stimulate your brain, you tend to feel less alive. Thus seek any activity which can break your repeated routine in order to stimulate the neurons of your brain.

Additionally, the new activity reduces your boredom. Psychologist Vivian Diller says that boredom most often results from repetition of routine and laziness. Thus, have patience so that your experience may reflect on, and you may reap the benefits and apply such new activities in day – to-day life. Anyhow, after developing these activities in habit, change the activities again and always try to do something new and interesting daily, weekly and monthly. In addition, always embrace the diversity of challenges so that you may push the boundaries of your comfort zone in all directions.

Dr. Lombardo says, "Do something new on regular basis—the more comfortable you get with trying new things, the less you are going to avoid it and the more you are going to say yes to new challenges". "Doing something that challenges you, gives you a whole different outlook and makes you more receptive to change" she says further.

Corrine Lin an Author describes, "Say yes even when you don't think you are ready". If you are working, say yes to new project, new assignments, and new roles—even when you have not done it before. It opens up huge opportunities in your career. Who knows you might find yourself enjoying something you never got the chance to explore earlier. Make a list of all the things that you feel uncomfortable doing, and start doing them like hobby.

Gordon Ritter a Triathlete founder of Emergence Capital says, "I continue to find ways to get out of my comfort zone". "If you go too long without pushing boundaries, you get stale", he further says. Thus make a role model who overcame big hurdles to do what you want to do. Then it will be easy for you if you follow someone who has paved the way.

Nicholas Turiano who is National Research Service Award post-doctoral fellow at the University of Rochester Medical Center's Psychiatry Department says, "When confronted with problem, don't stress out; think creatively about how to solve it. There isn't one specific type of creative person". "You can become more creative just by trying new things. Keeping the brain healthy may be one of the most important aspects of aging successfully—a fact shown by creative persons living longer in our study," he further says.

The study of Turiano found a link between a longer life and creative thinking. Since the brain is the powerhouse or commanding center for all functions of in the body, there is definitely an advantage to continually exercise the brain—which is hallmark of those high in creativity.

Thus, it is concluded that the only way to change our circumstances is to venture out of our comfort zone. However, it is the exact place where you will find everything you have ever wanted. Whether it is joy, love, prosperity, excitement, thrilling or anything regarding your personal goal can only be found only out of your comfort zone. Therefore, do not confine yourself in the cocoon of comfort zone, break it and embrace the unknown.

I admit that initially, to leave the comfort zone and enter in unknown zone may be uncomfortable and difficult. However, I noticed throughout my life that whatever we feel uncomfortable in new situation becomes more comfortable after some period than previous comfortable zone which we had left reluctantly. Generally, in the busy schedule we forget that there may be any another place and other people we might meet if we break this identical routine. Therefore, with repeated efforts our comfort zone expands to include the things that we really want from life.

Thus, the life you want is waiting for you outside of your comfort zone and you need not to travel very far away. However, you have only step out of the person you normally are and find the new 'you'. Therefore, dive in uncertainty and embrace the unknown so that you may remain fresh and you always feel alive and cheerful.

Chapter 12

Develop a positive attitude

"Keep your face to the sunshine and you cannot see the shadow"—Helen Keller.

Generally, we are taught since our childhood that we are born with destiny that cannot be changed. However, first of all we have to change this prejudice. Man comes in this world, in fact, with a clean slate. Mean to say, human's mind is complete blank at the time of birth. However, as we grow, we start learning informally as well as formally. In addition, we experience some good and bad events, and the phenomena of their occurrence are explained and described to us by our parents and other elders related to our family or society in which we are brought up according to their own beliefs.

Thus in this way whatever is taught to us, start accumulating in our unconscious mind as belief. According to those beliefs, our thoughts start to develop. Thus thoughts are nothing but mind stuff filled through the informal teaching process by our parents and other elders according to their own point of views. Thus whatever we learn from them, every bit of information start to pile up in our mind known as minds stuff. It can also be said that our basic mind stuff is developed on the basis of the beliefs of our parents, relatives or other elders. So there is no guarantee that these beliefs are true. If the beliefs are true then our basic mind stuff is real, and our attitudes develop accordingly.

On the contrary, if the beliefs are false then our mind filled with wrong mind stuff which may leads to prejudices and superstition. This feedback is going on....and our attitude develops accordingly. Thus it is our attitude which makes us optimist or pessimist; coward or courageous; selfish or selfless; kind or unkind, or whatever we are, even our habits develop accordingly. Then set of habits make our character. Therefore, our attitude plays an important role in developing our personality, even our destiny forms accordingly. Anyhow, before knowing the importance of attitude in our life, it is necessary to know what the attitude is exactly.

What is Attitude?

According to Business Dictionary, "Attitude is a predisposition or a tendency to respond positively or negatively towards a certain idea, object, person, or situation".

Whilst according to founder of analytical psychology Swiss psychiatrist and psychologist Carl Jung, "Attitude is a readiness of the psyche to act or react in a certain way."

Social psychologists Eagly and Chaiken define an attitude as a psychological tendency that is expressed by evaluating a particular entity with some degree of favor or disfavor.

Actually attitudes are combined results of our experiences and upbringing, and they are powerful experiences over behavior. It can also be said that our attitudes are formed by our basic mind stuff which have been stuffed in our mind at the time of our upbringing and then shaped by our own experiences. Thus our attitude is constantly changing with the experiences. Therefore, as we experience something new, our attitude may be changed. Thus psychologists define attitude a learned tendency to evaluate things in a particular way. Such evaluation may be positive or negative.

Therefore, attitude can be described as a tendency to react positively or negatively to a person or circumstances. It can also be said that an attitude refers to a set of positive or negative emotions, beliefs and behaviors towards a particular object, person, thing or event.

Dr. Richard W Scholl, a professor of the University of Rhode Island, says that attitudes are the 'mental folders' where attitudes' objects such as perceptions, beliefs, feelings and expectations about the environment are stored. So attitudes are such mind stuff which decide thinking pattern and they shape how to relate to the society. It can also be said that it is the way of act and behavior of the individual. In other words, it is a way of person's response to his or her environment either positively or negatively.

According to Robert Jeffress Baptist Pastor, "We can say that attitude is a mental and emotional response to the variety of circumstances that occur in life. They are not specifically behaviors but mods or forms of conduct or performance. It is express outwardly, through gestures, movements, words, cries, laughs, tears, or sometimes stillness and apathy. However it is also responds to internal, cognitive and effective stimuli, you cannot have an attitude to what is not known or is not valued as good or bad".

Thus, from all above definitions, it can be concluded that we see the world according to our mind stuff developed so far. Mean to say, we do not see the world as it is rather we see it as we are. Therefore, in order to see the reality, we have to fill our mind with the real stuff because it is mind stuff which affects our behavior. However, if our mind stuff is already developed positively, no need to change it. On the other hand, negative mind stuff should be changed in order to develop positive attitude. Therefore, it is necessary to know what positive attitude is and what is negative.

A positive attitude indicates the strong will and optimistic reaction to adversity. It develops optimistic thinking and avoids worried and negative thinking. With positive attitudes day-to-day affairs can deal better because it brings optimistic view in handling life's situation. Thus when you demonstrate the positive attitude, you are optimistic and expect favorable outcome.

On the contrary, negative attitude is a harrowing vision, living in the state of apprehension with the consequent reaction apathetic or aggressive so it pushes us towards dark side of life. Means negative attitude develops pessimistic thinking which sees negativity in each situation.

How to Develop Positive Attitude

It has been already described that attitude is the result of mind stuff developed in the process of learning in childhood of an individual. Whether it is positive or negative, in both cases, it works as feedback to develop further attitudes. Mind stuff decides the mode of action which further develops the pattern of thoughts. Eventually, these thoughts become the parts mind stuff, and this system of feedback is going on.......continually until the mind stuff is changed.

I would like to clarify this theory with an example of child. Suppose a five years old child likes a beautiful flower and wants to achieve it. Then the child thinks all option of getting it. Either he can ask to gardener for plucking the flower or he can steal it. Ultimately, he decides according to his mind stuff which has been developed so far. The action of achieving the flower will affect his mind stuff and thought pattern accordingly. If his mind stuff is positive, he will take permission from gardener before plucking the flower. On the contrary, if his mind stuff is negative, he will steal the flower.

Thus in both ways, this action of plucking the flower, enhances his mind stuff accordingly. Mean to say, this event of his life either leads him towards greatness or it may pushes him towards a professional thief. Thus each and every childhood's action provides a feedback to develop the mind stuff at either side. Thus whatever is the mind stuff, it enhances the thought pattern and whatever is the thought pattern, it enhances action. And whatever is the action, it enhances the mind stuff. Then this circle completes and it is going on constantly. So each and every action provides feedback to make it stronger. Thus, attitude develops accordingly.

In other words, mind stuff (attitude), thought pattern and action are linked to each another and they altogether make a triangular feedback which enhances continuously either side. Actually, action is decided according to ones thought pattern, thus accomplishment of action develops attitude. Then attitude enhances the thought pattern, and thought pattern again effect ones action. If thoughts are positive, individual will act positively, and positive action develops positive attitude. Thus positive attitude further enhances the positive thoughts and the process is going on. On the contrary same phenomenon is applied in developing negative attitude. Mean to say, origination point of each and every act irrespective to evil or good is—mind.

In order to develop positive attitude, first of all it is necessary to recognize your mind stuff. If your mind stuff is already positive then you have to only improve it which is not much difficult. On the contrary, if your mind stuff is negative then you have to reverse it. However, it may be difficult to reverse, but it is not impossible. Anyway, first of all, you have to control your desires, and choose them according to their need. If you make reasonable choices and act accordingly, you will get satisfying results.

William Glassner, psychiatrist wrote in his book *'Choice Theory'*, "We choose everything we do including misery. Other people can make us neither miserable nor happy. We are very much in control of our lives than we believe. Therefore, we should change the myth that our sufferings are due to our fate".

Actually, we write our fate daily. We should know that we have the ability to shape our destiny like potter shapes clay. We are architect of our lives. We can make our lives as beautiful as we think. If there are any limits to this, those are self-imposed. When we change our self- image, limits will be crossed automatically.

Therefore, to develop positive attitude, we have to change our subconscious mind stuff. And for changing the mind stuff, we have to analyze each and every thought. Thus through this analyzing process, we will be able to convert negative thinking into positive thinking. Thinking is habit whether it is negative or positive. Therefore, always think positively so that it becomes habit after some period. Actually, situations or circumstances are not positive or negative they are only real, only our reactions to them make differences.

Thus, instead of remains control in your attitude, take control of your attitude in your hand by reacting positively to the situation. After controlling the reactions, result will also be controlled. Positive thoughts lead to positive attitude. In order to develop the positive thoughts, fill the brain with positive messages with the help of optimistic books, articles, movies, songs, etc. Read inspiring stories and biography of successful persons. Avoid negative social media's messages which are too much in circulation for spreading panic and rumors.

In addition, always try to surround with positive thinking people who inspire and encourage you rather with toxic people who discourage you. Program your mind with positive vocabulary and use positive words in your conversation. When you face any problem, break down the problem in various parts. As you know that a huge log cannot be lifted from road to clear the road, the road can be cleared after cutting the log into pieces. Then small pieces can be removed easily. Mean to say, solve the problem step by step.

Additionally, consider the adversity as challenge and sustain positive emotions to face the adverse situation. Actually, there are no dead ends but only re-directions. Therefore, instead of frustration, change your strategy when you do not get success. Changing of strategies and methods may bring success for you. So do not quit and have patience!

Accept the failure because failure gives you valuable experiences which make you enable to judge the situation wisely. Eventually, good judgments lead you towards success. So consider failure only an ingredient of success. Everyone experience failure or rejection in his or her life. No one can achieve maturity without failure. So instead of discouraging by failure, take it as positively.

Failure, in fact, is nothing but one more bitter experience which adds in your treasury of wisdom which helps you in future for taking right decision. However, failure is in sense is a gateway to success, in as much as every discovery of what is false leads us to seek earnestly after what is true. Thus every fresh experience points out some form of error which we shall afterwards avoid carefully. Therefore, do not afraid to be failures. They will only lead you towards wisdom.

Robert Toru Kiyosaki an Author also says, "Have fun with challenges, embrace them as adventures instead of attempting to resist an experiences for growth. Sometimes you win and sometimes you learn".

Thus, neither blames others for any particular circumstances nor comparison yourself with others in any critical situation. You and only you can surmount your problem with the help of your positive attitude. So seek solution rather than point out the problem. A study done at Warsaw School of Social Psychology shows that complaining leads to lower moods and increase negative emotions, decrease life satisfaction and optimism.

In addition, you can practice being positive, all of us know that practices make man perfect. Love yourself and accept yourself fully as you are. Seek good characteristics in your style, your looking, your dressing, your behavior, your conversation, modus operands of your work etc. Share your positive thoughts with others, appreciate others and support them rather than criticism. Make a worthy goal in your life, even set a goal for each day to make someone else smile, and seek the reason of your own smiling. Be kind, sympathetic and compassionate to everyone. Express gratitude wherever and whenever it is required.

Above all, search your mind stuff with the help of retrospection or meditation. When you are searching your mind deeply, a visceral change occurs. Your attitude shifts towards positivity. Such as—you go from seeing problem to seeing solution; you go from a mind that's focus on the dark side of the world to focus on bright side; you go from shrinking the challenges to face them boldly and go towards seeing silver line in each and every adversity.

Positive attitude enhances our overall well-being and Personality

Actually, positive attitude, optimism, expectancy and enthusiasm make day-to- day activities easier. Positive attitude boost your mood up when you feel gloomy. The people of positive attitude see something good in each and every event. Whatever the terrible situation may be, they look only bright side of it. So they find something good in every situation and every person. Thus people with positive attitude are able to look through the difficulties they face and believe they can find a way through those difficulties.

Jeff Keller Author of '*Attitude is everything*' said, "Attitude does not emerge from what happens to you but instead from how you decide to interpret what happens to you". As you start thinking positively, you start to learn from each and every adverse situation. Thus you can deal the stress easily.

Dr. Ronald Rubenzer of the, Midwest center for Stress and Anxiety suggests that you can convert bad stress into good stress through your thoughts. Instead of feeling 'stressed out', turn the situation into an exciting opportunity for growth and achievement. People who have positive attitude can maintain physical and mental health in good condition. Thus overall well-being can improve by learning how to hold a positive state of mind.

Dr. Charles Raison, Director of Behavioral Immunology Program at the Emory University School of Medicine also says, "When people have positive attitude they do not perceive stress as intensely dangerous or as difficult as they would if they had a more negative attitude. Positive attitude provides improved coping skills when you are faced with challenges or adversity".

The Mayo clinic also states that a positive attitude can lower your stress level, which is good for your mental and physical health. In other words, it is how people respond to stress that determines whether they will profit from misfortune or be miserable.

Immune system has been found better in those people who have positive attitude. David B Beaton of the Rochester Institute of Technology has conducted a review of the field of Psychoneuroimmunology and how psychopathology may impact the body's immune system. What Beaton found were correlation between a positive attitude and body's immune system. In other words, positive attitude play an important part in helping the body fight to illness and disease.

A study conducted by Carver et al. 1993 found that optimist people experience less distress when faced with potentially life-threatening cancer diagnoses.

Kohat Cooper Nicklaus Russell and Cunnick also conducted a study in 2012, in that study; elderly adults were immunized for influenza. Two weeks later, their immune response to the vaccination was measured. Greater optimism predicted greater antibody production and better immune outcomes. It means positive attitude's people recover rapidly from illness and disease.

The positive attitude's people have the ability to 'bounce back' from difficult circumstances. The American Psychological Associate found that resiliency, or hardiness has three attitudinal components: commitment, control and challenge. Commitment is the willingness to stay engaged rather than become isolated during hard times, choosing to be involved in life's next step. Second one is control, here the meaning of control is willingness to try and influence the outcome of challenging circumstances. Third one, challenging is the ability to view each situation as an opportunity to learn.

Additionally, the people who have positive attitude produce more energy and they save energy which negative attitude's people spent in unnecessary thinking. People who have positive attitude are more confident and have faith in their abilities. They are able to inspire and motivate themselves and others. Therefore, they get more respect and love from others. They achieve their goal easily, and success in their lives because they are creative, capable in taking better decision and choose better options. They are humble, charming, affectionate, caring and self-disciplined.

Thus positive attitude helps the persons to overcome the obstacles and make them mature to solve the problems. Actually, the way we think affects the things that are going to happen in our lives. Moreover, the positive attitude is the way that we behave and the way we react to the daily activities. Eventually positive attitude influence our lives in a deep way such as how we think, act, socialize etc. Mean to say, our whole personality is determined by our attitude.

In this context Thomas Jefferson 3rd U S president said, "Nothing can stop the man with the right mental attitude from achicving his goal while nothing on earth can help the man with wrong mental attitude".

Positive attitude reduces suffering and enhances happiness

Suffering and happiness are relative terms rather than absolute. Some people suffer even in good conditions while some people remain happy even in bad conditions. In this context Frederick Lang bridge Poet and Author said, "Two men look out through same bars: one sees the mud and another sees the stars". It can also be said that all that we are, is the result of are our thoughts. If a man speaks or acts with an evil thought, pain follows him. On the contrary, if a man speaks or acts with pure thought, happiness follows him.

Suffering and happiness depend on our attitude. We cannot control events because they are beyond our control. Only our mind can be brought under control, remaining world such as—behavior of the other people, events, calamities etc. are beyond our control. Thus we should differentiate between what can be controlled and what cannot be controlled. Otherwise any type of confusion will create only sorrow.

Therefore, we should always remember that what is beyond our control will happen definitely whether we like or not. If we set our mind accordingly, we will be less miserable on happenings otherwise we will suffer more. How much tragedy effects any person is entirely depends on the individual's attitude. Some people react too much even on small matters while some react less even on big matters. Thus some are capable to bear big tragedy while some breakdown on occurring of even small happening. It is all matter of the individual's attitude.

In this context Marcus Aurelius Antonius Roman Emperor and a Stoic Philosopher said, "If you are distressed by anything external, the pain is not due to the thing itself, but to your estimate of it and you have the power to revoke at any moment" It means it is not external things that disturb you but your own judgment about them, and you can wipe out that judgment any time if you want to do so.

Thus, suffering can be reduced to some extent by changing the attitude. After happening of any event, crying and irritation make no difference. How much we cry, how much we irritate, the event which has been already happened will not reverse. However, only our reaction toward any event is in our control. Happiness comes if we accept the tragedy with tranquility while our resentment towards event makes us misery.

Thus with right attitude we can reduce the burden of misery. Therefore, you can choose to be happy or sad. Whichever you choose that is what you get. Johan Milton English Poet and Author also said that the mind can make a heaven of hell and a hell of heaven. Actually, suffering conveys us that time has come to change our attitude. If we don't change ourselves, we experience more suffering. Thus, in order to choose happiness, changing is necessary.

Actually, every bitter experience is a signal for us and has a hidden message. However, often we fail to understand this message. All events happen to us so that we may learn some lesson. If we do not learn the lesson at first time, the life repeats it again and again, like a teacher of classroom, until we change our attitude. Suffering is like holding a piping hot bowl in hand. When we realize pain in our hand, we either shift it in another hand or put dawn to relieve the pain. Thus we should understand that suffering befalls on us in order to change our response regarding any happening. It can also be said that suffering is a turning point in our lives.

All tragedies, in fact, have some hidden message for us so that we may change our current way to handle the situation. Therefore, they happened to us so that our attitude might be changed in order to live a better life. If we change our attitude earlier, we will suffer less otherwise we have to get experience of suffering again and again until we change our attitude.

In this context Peter McWilliams Author said, "The more severe the pain or illness, the more severe will be the necessary changes. These may involve breaking bad habits or acquiring some new and better ones".

Thus no one is really responsible to make someone else happy or sad. You have the power to be whatever you want to be. You choose to be happy, joyous and peaceful. Only your affirmation can make you whatever you want to be. You can create yourself happy and joyous when you consciously choose to be blissful personality and let go of your grief.

The greatest cosmic law is that whatever you hold in your thought will come true in your experience. When you hold something in your thought, then somehow coincidence leads you in the direction you have been wishing to lead yourself. Thus it is our own choice whether we want to go towards sadness or happiness.

Actually, whole of existence is just a reverberation of energy in the form of vibrations. Thus our thought is also vibrational energy. If we generate a powerful thought and let it out, it will always manifest itself, and anything that we wish will definitely happen. Thus in order to live joyfully and peacefully, we have to think accordingly. However, first of all, what we want must be well manifest in our mind. Once we maintain a study stream of thought, then its manifestation as reality in our life will not be far away.

Thus to avoid sorrow, we have to resist ourselves from focusing our thought on it. On the contrary, to attain happiness we have to hold the thought which focus only on happiness. The way we think lead to the way we feel so unorganized mind organizes our emotions. Once our thought and emotions organized, our energies will go to the same way. Then our body will also get organized accordingly. Once all these four factors (thoughts, emotions, energy and physical body) are organized in one direction, our ability to create and manifest what we want is phenomenal.

In this context, Sadguru, founder of Isha Yoga says, "If you organize your mind to certain level, it in turn organizes the whole system. Your body, your emotions, your energies, everything gets organized in that direction. If life has to happen the way you think, it should happen accordingly how you think; how much stability is there in your thought and how much reverberation is there in your thought process".

Thus we are creator of happiness by holding our thought accordingly and tune our mind to the extent to attain happiness. We should understand that we are the chooser of our response to the situation at any given moment. Blaming others for any situation only increase the suffering. Excuses are created only for self-defense so they cannot give us happiness.

Therefore, we should understand the truth that happiness is created by ourselves so we and only we can generate happiness for us but none of else. And no any outer object is required to generate it. Means, it is generated from within rather than without. However, to generate happiness, we have to develop such positive attitude which focuses only on blessing rather than woes. Thus we ourselves have the power to transform our grief into bliss.

CHAPTER 13

Trust yourself and have faith in God!

"As soon as you trust yourself, you will know how to live."—John Wolfgang Von Goethe.

Many people believe more on others than themselves because they do not trust on their own ability. Thus, due to lack of their self-trust, their personality cannot develop thoroughly. However, before taking the suggestion on any issue, we should confirm properly whether the person who is giving advice is applying the same on himself or herself. A person who becomes irritate when the train or bus is slightly late but teaches you a lesson on patience. A bankrupt gives you the suggestion regarding saving and investment. An unhealthy person gives lecture on health and diet. Means, in each and every field you may meet such so- called specialists who advise you in every step but they themselves do not follow their own advice.

There is an African saying, "Be careful when a naked person offers you a shirt." Mean to say, if anyone is unable to use his or her strategy, policy or suggestion on himself or herself, the advice should be ignored. Therefore, to avoid such unnecessary advices, we have to develop trust in ourselves. Instead of trusting on any novice's advice, take decisions according to your own experiences. Therefore, before taking any decision, ask yourself and decide whatever your intellect and intuition say.

Meaning of self-trust

Buddhism describes about self-trust, "Self-trust means dedication to and conviction in one's own wisdom, which permits one's own intellect to begin to manifest as one's *guru*, teacher and spiritual friend. Moreover, when you will understand this truth, you will be able to trust on yourself confidently." Anyhow, when you develop self-trust in you, others will also start trusting on you.

Cynthia Wall LCSW a psychotherapist in private practice in northern California said, "Self-trust means that you can take care of your needs and safety," It means you first yourself to survive situations, and then practice kindness, and perfection. Thus in order to do something for others, you have to know yourself; trust yourself and love yourself.

In the courage to Trust Wall lists other components that encompass self-trust. They include: Being aware of your thoughts and feelings, and expressing them; following your personal standards not ethical code; knowing when you need to care for yourself first; knowing you can survive mistakes, get up and try again; and pursuing what you want without stopping or limiting others.

Self-trust, in fact, requires a deep understanding acceptance of who we are. If we really trust ourselves, it means that we are bringing our authentic self to work every day in everything we did and how we do it. When we trust on ourselves, we become so capable that we can share our knowledge, wisdom and secrets with others. It can also be said that self-trust is much more than just self- confidence.

Importance of self-trust in human's life.

We need strength, courage and wisdom to cope with day-to-day difficulties, in life's critical situations and during adversities. These qualities neither can be bought nor borrowed from someone. There is one and only one source—and that is our own inner wisdom. However, there is unlimited strength within us but we fail to recognize it. Therefore, we should recognize it and have to harness this energy. Thus trust more on yourself than any outer source. Then not only you can get rid of from your own problems but you can help other people also in solving their problems.

You have so much energy that you can change the world and your actions make this world very beautiful. Swami Vivekananda said, "Never lose faith in yourself: you can do anything in the Universe." He further said that history of the world is the history of a few men who had trust themselves. That trust calls out the dignity within. You can do anything. Your failure is only due to not striving sufficiently to manifest infinite power.

According to Vivekananda, whatever we think, we will be. If we think ourselves weak, we will be weak; if we think we are in misery, we will be in miserable condition. If we think, the way will never work out. Then at that instant every cell in our being will be deflated and give up the fight, and then everything really will move in the direction of failure. On the contrary, if we think we are strong, strong we will be; if we think we are happy, happy we will be. Thus, optimistic nature and will power is necessary to attain success in life.

R W Emerson also said that self-trust is the first secret of success. Actually, self-trust is often overlooked yet it is the most powerful quality we have.

In order to succeed in anything, we must possess this ability. Then we can only become capable of achieving things which we want to achieve. We feel more powerful and stronger as and when we achieve our targets.

Trusting ourselves more and more leads us towards acquiring more confidence to do any difficult task. Eventually, these accomplishments realize us a successful personality. Thus, self-trust is most important factor in our life, and our whole personality can be defined according to our degree of self-trust. In other words, it is the core of our personality.

Alan Alda a prominent American screenwriter and Author explained creativity as going into the place where no one else has ever been. He said, "You have to leave the city of your comfort and go into the wilderness of your intuition. A child with healthy sense of self-trust is more akin to freely explore his creative abilities".

Author Rita Mae Brown an American writer and activist also has similar views regarding creativity. She explained that creativity comes from self-trust so self-trust appears to be precursor to creativity. Therefore, the people who trust themselves are generally more creative than those who are lack in self-trust.

Additionally, self-trust frees us from self-doubt and leads in right direction. It frees us from fear and anxiety so we feel more relax and feel high self-esteem. Self-trust makes us feel more worthy irrespective to others' opinions about us. Thus we become more confident to face challenges and difficulties rather than feeling crippled and defeated.

Christel Nani RN Medical Intuitive wrote in her book *'Sacred Choices,* "A limiting belief will severely hamper your ability to follow your guidance or inner knowing."

When we trust ourselves we are first of all keeping our power, as opposed to giving our power away to outside sources. Thus we gain more energy and motivation to act. When we experience happiness or assurance on the approval of others, the happiness dissipates as and when the approval has been removed. It means these feelings are short-lived due to conditional. On the contrary, when we trust ourselves we won't fear failure and making mistake because our sense of self is not externally derived.

Therefore, we feel more comfortable with others and in return, they also respect us more and have more trust on us. If you do not trust on yourself, no one will trust on you. Thus, in order to make people trust you, understand your worth and value—trust on yourself. Then your self-trust will attract the trust of others spontaneously. Naturally, your self-trust leads you towards success, happiness and peace of mind.

How to develop self-trust?

First of all, you have to recognize your inner strength and remain honest to yourselves what you do. Thus recognize your inner strength, build it and use it wherever it is required. Honor your self-esteem, position and achievements. Your achievements themselves are a big source of your motivation. On introspecting in yourself, you will find that you have achieved all goals in your life only due to trusting on yourself rather than depending on others. Therefore, you have to only believe in yourself that the self-trust which did not betray you so far will not betray you in future also.

Actually, everyone in our life has the tendency to betray you. Some have left you in the middle of the way; some have ignored you; leave you; some have commented you in sarcastic way and some have told lie to you. Even some of them cheated you one way or another and have hurt you in many different ways. Anyhow, you have been disappointed by them; you have noticed yourself that there is only one person who has not betrayed you so far and that is—you. So first of all, trust on yourself then others will also trust on you.

In this context, Cynthia Wall a psychotherapist describes in her book, *The Courage to Trust: A guide to building deep and lasting relationship, the person you need to trust first is yourself.* "We can't count anybody hundred percent but this does not mean we should isolate ourselves or harden our hearts. But it does stress the importance of being able to trust the one person we know we can count on—'ourselves'." Thus no one can be as consistently, supportive of you as you can learn to be. When you introspect, you encounter with unique and bold self who crossed all hurdles of life. It was only your self-trust which made you so capable to face such problems.

Lea Brovedani, The Trust Architect, and The Author of *'Trusted: A Leader's Lesson* 'said, "Each situation has its own unique demands—if you meet them first, others fits into places. Self-trust is based on our ability to be true to ourselves and follow through on what we commit to. It is based on building our confidence in overcoming certain obstacles and consistently doing."

Thus instead of hiding yourself behind masks, you have to show yourselves what you really are. Showing the vulnerabilities, in fact, is sign of strength rather than weakness. Lack of self-trust pushes you towards become someone else. When you reveal your shortcomings and accept them without any hesitation, your self-trust start to develop. Thus you should always be ready to face any consequences for what you say and do. Therefore, accept yourself what you're now irrespective to your negative or positive traits.

On the other hand, if we think about result and fear of consequences, we will be unable to do good enough. Even we will afraid to face challenges and to take courageous steps. Thus without taking bold decisions, our self-trust cannot be developed. On the contrary, lacks of courage not only lose opportunities but it diminishes our self-trust also.

Like other skills, self-trust can also be developed with constant practice. Therefore, being kind to yourself; increases self-confidence and lessens your need for approval. Loving and caring for yourself not only increases self-trust but also deepens your connection with others. Thus care yourself and spare some time for yourself for engaging in yoga, aerobic exercise, morning walk etc. When practiced every day, these activities alone help you redirect the focus of your attention from external to internal and will change your life.

In addition, spend some time alone with Nature, and be mindful. When you will remain in mindful state, your intuition will take over the command from incessant thoughts. Thoughts cannot be trusted so they must be ceased in order to take right decisions. Thus thoughts can be ceased only in mindfulness. As mindfulness stabilizes the emotions, it plays very important role to enhance the self-trust. In other words, logic may fail but intuition never fails.

In this context, John Prendergast a psychotherapist also has same view. He states, "As we learn to slow down, tune in it our inner guidance, and act on it, our self-trust grows. We increasingly get the feel for when something resonates as being true or false for us, in or out of accord. This sense of inner resonance becomes our inner authority. To me, it is rather amazing that the body has this innate sense of the truth, as if the body is hardwired for it". Thus honor your sensitivity. Actually, as we learn to recognize and understand the body's subtle sensations, and then act on them, our self-trust will grow tremendously.

We must avoid such people who undermine us. Such people use us and don't want us to succeed. They are dream smashers and feel pleasure when they see us in suffering. Thus, such toxic people drag us right down with them. So in order to develop self-trust, avoid such people. On the contrary, the people who have unconditional self-regard for us enhance our self-trust.

Thus self-trust is not static. It can be lost and restored. Some people pull you down while some push you forward. And this tug of war is going on throughout our whole life. However, this pull and push lead us towards growth. Thus our evolution is the result of this tug of war. Therefore, the path of evolution of self-trust is zigzag rather than straightforward.

Meantime, we commit some mistakes. Then instead of regretting on mistakes, learn lesson from them. Actually, mistakes are not really errors, but gifts to help us direct our focus as we choose. Actually, betrayals and mistakes are valuable lessons in the process of restoring self-trust. Thus betrayals and mistakes are the turning points for taking right decisions.

In addition, avoid such promises which you cannot keep. Only make promises which are guided by your intuition to make. If you feel right, say yes and if something does not feel comfortable or right to you, say no, and do not feel guilty about it.

Herbert Fensterheim Author of the book, *'Don't Say Yes When You Want to Say No'* describes, "People who don't recognize their own strengths are unable to express their emotions and hold their own desires. They have inferior self-image and possess no control of their own life. When they start to say 'no' in which they feel uncomfortable, they start controlling their own life. Eventually, self-trust developed.

Embrace your intelligence and skills. So try new things which you previously think you are unable to do. Such as—make budget beyond your limit, accept the projects beyond your capacity, try to learn new skills, choose critical situations comparison to comfortable, change the way of doing things etc. Mean to say, try to get new experiences whenever and wherever you found any chance. When you try to do such new and hard things, you might really surprise yourself and you found that everything is accomplished in a miraculous way. Actually, this miracle happens due to your self-trust.

True Meaning of Faith in God

Once there was long dry spell due to draught in an area and many villages were affected of this dry spell. Then one village from those villages organized big prayer in a common place in the center of a village in order to please the rain-god. The priest appealed the villagers to bring any items whatever they like at the site of prayer. Mean to say, no one would come empty handed for worship to rain-god. On the stipulated day at auspicious time of worship each villagers brought some items. Some brought flowers; some brought garland; some fruit; some coconut; some sandalwood etc.

Thus, each and every one brought the items for worship according to his or her faith so that worship can be performed with full rituals so that rain-god may be pleased and rain may be started. However, a little girl brought only an umbrella. As it was the condition of priest that no one would attend the rituals with empty handed rather the condition was that everyone has to carry the ingredients of worship. Thus instead of bringing any ritual's items, the girl carried only an umbrella with her because she has much faith on rain-god. As she had full faith in the god that as and when the prayer would be completed, the rain would definitely start. That's why she decided to carry an umbrella so that she may protect herself from rain. Actually, this is the true faith in God. Thus it is very important to have full faith in God.

Thus, it is not enough saying you have faith rather you have to faith wholeheartedly. Half faith never works because it shows doubt on God, even fraction of doubt may resist your wishes to be fulfilled. Thus, faith in God means we rely on Him and depend on His reliability.

Faith in God also realizes us that there is some Supreme Power above us. God is always hundred percent right. His wisdom is unlimited. He understands all the elements of any situation. We need not to update Him, counsel Him or persuade Him to do the right things. He does always right thing at right time because He himself does everything according to cosmic plan. So, no need to lose the patience. At first place we are unable to understand cosmic plan, it may feel us painful. However, ultimately we are benefited from Divine's plan because motives of that plan are pure. Thus they are always in favor of human beings.

If we will have full faith in God, He will never make a mistake, never undercut us or deceive us. He can be fully trusted to do what is right, in all circumstances, at all times .He knows what we need and He wants to meet those needs. That's why God is known as omnipotent and omnipresent.

Thus we should faith in God as a child trust on his father. At the time of playing, when a child asks to jump from height, he never think even for a while, and jump immediately because he knows that his father will catch him before falling on the ground. So God is fully reliable and sovereign over everything.

According to Bhagwad Gita, "None can go a day out of my faith. All have to come to me. Whosoever wants to worship in whatsoever form, I gave my faith in that form, and through that I meet him." Along with the faith, Bhagwad Gita emphasizes on karma also. It says, "Your right is only doing work, but never to the fruit; let not the fruit of action be your motive, neither let there be in you any attachment to inaction." On seeing the both above quotes it seems that both are contradictory because in the first quote, Lord Krishna emphasizes on faith only while in second He stresses on deeds only. But both are not are contradictory rather they are complementary to each other that can be understood with following another quote of Bhagwad Gita.

"Whatever you do not wish to do because of your delusion, you will do even against your will bound by your natural duty or *karma*. The Lord is present inside all beings; moving them like puppets by His magic power." Here Lord Krishna wants to convey that man is like a puppet that has to perform the duty and leave the fruition to the God. That's why He gave priority to the Karma so that only after completion of the duty, fruition should be left for God. Thus, leaving everything for God denotes full faith in God. It means duty and faith are here complementary to each other.

People have faith in God to fulfill their desire, and God fulfill their desire through human beings. In other words, according to Bhagwad Gita faith does not mean that we should stop doing our deeds. Instead we have to play our role. As a human being we come in this world to do something concrete. God complete His mission through human beings and Lord is present inside all beings as mentioned in above quotation. So everyone has to do his deed whatever has been allotted by God for individual to complete His mission. So question does not arise to think that whatever we are doing here, we are doing with our will or against our will rather we should understand the truth that we are bound by our natural duty or *karma* as mentioned above quote of Bhagwad Gita.

It can be said that meaning of true faith in God is to do our duty selflessly so we must work as much as we can, and leave its results to God. Results are not in our hands only our actions are in our hands. So forget about results because God of faith never lets us down. To those who have strong faith on Him, He promises an eternity of hope resting in Him. After doing our duty with best performance, we should leave remain to God who is our protector. So have patience and maintain strong faith in God. We will get our reward at most suitable time better known to God.

How does faith in God transform us?

Faith is a positive emotion which involves a transformation of one's approach to life and one's awareness of the truth for one's life. Faith gives us potency, it empowers us to act, to step out of the known and to taste to the freedom of unknown. It can be said that faith is openness to new experience, openness to possibilities and potentials beyond what we already know. Faith provides us the energy which awakens us to our deep obligation to life. It also energizes our commitment to the welfare of others which is, in real, the foundation of living.

Thus faith is a key factor in spiritual aspect so it helps in enlightenment together with the related states of joy and bliss. Emotionally it is an attitude of serenity and joy which frees one from discomfort of doubt and prepares the mind for meditation. Thus through such faith along with other spiritual practices, Buddhist aspirants become enable to attain Nirvana. So faith is the first step in path of Nirvana.

Faith purifies reason, strengthens it and elevates it, and is an engine for continuous self-improvement. God always tests us whether we have faith in Him or not through miseries and sufferings. Sometimes we face such grim situation in our life that seems to be too difficult to improve. Eventually, the problem solves in a miraculous way. When we have full faith in God, we came to know that even small events are parts of cosmic plan, and all events are happened in our favor. However, we are unable to understand the mystery of such events which give us agony but ultimately they lead us towards joy and happiness.

The process and methods of God may be painful and passes through a hard way. However, without overcoming of a hurdle, we cannot enter in the realm of joy because God want to know how much faith we have in Him. It doesn't matter whether we lose faith in Him at the time of most suffering days or we are capable to overcome the hurdle. If we maintain patience and cross the hurdle, we come to know that some Invisible Force gave us that strength to overcome. Actually, the energy which has been used to rid of the problem is part of cosmic energy.

In fact, each and every moment we are linked to Divine in one way or another, and whatever we do, accomplished due to that Divine's roll. It is not the matter how it happens but when we do something wholeheartedly, the Universe conspires to make it happen. Thus God is always with us whether we are in awakening state or sleep state.

Janina Gomesa well-known philosopher of India compares God with gardener who keeps us trim and fit for His kingdom by a continual pruning process. That's why we go through affliction and sorrow. According to Gomes, God's secrets and His plans for our lives may have been revealed through a long-drawn sequence of events which are mysterious for us. However, God has the master key to solve all these mysteries.

When we allow God to take first place in our lives or when we have full faith in God, we enable to know that He gives us the keys not only to our present but future also. Moreover, God also entrusts us with the keys to other people's lives, especially, those who may come under our influence or who have been touched by us. However the key is not given to us on a platter. Instead we have to be seekers and do our part in every Divine's transection.

Daisaku Ikedu explains the teaching of Nichiren Daishonin's Buddhism that the first thing is to cultivate the faith in divine's power. From the moment we begin to believe in divine's power, things start moving; the sun begin to shine in our hearts; problems start solving and difficulties start overcoming. Mean to say, the conditions of our lives start elevating. Thus this is the real path of changing earthly desire into enlightenment. However, when our determination changes, everything else will move in the direction we desire.

Actually, every moment we resolve to be victorious, every nerve and fiber of our being will immediately orient itself towards our success. Once we cultivate a divine perspective, things start falling at their suitable place. Like the flourishing and verdant trees and flowers in full blossom, our lives are transformed. This transformation sometimes takes time while at other times it happens in the twinkling of an eye.

Chapter 14

Ignore the society's unjust and unfair norms

"You can either hold yourself up to the unrealistic standards of others, or ignore them and concentrate on being happy with yourself as you are."—Jeph Jacques.

People who are always bothered about their respect, honor, prestige, position etc. are bound to follow society's norms irrespective to just or unjust; fair or unfair and realistic or unrealistic. They remain engage in performing formalities which are, in fact, very far away from realities. For them, formalities become burden rather than source of joy. They are obedient of others rather than their own Self in order to comply the society's unrealistic standards. Mean to say, they ignore their inner voice in order to follow unfair and unjust norms. Thus they suppress their conscience.

However, when you suppress conscience, whatever may be the reason, you feel suffocation which brings more suffering for you. Moreover, whatever you do, you cannot attain happiness and peace unless you feel your own conscience comfortable. Therefore, you should always do those things whichever you feel right to do. Thus only when your conscience will be comfortable, you can achieve happiness.

However, the people who are compelled to obey the unjust and unfair norms of society suffer throughout their lives. They always try to please others even on the cost of their own comforts and happiness. Anyhow, if you want to be happy, you have to get rid of these touting norms. You should never bother about these petty society's norms. No doubt that by doing this; you will be labeled deviant, individualist, disobedient, revolutionary, rebellious, etc. However, these labels will liberate you from unnecessary burden, and ultimately provide you happiness and peace.

What are norms?

Actually, social norms are unwritten rules about how to behave. Means, they are guidelines for behavior. Therefore, every society has expectations from its members that how should they behave.

Each society makes up its own guidelines for behavior, and also decides what can be done on violation of these norms. Moreover, norms are remain changing constantly, and differ widely among community or culture even the norms can differ from group to group within same society. Thus norms define appropriate behavior for every social group. So the behavior generally changes when the individual moves from one group to another.

Norms are cultural products including values, customs and traditions. Sociologists describe norms as informal understanding and governing behavior of the individual. In other words, social norms are the accepted behavior that an individual is expected to conform to in a particular group, community or culture. Here, I do not advocate about ignoring such norms which are used for creating the foundation of correct behaviors. Actually, without any rule regulations, no society can be operated peacefully.

I admit that human beings need some guidelines so that their behaviors can be directed. Otherwise the society cannot be kept in order, and it becomes hotchpotch and chaos. That's why communities shunned the people who do not follow their norms so that they may suffer some kind of consequences.

However, it is also equally justifiable that these guidelines of societies should be changed timely according to situations and environment. Therefore, norms should be modified according to the necessities of the members of community rather than to satisfy the ego of dominant people of the community.

Therefore, only those norms should be ignored which are unjust, unfair, unrealistic and rigid, and are still continue in the communities. For example, in many culture, working of women outside from their home is still prohibited thus they are considered only housewives. Thus, gender inequality and racism are still existed in almost all communities. There are such other norms also that should be changed as the people progress. Therefore, following such rigid and old norms which resist the freedom and progress of the individual only pushes towards problems and suffering. Thus such norms should be discarded.

In addition, there are some more norms which are introduced and set up in the society by few dominant people for their own interest. Actually, norms are very effective means to keep the community in order. However, dominant people misuse this means by maintaining the wrong old norms or by creating wrong norms so that they may remain in power. Thus such norms are imposed on the members of community on the pretext of protection the moral values in the community. However, the freedom and emotions of the individuals have been ignored completely by imposing such norms. These norms, in fact, not only hamper the individual growth but also resist the progress of whole society. Even sometimes laws of the country are also violated through these norms. So such unjust and unfair norms are also to be ignored.

Hardly anyone dare to go beyond the norms because social norms are accepted behavior of social groups. Actually, the idea of norms provides a key to understanding social influence in general and conformity in particular. However, the norms are powerful ways of understanding and predicting what people will do. Though the norms are not part of the law, they play very important role in any community or culture.

How to be courageous for ignoring society's unjust and unfair norms

Nothing changes easily and overnight even seasons change slowly. Therefore, in order to ignore such unjust and unfair norms, some traits such as— courage, patience and tolerance are required. Anyhow, these positive traits in human beings are developed either after experiencing grief related to that particular norm or on facing any critical situation regarding the norm. Without facing any problematic circumstances, no one can dare to ignore these norms. However, we should always ready to face each and every adverse situation boldly because no one is spared by unjust, unfair and unrealistic norms. Mean to say, critical circumstances can befall to anyone and any time.

Anyhow, we have to be daring to stand against such cruel norms. We have to dare to struggle against injustice and have to raise our voice to oppose double standards practicing in society so that social evils may be abolished. Anyhow, History is full of such courageous people like Raja Ram Mohan Roy, Ishwar Chandra Vidyasagar, Galileo, Abraham Lincoln, Martin Luther king Jr., Swami Dayanand etc.

Up to early 19th century, *sati pratha* in India was a forceful unjust norm to immolate Hindu widow on the funeral pyre of her deceased husband. However, with the sincere efforts of Raja Ram Mohan Roy, in 1829 this practice of *sati* could be abolished by enacted the Bengal Sati Regulation.

Additionally, the critical lifestyle of widows was also another example of such unjust norms. The condition of Hindu Widows in the 19th century was very horrible. However, this norm also had been discarded due to courage of social reformer Ishwar Chandra Vidyasagar. His efforts regarding reforms in the status of women forced the British Authorities to bring the Hindu Widows' Remarriage Act. The convinced British authorities brought the decree on 26, July 1856, about the 'Widows Remarriage Act. Thus an unjust and unfair norm of the society came to end.

Anyhow, you must analysis each and every norm before practicing it. If you found it unrealistic, you should not comply with it. Buddha also said in this context, "As the wise test the gold by burning, cutting and rubbing it, so students should you accept my words—after testing them, and not merely out of respect." He further elaborates that it is not enough just to have faith in something because a priest or great person said so. You must use your own intelligence and analysis it critically to decide yourself if this great person is speaking something factual.

Dr. S Radhakrishnan also had similar views regarding rigid tradition. He said, "If we reach ready-made doctrines and see in any system of thought perfection and completeness, we miss the true spirit of enquiry." Thus if we have no question about prevalent opinions, we cannot set up a society based on justice. It means, to follow each and every norm blindly of any society may lead us towards unjust and unfair. Lord Krishna also advised to Arjuna in Bhagavad Gitathat he should think himself and do as he chooses rather than obey trodden path blindly.

In addition, we should always be aware about what we are doing. Generally, we are doing rituals, ceremonies, celebrations, etc. without awareness. It means, we hardly think on such occasions whether they are necessary or mere formalities. Moreover, by doing such formalities, we reach very far away from realities. Though we do not know the real reason and meaning of such ceremonies, we are continuously performing them. Actually, we comply the norms because we want to please the leaders of community who are sustaining such norms for their own interest.

The particular cultures are practicing such norms for long times, and instead of discarding them; members of society follow them blindly. Thus by following them blindly, the behavior of the members of society has become almost paradox. For example—our principles are very high but in reality our moral values are very low; many rituals and ceremonies are practices during worship but the persons who perform them are not religious in real sense; celebrations are being organized in each and every occasion but hardly any one enjoys them. There are some other ceremonies which have to perform blindly on occasion of marriages.   So there is no use of performing such formalities on the pretext of only being a part of norms. Thus in order to achieve happiness, we have to avoid such formalities.

We waste much energy and spent huge amount of money on such rituals, ceremonies etc. because we have no courage to discard them. In early 20th century, Munsi Premchand prominent writer of Hindi literature had done great efforts to abolish such rituals and ceremonies. He wrote many stories and other such literature which arouse public awareness about such social issues.

Thus we should ignore such norms which resist our progress on the name of traditions. However, in order to ignore unjust and unfair norms, you should maintain your uniqueness. Thus instead of becoming someone else, live with your originality and dare to deny to become the part of herd-mentality. Thus try to be individualist.

Dr. Abdul Kalam also said in this context, "Never change your originality for the sake of others because no one can play your role better than you. So be yourself. You are the best."

However, if you preserve your originality, your conscience will not allow you to accept society's unjust and unfair norms. Anyhow, when you will start listening your inner voice irrespective to society's pressure, you can easily ignore such unjust and unfair norms.

Actually, social norms have not a specific reasoning behind them rather they are linked with emotional sentiments of the society. In addition, religious sentiments of the community make them more conservative. That's why they are not only difficult to ignore but also more difficult to change than explicit rules such as laws. However, the people who have strong will power get success to provide a way in which some individuals and group can introduce their agendas to the rest of society.

Therefore, do not afraid of criticism rather do whatever your conscience allows to do. Swami Vivekananda had written in his diary about criticism on 01 February 1885 in New York when he got a letter from a friend from India which was full of criticism. He wrote, "I just received your beautiful note.........I am very glad of your criticism and I am not sorry at all. I know full well how good it is for one's worldly prospects to be *sweet*. I do everything to be *sweet*, but when it comes to a horrible compromise with the truth within, and then I stop".

He further described that the duty of ordinary man is to obey to command His (God) society; but the children of light never do so. This is an eternal law.

One accommodates himself to surroundings and social opinion and gets all good things from society, the giver of all good to such. The other stands alone and draws society up towards him. The accommodating man finds a path of roses; the non-accommodating, one thorns. But the worshippers of "Voxpopuli" go to annihilation in a moment; the children of truth *live forever.*

Thus, many social norms which had been converted in social evils and had been become unfit for the contemporary society were discarded by courageous people time to time. So you should also show courage for discarding such norms which are not suitable for the current progressive society.

Meaning of conformity, and how does conformity hamper our personality?

There are so many things in every community that are unjust and unfair. Thus following blindly any system without any question may be dangerous. It is not only bad for members who live there but also for whole community. A check and balance method is very healthy in any system let the system is huge or small. Moreover, check and balance system within a society or culture can help to point out what is unfair and unjust in the society.

However, the system cannot be maintained through conformation because if everyone conforms to society and does not question the rules then there will be no change. Therefore, non-conformist are the people who change society otherwise the society would have been stagnant so far.

First of all, I would like to clarify the term conformity. American Heritage Dictionary defines, "Conformity is the action or behavior in correspondence with socially accepted standards, conventions, rules or laws." It can also be said that conformity is a process by which a person's attitudes and beliefs become influenced by other people. Means conformity is the act of behaving, thinking, talking or appearing in ways similar to other people, whether it is through conscious change in behavior or beliefs or form an unconscious attempt to adapt to pressure real or imagined from a group. In brief, it can be said that it is herd-mentality that follow sheep- like belief.

Actually, by conforming to a group, you are either changing who you are to fit in, or you are masking your true self by the veil of conformity. By conforming to a 'socially accepted standards' you are not allowing yourself actually be yourself. Thus the pressure of conformity compel people to change who they are and never let them get opportunity to get to know who they really are in the first place. They change simply so that they can fit into a society or a group of friends.

People hesitate to question whether it is right or wrong, and they just follow the crowd. They don't stop to think about what they are doing because everyone else is doing it. So everyone wants to look, act and sound like others even cost of individuality. Thus when someone follows the crowd, he or she is not being true to himself or herself, they are really is denying themselves the essential individuality that each person has. Actually, society taught us to suppress this individuality in ourselves from childhood, and replace it with an accepted way to talk, act and think.

Thus conformity makes us coward. By following the conformity, people become so timid that they do not dare to ask any question to their leader even they know they are right. So by not questioning and arguing with leader, turn the leader towards dictatorship which ultimately end up with serious consequences. Moreover, people have spent their whole life conformity to an ideal that in actual they don't agree with.

Thus we conform to things due to our fear because other people want to us to do the same. We have adjusted in this environment of fear, and live in it throughout our whole life. We are afraid to be straightforward and afraid to be different. Thus we are afraid to think of ourselves. It seems that whatever we are doing is being done in hypnotism.

In each society, there may be various categories of the people. For example, first category's people are those people who are not in favor of conformation. However, simultaneously they have not so much courage to deny the conformation. In second category, some people may be in confusion what to do in that particular situation. Mean to say, mostly cannot decide whether they should go with conformists or with non-conformists. So people often continue to do things the way they have always done rather than respond to new information or ideas in a changing society.

Conformists can have significant impact on both these categories. Therefore, those who are afraid to deny the conformation and those who are in confusion, both may go to the side of conformists. Thus, it can also be said that only few conservative people dominate the society because many people of the community are afraid to go against them. They not only have the hold on mass population but victimize them also. They pressurize even threaten the members of the society to agree with them.

In reality, the social norms were introduced for guidance and direction to provide order and harmony in the society so that relation between each group within the community may intact. However, few dominative people have twisted this purpose in their own favor. Even in the long run, social norms have become the puppet of few conservative people, and social norms are no longer providing peace and harmony in the society rather these norms have been converted into social evils.

Thus these norms create conflict between members; suppress the individuality; reduce the diversity; giving too much power to leaders over the people and divide the community in many different ideological groups. Thus, conformity is not only hampering the individual's personality but also resists the progress of whole society. A progressive society cannot be conservative rather its norms and standards should be remaining in change accordingly.

As people do not want to leave any comfort zone, they become conformists. Naturally, everyone wants to live along with the herd whatever suffocation may he/she feels in it. However, sometimes people want to freedom from such suffocation which they feel in this crowd but their fear and herd-mentality resist them to be different. So they are always going with this flow, and maintain the status-quo rather than stickling up their own belief. The conformity to unjust society's norms not only resists the development of humans' personality but also effect on their health and mood which can be proved by following study.

Mark Seery, Ph. D. an associate professor in the Department of Psychology at the University of Buffalo along with his colleagues measured cardiovascular responses, and they were able to gauge how the bodies of persons responded while in the act of conformity or being non-conformist. In a statement Mark Seery head of the team said, "People can show conformity, but going along with the group doesn't mean they are going along happily. The external behavior isn't necessarily a good indication of their internal experience."

The researchers found that low resources and high demands lead to less confidence and feeling of threat which often produce anxiety. Conversely, while trying to reach a goal by stickling up for yourself, the combination of high resources and low demands lead to more positive, invigorating experience. This is described as 'challenge' which corresponds with feeling more confident.

Thus, non-conformist are ready to accept all type of challenges due to more confident than conformist. They don't fear to open their mouth against unjust and unfair while on the contrary, unjust actions by the society are mainly fueled by conformist. Therefore, be straightforward and take the road less travelled so that you can attain internal peace rather than feel good artificially by conforming to unjust and unfair society's norms along with the crowd.

PART III

In the last part of book, such type of content is included which leads the readers towards bliss. Peace of mind and bliss both may be used as synonymous because without attaining peace of mind, bliss cannot be realized. Thus in this part emphasis is completely given on spiritual aspect. In order to live happily and peacefully, it is necessary that a person has some noble purpose to live, and one must detach from worldly affairs. So how we can detach ourselves from materialistic world and what is the role of noble purpose to enhance spirituality is theme of this part.

Only after detaching oneself, one can go towards Nature which is essential requirement to get intuition. However, without intuition, it is very difficult to hear inner voice which is real voice of divine. Thus along with the role of intuition, love and compassion in blessed life is also included in the last and third part of the book. I think living in present moment and meditation is the gate-way to attain peace of mind and bliss. So mindfulness and meditation are also included in this part.

Actually, Peace of mind, joy and bliss including Supreme Power are already exist within us which can only be realized when we enter into the state of thoughtlessness. So the content of thoughtlessness is also included in this part. However, you cannot attain thoughtlessness without going within yourself. Thus last chapter is about going within.

Chapter 15

Detach yourself

"If you want to fly, give up everything that weighs you down"—Buddha.

As long as you seek happiness in objects such as relationship, wine, sex religion, power, property, position, name, fame etc., you cannot attain permanent happiness. Actually, all these objects are transitory and cannot fill the emptiness exists within you. You are changing your friendship frequently; you are changing materialistic objects quickly as a child changes the toys; you want to change your relations it does not fit according to your demands. Mean to say, you always feel boredom in spite of having everything.

Actually, you are running after mirage which is impossible to achieve. Moreover, this process is going on throughout your life or till you understand the truth that happiness cannot be achieved in these worldly objects. On the contrary, as and when you become free from all type of attachments, you enter into the realm of bliss. Actually, all attachments are shackles which bind us in hopes and expectations.

However, you expect from others to do the same what you do to the others which is, in fact, almost impossible. Actually, neither can you change the behavior of other people nor can you develop moral values in them. Whatever you do for others, is done according to your moral values while whatever others do, is also done according to their moral values. Therefore, such expectation is meaningless. So do whatever you feel right and let them do whatever they think right. In brief, you should not depend on attitudes or behaviors of other people for your happiness.

Actually, for obtaining psychological security, we want to link with someone or something otherwise we feel completely insecure. However, maintaining the relationship or friendship; joining any club or community; possessing of any post or wealth etc. is neither the guarantee of psychological security nor they can provide us permanent happiness. Actually, everything how much big it may be, lose its charm after some period. Moreover, every interaction with another human being becomes sorrowful after certain period. Or you can say that there is no any psychological security in external world.

Therefore, you should remember that any type of relation cannot make you happy. Thus, instead of seeking happiness in your relationship; your external identity or in materialistic things, you should seek it within yourself. You are yourself source of your happiness but you are wandering here and there throughout life like musk deer. Once you will dive within yourself, you will not only find peace and happiness there but you will also feel secure in all aspects. So detach yourself from each and everything which you have been clung so far including your thoughts, ideas, beliefs, principles etc. whatever it may be.

What is detachment?

Actually, to leave the family and society is not detachment. Mean to say; to renounce this world is not real detachment. Such type of detachment is only run away from your duties. In other words, by doing this, you will become only deserter. You are here to do your worldly duty rather than for wandering in jungles to seek the Almighty.

On the contrary, such Entity can be found only here in this world by doing your duty. As you are unable to perform your worldly duties, you abscond and renounce the world. If you are unable to adjust yourself here then how can you adjust yourself there? Mean to say, if you fail in current situation, you will also fail everywhere wherever you will go whatever may be the situation. Thus run away from your duty is neither solution of any problem nor is it detachment.

Instead, to see the whole world as a drama without personal involvement is detachment. It means, do your duty without emotional involvement. So perform your worldly duties in this world here and now, and forget about relationships which are based on conditions. Then such detachment will be actual detachment. Mean to say, performing the worldly duties; doing *karma* without any expectation is real detachment.

In *Mahabharata*, when Arjuna put down his weapons and refuse to fight on saying that he could not kill the warriors of opposite side because they are all his close relatives rather than enemies. Then Lord Krishna motivated the Arjuna, "Here, don't consider them your cousins, uncles, granduncle, nephew etc. rather consider them soldier of opposite army, and you are warrior here so being warier it is your duty to fight. So forget about relation and do your duty." Therefore, doing your *karma* whatever it may be with sincerity without its fruition is real meaning of detachment.

Buddhism also resists the practice of runaway from work. In Buddhist view, detachment does not mean that we have to leave this world to sit in secluded place in forest or somewhere on mountains. Actually, this practice is only escaping from your duty. Whilst renunciation can be get only in this world while living the humdrum existence of daily life. It is just like wick of lamp which can only burn when its half parts remain in oil and another tip of the wick remain at outside of the oil. If the wick is removed from the oil, it will extinguish. On the other hand, if it is dipped completely in the oil, in that case also it will extinguish.

Thus like a wick of the lamp, only those persons get renunciation that detach themselves from the worldly affairs and continue their mundane duties in this world rather than going in isolation. In isolation, everyone can become a saint but in the web of social structure who can maintain the inner tranquility is real saint. In our relationship with others while living in this hotchpotch society irrespective of people's behavior and their response maintaining the inner tranquility is the real renouncement. Thus both duty and detachment should go simultaneously.

Hindu Philosophy is completely based on selfless work. According to the chapter six Verse 1 of Bhagwad Gita, "He is the real renouncer of the world who does his work without desiring for the fruits of his actions, certainly not the one who renounce actions and worship the sacred fire". Thus it can be said that the action which is regulated and which is performed without attachment, without love or hatred and without desire of result is said to be true renouncement.

Remez Sasson author of *'Emotional Detachment for Happier Life'* explains that detachment is a state of calmness and the ability not to be emotionally agitated by people, events and your own thoughts. This is not a state of indifference; lack of interest or lack of feelings. Rather it is an attitude of common sense, open minded and practical behavior.

It can also be said that detachment is a positive behavior which allows person to react calmly to highly emotional circumstances. Thus detachment in this sense is a decision to avoid engaging emotional connections rather than an inability or difficulty in doing so. However, detachment does not necessarily mean avoid empathy; rather it allows the person to choose rationally whether or not to be overwhelmed or manipulated by such feelings.

In this sense, it can allow people to maintain boundaries, psychic integrity and avoid undesired impact by or upon others, related to emotional demands. Spiritual Author Ron W Rathbun wrote, "True detachment isn't a separation from life but the absolute freedom within your mind to explore living. "It can be said that the people who are detached are free from emotional disturbances because after detachment they no longer have to worry, wonder or even think about happenings. Thus, to attain this clam attitude is detachment.

Even some people consider the detachment synonym of non-attachment thus they avoid the entanglement. However, non-attachment is somewhat different from detachment. If you remain aloof from anything or any relation, you would not be able to know dark side of that attachment. However, after attaching to someone, you gain the experiences either pleasurable or bitter one. Thus, after attaining the experiences, distancing from the object provides you mental satisfaction while remaining aloof from an object or person without gaining any experience—provides the feeling of lacking which is, in fact, a hidden desire. Therefore, hidden desire cannot be detachment rather ending of all type of desires is real detachment.

Anyway, differentiate between detachment and non-attachment can be understood better by the description of Frank Ostaseski Author of 'The Five Invitations 'who describes about detachment and non-attachment by differentiating between them. He differentiates, "Detachment implies distancing from a particular object or experience. It can feel cool, like we are withdrawing or pulling away while non-attachment simply means not holding onto, not grasping, not getting entangled. There is no need for distancing oneself".

Thus in order to attain tranquility, we have to not only detach from relations but also have to detach from such attitude and traditions which resist our freedom and development. For example—ego and pride; blind faith and beliefs; unnecessary rituals; unrealistic society's norms and standards; desire to become someone else; hoarding of stuff; desire to achieve power, prestige, position, property, name, fame etc. are also attachments in one form or another. Means, we should live our simple and original life without seeking unnecessary recognition or identity. Therefore, free from all these desires is real detachment.

According to Buddha, clinging to impermanent aspects to this world is attachment. And it is not just attaching to things we like but disliking is also attachment. Thus, an aversion to some aspect of the world—for example the dislike of a person, place or idea—is an attachment, since the aversion itself binds us to the things we dislike. Things are what they are, and no amount of pretending will make them otherwise. Thus both liking as well as disliking is attachment in view of Buddha. So, detach yourself from each type of liking and disliking. Thus the term detachment is used in very broad sense in Buddhism.

How to detach yourself

Actually, attachment to objects such as—relation, society, idea, belief, things etc. are interrelated. For example when we start to detach from relationship, detachment from society also becomes easy. Actually, most people are generally not aware that they are attached to someone or something. Even they are unaware that attachment resists their growth. Thus the awareness is the first step in the direction of detachment. After awareness regarding anything, its implication becomes easy.

Actually, attachment is like a rope whose one end is tied with you and another with a peg. You can go round and round in a circle but you cannot go beyond the radius. However, you have become habitual of this attachment because you feel secure in it. You fear to leave this secure zone so you avoid facing the struggle. Therefore, instead of trying to detach yourself, you remain in that attachment deliberately because you feel comfortable there. Thus, attachment remains a secure state for you till you confront with any bitter experience.

Actually, it is too difficult to hide your craving for relationship with another person. Therefore, knowing this weakness, another person exploits you, and you feel hurt. However, when someone hurts you, you realize that this attachment is painful rather than security and comfortable. Then this bitter experience pushes you away from the person who has hurt you. Eventually, this hurting becomes the reason of detachment. So due to this hurting, you decide to go away from the person who has hurt you otherwise you remain attach to that person.

Actually, nothing is perfect in this world but we always seek perfection in each and every field. We expect perfectionism in each relation. However, we should not expect from others to do the same what we do for them. As human relationship is generally revolves around selfishness, the consequence will be sorrow and unhappiness. In other words, our expectation remains unfulfilled and we always remain discontent everywhere how much we possess. Thus as long as we tend to be perfect and require more things for being happy, we lead towards suffering rather than happiness.

Therefore, we have to turn back from materialistic world to spirituality. In order to detachment, we have to be content not only in relations but also in things, power, position, etc. Once we become contented, detachment will be easy. Thus in order to obtain detachment, it is necessary that we accept the things as they are. Moreover, for acceptance, we must be able to respond to the clearly seen Universe as it is, not as we would prefer it to be.

Thus the ability to see things for what they really are, and respond to their true nature is real acceptance which enhances our alignment with the Universe. Actually, we cling to each and everything because we want to change its true nature but changing the true nature of things is not possible. For example—true nature of the things is that if some person or thing provides you happiness, same person or thing brings forth sorrow for you too. However, instead of accepting both aspects of attachments, you expect only happiness. So you are not mentally prepared for such type of unexpected outcomes. Therefore, you hurt again and again due to ignorance of understanding the true nature of things.

Therefore, do not forget that happiness and sorrow are two sides of the same coin. So, sorrow cannot be avoided until you stop chasing the desires. How much you cling to anything or any person, clinginess or attachments with them cannot provide you any type of security. Rather, be content in whatever you already have rather than desiring 'what should be' because desires only push you towards more sorrow.

According to the concept of Buddha, no one really does anything. Events happen, deeds are done, consequence happen, but no one does any deed. Everything happens according to the cosmic law;

how each any event affects whom and in what way—for better or worse—is also according to cosmic law. So instead of involving too much, it is better to see this cosmic process from outside.

In other words, if we remain entangle and attach in each and everything, we remain in sorrow. On the contrary, if we want to be happy, we have to be detached from everything, and for the detachment we have to accept each and every thing 'as it is'.

Additionally, in order to get detachment, you have to focus on yourself. You need to love yourself and forget about those people who have been part of your life. You need to love and respect yourself more than anyone, and give yourself the much deserved importance and esteem. If you value other persons' words and opinions more than you value your own, you will feel irritation which may lead you towards frustration. So ignore such opinions, and trust yourself. Your self-trust make you enable to take your own decision which ultimately decreases your dependence on others and leads towards detachment.

Finally, meditation is the best way to let go of emotions and attachment. When you start meditation practice, your insufficiency will fill up spontaneously, and you become complete on your own. Remez Sasson founder of SuccessConsciousness.Com said that in meditation, you strive to ignore thoughts and feelings. This develops the habit of staying calm and emotionally detached, not only during meditation but also in day-to-day life. Means tranquility can be obtained only by meditation.

Thus meditation leads you towards such spirituality where you become so enable that you can understand the world deeply and you may be able to solve the problems by different points of views. Means you become so wise that you may recognize the voice of God known as intuition. Moreover, when you start following your intuition, you will have no need of any outer source for any type of dependence. Then detachment will come naturally and that detachment will come from within rather than by any other means. Actually, the detachment which comes from within is real detachment.

Why is the detachment so hard?

Actually, we have become so dependent on worldly things that they have become the center point of our happiness. Thus in the absence of such things, our happiness shatters. We have not only become habitual but also addicted to the materialistic things. Giving up any addiction is not only difficult but painful also. Anyhow, if we want happiness, we have to give up these things. However, we are still unable to detach from these worldly affairs due to the painful process.

Anyhow, in order to live happily and cheerfully, we have to detach ourselves from everything, however beloved, however much the soul yearns for it. Actually, detachment requires positive assertiveness, willpower, and courage to say 'no' to needless entanglements, commitments and relationships. Thus developing willpower is very hard process and to be courageous is even harder. That's why detachment is so hard.

To break this chain of attachment, we have to remind ourselves that there is nothing stable in the human affairs. Everything in the Universe is transitive. Nothing is permanent forever but we still believe that materialistic achievement can lead us towards happiness. Therefore, first of all we have to change this myth. Thus the object of materialistic achievements can be replaced with spiritual aspects. We have to understand that worldly objects give only sensory pleasure. Thus, we are trapped in this illusion which is very difficult to break. That's why detachment is so hard.

Some people consider pleasure synonym of bliss, here bliss means extreme joy while pleasure is related to sensual gratification. Therefore, in the context of attachment, it is necessary to understand the difference between pleasure and bliss. Every attractive worldly object binds us in attachment and gives pleasure. Moreover, as the attachment increases, addiction to materialistic objects also increases. For the reason, we want that pleasure again and again. Thus addiction gives positive feedback to attachment, and this process is going on. Ultimately, the mind become intoxicated, and bliss remains mirage for such type of intoxicated mind.

On the contrary, when we detach from the worldly object, we experience such tranquility which leads us towards bliss. However, to give up the attractive objects is not as easy as to say. Means, attachment is such a strong chain that it is not only difficult to break but it requires lot of patience and time also. Like drugs and wine, our attachment is also a quick fix to feeling good. All such items which give intoxication including attachment require much effort and time to give up.

Thus detachment demands that you have to change your attitude, beliefs and behavior. And above all, detachment demands moral values. Therefore, to change these traits are not easy. That's why it is very hard to detach.

Being social creature, you have to make relation to certain people in certain times; at certain places for certain reasons. In addition, some relations are blood related. However, some relations need to be ended at a certain point. Thus you have to recognize that particular point so that you can detach yourself at suitable time. It is really such a long and hard process where you have to come out from the state of overwhelming. Getting rid of from overwhelming itself is a painful process so detachment also becomes painful and very hard.

Thus sometimes you may win while sometimes you may lose in this lengthy and painful process. Some relations give you smile while some others give you wound in your life. Moreover, out of those wounds some may be so deep which is too difficult to bear even seem impossible to heal. Life is itself a long process of attaining experiences where you experience pleasant as well as bitter experiences. Your life is complete cycle of trails and errors where you learn something daily. However, you learn more from bitter experiences than pleasant experiences.

Anyhow, once you realize that your relation gives you more wound than smile that is the exact point where you must detached. Actually, this hurting is the signal for you for detachment sent by some Higher Power. At this point how much painful it may be but if you will ignore this signal, you will suffer a lot in future in that particular relation.

Detachment is very difficult due to two more reasons. First one is your past which is, in fact, very crucial in this process. It is, in fact, a black hole that will sink you deep and leads you towards pessimism. You brood over again and again on the painful past events. Thus you cannot not detach until and unless you forget such painful memories. Moreover, forgetting the past bitter events is not as easy as to be said. It can also be said that not forgetting the past is main obstacle of detachment.

Second one is your deep seated avenge and ego which resist the forgiveness while forgiveness is very important ingredient for detachment. Therefore, in order to forgive, you have to overcome on your avenge and ego which is really difficult. Thus forgiveness to offenders who have hurt you is not as easy as saying. However, detachment cannot be attained until you forgive the offenders and forget your painful past fully.

Anyhow, detachment is mental state, and you are the only person whose thinking and feelings are within your power to control. In essence, the detachment demands a broad mind. However, when time comes for detachment, coincidences starts to happen in your life thus it seems that Cosmic Forces are working in favor of you. Then by the grace of Invisible Power, your mind achieves that state of broadness spontaneously. Thus the detachment which was really very hard earlier becomes easy and opens the gate of bliss for you.

How does detachment bring Bliss?

Actually, detachment should not be considered 'lack of love'. On the contrary, it is the real love because it is not related to any image or appearance. A fountain of love, in fact, arises only after detachment. We know that love with attachment is associated with ego however love associated with ego cannot be a selfless love. Rather such type of love is based on mutual 'give and take' policy. So it is based on condition and conditional love cannot be true love.

However, only unconditional love is pure love which can be found only in detached personalities such as—Buddha and Mother Teresa. Therefore, without detachment, you cannot be source of pure love which is very necessary for obtaining happiness and to attain bliss.

To be attached is to live in the fear that what you want will not materialize, and you remain trap in web of desires. Mean to say, in the state of attachments, your desires never come to end. Attachment gives your power away to external forces and circumstances. On the contrary, as and when you detach yourself from a specific person or thing, you feel more powerful and determined. Thus you found more clarity in your thoughts. In addition, detachment from anything or anyone transforms your fear into love; lust into affection; desire into purpose; doubt into belief and materialism into spiritualism.

Attachment to anything or anyone is to tell yourself that you are somehow incomplete without that thing or that particular person in your life. Whilst, after detaching from that thing or person, you feel complete on your own and become able to see divine perfection in what is as it is. And instead of trying to control the events and their consequences, you accept them being governed according to cosmic law.

Moreover, as and when you accept calmly whatever happens either good or bad equally, your mind reaches in a state of inner balance and peace. Naturally, when you attain 'peace of mind', bliss will not be far away from your reach. Mean to say, tranquility is necessary in order to attain bliss.

Remez Sasson says that detachment is an important quality that can save you a lot of emotional inconvenience and suffering. It is a state of calmness which helps you conserve your mental balance and peace of mind. It makes you enable not to take things too personally. Mean to say, after detachment, you become so capable that you can sublimate your agitated emotions without harming yourself and others. Additionally you can listen people's comments about you with patience, and can cease your wandering thoughts.

Deepak Chopra a well -known Author says, "Those who seek security in the exterior world chase it for life time. By letting go of your attachment to the illusion of security, which is really an attachment to the known, you step into the field of all possibilities. This is where you will find true happiness, abundance and fulfillment". Thus in order to achieve true happiness, joy and bliss, detachment is very essential.

Chapter 16

Develop love and compassion

"The greatest degree of inner tranquility comes from development of love and compassion. The more we care for the happiness of others, the greater is our own sense of well-being."—The Dalai Lama.

Actually, love is the energy which helps us to heal whether we give this love to ourselves or we receive it from others. So first of all, we should love the self and have to become whole to give it someone else. If we have something then only we will become capable to give it to anyone else. Thus it is necessary to become the source of love and compassion so that we can deliver them to those who live around us. It can also be said that we cannot love others unless we love ourselves.

Therefore, in order to love yourself, you should focus on your positive traits rather than self-criticism, self-judgment, guilt etc. Much of our suffering emerges from our self-critical and judgmental relationship with ourselves. Thus we cannot love ourselves until we learn to embrace ourselves with kindness and compassion. However, we remain engaged in so many activities that we have no time for ourselves even we have forgotten our own need.

So first of all we have to spare some time for ourselves. When we start to care ourselves, healing will occur. Then we can heal ourselves as well as others. Moreover, self-love is nothing but caring our body and mind along with our appearance. Therefore, we have to recognize our own worth and other positive traits within us in order to love ourselves.

Meaning of unconditional love

We have developed many relations but most of them are without love. Most of us pretend to love each other; even we know that this is not true love. Thus mostly our relations are based on 'give and take' or 'what's in-it-for-me' principle so this principle may be business but it cannot be true love. It can also be said that instead of loving with each other, we trade with each other. Thus most of people love with one another for one reason or another.

Generally, the base of friendship is expectations so love based on expectation is not true love. If offspring love their parents to get something from them, and if parents love their children in order to get security in old age then it is not true love. Moreover, if husband love with his wife to fulfill his personal needs, and if wife love her husband to get only financial and psychological security, it is also not true love. Thus such 'give and take' types of love are not true love because they are based on condition. In other words; only unconditional love is true love.

Actually, unconditional love is known as affection without any limitations or love without conditions. Whilst, in psychology, unconditional love refers to a state of mind in which one has the goal of increasing the welfare of another despite any evidence of benefit for oneself. It can also be said that unconditional love is caring about the happiness of another person without any thought for what we might get for ourselves. It is unconditional love when other people care about our happiness because unconditional love does not seek pleasure or gratification.

In conditional love: love is 'earned on the bases of conscious or unconscious conditions being met by lovers. It requires some kind of finite exchange. Conversely, unconditional love is given freely to the loved one and it is seen infinite and measureless. Means unconditional love separate the individual from his or her behaviors.

Carson Mc Culler Author says, "Love that is unconditional transcends time, place behavior, and worldly concerns. We don't decide whom we love, and sometimes don't know why, and the motives and reasons of the heart are unfathomable".

Author Trungpa Rinpoche says that unconditional love is mere a state of receptivity and allowing, which arises from our own basic 'goodness'. Actually, unconditional love is one type of love which has no limitation and is given continuously and unconditionally. In other words, unconditional love means loving others in their essence, as they are, no matter what they do or fail to do. In brief, it can be said that unconditional love is 'love in all conditions and circumstances'.

What is compassion?

Actually, before knowing the meaning of compassion, it is better to know the difference between the term compassion and other similar terms such as love, sympathy and empathy. However, compassion is closely associated with these terms but all these traits are different.

Actually, compassion is closely associated with love that's why it is used along with love. However, both are not synonyms rather somewhat different from each other. Thubten Chodron Buddhist nun and founder of Sravasti Abbey in Newport Washington differentiate between love and compassion. She describes that love is the wish for someone to have happiness and its causes while compassion is the wish for them to be free from suffering and its causes. Thus it can be said that compassion is 'love applied' to sufferer.

Some people consider the compassion as a synonymous of sympathy but there is also difference between both. Sympathy responds to suffering with sorrow and concern while the compassion responds with warmth and care. In other words, in compassion, only concerning regard suffering is not enough but taking action for help is also associated with it. Thus compassionate people are so motivated that they go out of their way to help the physical or emotional hurts and pains of another.

Additionally, many people confuse compassion with empathy. Thus, it is better to draw distinction between empathy and compassion also. Empathy is the capacity to feel as the sufferer feels while compassion is a strong motivation to reduce suffering and advance the other's well-being. Thus empathy is the ability to understand from the inside what the other person is thinking and feeling while in compassion, it is not the matter whether you share the feelings of sufferer or not but the matter is you move to work to end the suffering of sufferer without thinking of the consequences of your kind act. Thus compassionate people even take risk of their life in order to remove the suffering of sufferer.

Here, I would like to differentiate between both with an illustration of road accident. On seeing a wounded person on the road accident, the persons who feel empathy only cry and fill their eyes with tears because they feel the pain with wounded parson. Whilst, compassionate person immediately picks up the wounded person and send him/her in hospital for proper treatment. Mean to say, helping hand is more important in compassion. We can say that with empathy, we feel with the other person while in compassion we feel for the person.

Russell L. Kolts, Ph. Dclinical psychologist, professor at Eastern Washington University and co-author along with Thubten Chodronof book '*Living with an Open Heart: How to Cultivate Compassion in Everyday Life*' clarifies the distinction as well as interrelation between both terms, "Empathy is a core component of compassion. Empathy enables us to understand what another person is feeling.

Without empathy our efforts to act with compassion will likely doomed to fail because without understanding the experience of others, it is almost impossible to give them what they need". Thus empathy requires from us 'to be emotionally attuned to another person' while compassion requires timely 'helping hand'.

Actually, empathy is the base of compassion so in order to be a compassionate, it is necessary to be empathetic. However, in compassion, feeling concern for another's suffering is not enough but a motivation to help the sufferer is also necessary. Or it can be said that compassion is the next step of empathy. In empathy the distance from the person is maintained as a psychotherapist maintains from patient but it is not necessary in the relationship of compassion. Thus empathy requires a certain distance but it disappears in the case of compassion.

Thus without the presence of compassion, we cannot be open to suffering. Therefore, compassion is the exact force which serves as a healer of sufferer because everything such as—sympathy, empathy, love, altruism etc. are involved in it.

According to Tibetan Buddhism, compassion is a mind that is motivated by cherishing other living beings and wishes to release them from their suffering. Here the meaning of 'other' is not refers for friends and relatives but generally for strangers.

Sometimes out of selfish intention, we can wish for other persons to be free from their sufferings this is quite common in relationship that are based on principally on attachment. This wish is basically on self-centered and is not true compassion. Thus, true compassion is based on cherishing anyone else whom we have no connection.

Buddhist Monk Kelsang Gyasto says, "Although we already have some degree of some compassion, at present it is very biased and limited, when our family and friends are suffering, we easily develop compassion for them, but we find it far more difficult to feel sympathy for people we find unpleasant or strangers". "Thus if we genuinely want to realize our potential by allowing by full enlightenment, we need to increase the scope of our compassion till it embraces all living beings without exception. This universal compassion is the heart of Mahayana Buddhism", Gyasto further explained.

Buddha put the compassion, a strong sympathy and empathy for all living beings without exception. So Buddha's compassion extended to all beings equally. It is the impartial, unconditional and all-inclusive compassion that the Buddha imparted to his followers. From Buddhist perspective, compassion is the foundation of emotional healing. Thus we sense others' suffering as like our own and naturally wish them free from this suffering.

Bokar Rinpoche wrote about compassion in *'Chenrezig: Lord of Love'*. Hedescribes,"Every person whose heart is moved by love and compassion, who deeply and sincerely acts for the benefit of others without concern for fame, profit, social position or recognition express the activity of Chenrezig is true compassionate person."

Indian and Tibetan Buddhist Scholar John Markransky says, "Compassion is characterized as a mental capacity that, when cultivated and strengthen, empowers all positive states of mind as we awaken to our fullest human potential".

The Dalai Lama clarifies this concept of true compassion and says that compassion without attachment is possible. Therefore we need to clarify the distinction between compassion and attachment. True compassion is not just an emotional response but a firm foundation, a truly compassionate attitude towards others does not change even if they behave negatively. Thus genuine compassion is not based on our own projections and expectations but rather on the needs of others: irrespective of whether other person is close friend or an enemy, as long as that person wishes for peace and happiness, and wishes to overcome suffering then on that basis, we develop genuine concern for their problem.

Thus compassion is not only empathy or sympathy but also actively efforts to free others from suffering. It can also be said that it is empathetic altruism which is done without any reward or expectation. Thus Buddhist perceptiveness requires two main traits regarding true compassion.

First one is wisdom and second one is loving kindness. When one must understand the nature of suffering from which wish to free others, this is wisdom. And when one must experience deep intimacy and empathy with others sentient beings, this is loving kindness.

In essence, compassion is a—strong aspiration; a passion to suffer along with sufferer; a wisdom to recognize the suffering of others; a kindness to feel interconnectedness; deep feelings to feel the hurt and pain of others; and above all, sincere efforts and acts in order to remove the suffering by all means.

How to develop love and compassion

Like other traits, love and compassion can also be developed by practice. Thus, as much as we practice compassion, as easier as it can be achieved. Actually, as we perform compassionate actions over and over again, we become habitual of such actions. Psychologists call this process 'Habituation'. So the habituation makes it easier for us to be compassionate. However, it will be better if we start it with ourselves. Bodhicitta also said, "If I really want to change the world, I need to start with myself". Mean to say, whatever you want to do, start from yourself.

In this context, Nun and teacher Pema Chodron said, "In order to have compassion for others, we must have compassion for ourselves, and as our self-delusions dissolve, we become more sensitive to the suffering of others, and as we are more sensitive to the suffering of others, our self-delusions dissolve further." "Start where you are, whatever mess your life is right now is the soil from which enlightenment may grow", she says further.

Thus you can begin better by understanding your own suffering, which takes you back to wisdom then compassion arise from wisdom. So by using your own grieving experience towards the healing of other's grief, you can cultivate much love and compassion which further can be utilize in more positive way. Therefore, your suffering can be boon for others because it enables you to easily feel the pain of others.

The Dalai Lama says, "Every human being has the same potential for compassion; The only question is whether we really take any care of that potential, and develop and implement it in our daily life. My hope is that more and more people will realize the value of compassion, and so follow the path of altruism." Thus, if we serve others with pure heart, and not expect gratitude, payment or recognition, more love and compassion will be developed and we will become source of love and compassion.

Usually meditation or other mindfulness practices are the means to develop this understanding. In Tibetan Buddhism there is a practice called Tonglen which is a kind of meditation practice for helping us connect to our own suffering and the suffering of others. In the process of Tonglen, we begin to feel love and start to take care of both for ourselves and others. It awakens our compassion and it also introduces us to a far larger view of reality.

Actually, the Tonglen is one type of breath-based meditation in which the meditator visualize taking the pain of others in every in-breath and sending out whatever will benefit on the out-breath. Means meditator imagines receiving the suffering of others in each inhalation and imagines giving the happiness, joy and loving to them in each exhalation. However, this practice should start from ourselves. Mean to say, first we practice to visualize taking our own pain in each inhalation and visualize giving away love, happiness and joy for ourselves in each exhalation. Thus, in this practice of Tonglen meditation, we will be able to evoke compassion in ourselves.

Then we can start practice by for other sufferers. Actually, the sensation of Tonglen meditation is not only a symbolic visualization but a process of transforming pain and suffering. A practitioner becomes aware of tapping into an endless well of love and compassion that is available not only to others but also to ourselves. It is, therefore, a very good meditation practice to practice during times when you are most vulnerable yourself.

Actually, when we undergo sufferings, we sense right through our own suffering the analogues to suffering that may others undergo, and then imagine joyfully relieving those others of their suffering by undergoing our own on their behalf. Thus Tonglen practice is a method for connecting with suffering our own and that which is all around us, everywhere we go.

Generally, people tend to experience the grief of loss, for example as an isolating them from others. But in this practice, through our own feelings of loss and grief, we sense what others may fail, making a strong empathetic connection to them. Thus by familiarizing with applied Tonglen in this way, we can generally learn to take all of our suffering into the path of compassion and wisdom.

For developing love and compassion, The Dalai Lama uses some assertive affirmations and he also suggests all of us to use them. He suggests, "Today I am fortunate to have woken up, I am alive, I have precious human life, I am not going to waste it. I am going to use all my energies to develop myself, to expand my heart out to others, to achieve enlightenment for the benefit of all beings, I am going to have kind thoughts for others, I am not going to get angry or think badly about others. I am going to benefit others as much as I can." So by repeating this affirmation, love and compassion can be developed up to very high level.

According to Thubten Chodron, compassion is a quality of mind that can be deliberately cultivated. Unlike mental states that are caused by distorted perceptions and misconceptions, such as anger and greed, Compassion is developed with a more rational state of mind that does not exaggerate either the positive or negative aspects of a person, object, idea or situation. Moreover, compassion influences our other thoughts and emotions also. Thus generous heart, patience, effort, acting ethically and making wise decisions can gradually lead us towards cultivation of love and compassion.

Additionally, forgiveness is also an effective way for developing love and compassion. A profound love comes when we first forgive and accept ourselves for all our shortcomings, misunderstandings, limiting beliefs etc. So forgiveness is the most powerful act of kindness we can make. Thus by forgiving ourselves as well as others, we can promote unity, peace and harmony. When we forgive and accept others as they are, such kindness activity develops the love and compassion. Therefore, in order to develop love and compassion, we have to be broad minded.

Impact of love and compassion on healing process

Love is basic requirement of human beings like food and shelter. The need for love lies at the very foundation of human existence. How much wealthy and independent one may be, however capable and skillful anyone may be, no individual can live happily without love. Anyhow, some duration may be passed but at a certain stage such as illness or at the time of sorrow, individual realizes the deprivation of love.

Actually, love and compassion are much effective for healing the illness especially mental illness. Thus mental illness can be reduced to some extent if we love one other and deal compassionately. In other words, love and compassion are better anti-depressant than medicines. Thus these positive emotions have been proved more relaxant than any other tranquilizers.

Counselor and psychiatrist Dr. Dean Ornish believe that love and intimacy are at the root of what makes us sick and depressive, and what makes us well and happy. He wrote in his book '*Love and Survival: The Scientific basis for healing power of the intimacy*', "Personal intimacy and other aspects of emotional well-being—all the elements of what we call 'love' are important to physical and emotional health. Not only love and compassion help us to make better life style choices, they also have a direct effect on our bodies, giving us stronger immune system."

Even only touching anybody with loving hand can feel him or her relax and comfortable. Actually, love and compassion boost chemicals in the body that protect from physical and mental disease. Most of the therapists and researchers are agreed on this point that love and compassion are great healers.

According to Darlen Lancer a Marriage and Family Therapist, when we delight in another's being-ness, boundaries may dissolve in what feels like spiritual experience. This allows energy to flow into places of resistance that surround our heart and can be deeply healing. It can happen during moments of vulnerability during therapy.

Dr. Theresa Larsen Crenshaw who researched the role of hormones in the body believed that physical touch with love and compassion increases the body's oxytocin promotes feeling of affection and care taking behavior. Actually oxytocin is a hormone but acts as a neurotransmitter to the brain, and synthetic oxytocin, in fact, has been used to treat depression and obsessive-compulsive disorders. Thus physical touch with affection helps in curing mental disease.

Dr. Robert Lusting MD MSL and Author of *'Hacking of American Mind'* says, "You are a set of neurons in your brain, and when you adapt the emotions of sufferer generates empathy. Moreover empathy is necessary for producing serotonin a hormone which enhances happiness". Therefore, touching someone with tenderness during painful moment reduce the sufferer's pain but also comfort you. So touch affectionately; hold the hand tenderly and even hug someone in need.

In this context, Dr. Pearsall who is an innovator in the science of psychoneurosexuality believes that people engaged in mutually fulfilling relationships are healthier and more resistant to serious illness. He wrote in his book, *'A Healing Intimacy: The power of loving connections'* that a relationship results in healing intimacy when there is less emphasis on self-fulfillment and more emphasis on mutual support and respect. Means, selflessness pays a big role in any relationship.

From the finding of these researchers, it can be concluded that love and compassion have the potential to be great reduces of stress. When people get love and compassion, they feel less alone, less depressive and less threatened. Instead, they feel more confident in facing stress. Thus, this loving care is the great antidote to stress.

Author James Lynch explained the importance of love in '*The Broken Heart: The Medical Consequences of Loneliness* 'that the mandate of love your neighbor as you love yourself is not just moral—it is physiological.

When people witnesses our loving kindness, they see new way of responding anger and aggression. Thus, anger and aggression can be diverted towards construction rather than destruction. Therefore, we should understand that love and compassion not only heal the people but also turn them towards creativity.

The Dalai Lama said that there is no denying that our happiness is inextricably bound up with the happiness of others. There is no denying that if society suffers, we ourselves suffer. Nor is there any denying that the more our hearts and minds are afflicted with ill-will, the more miserable we become.   Thus we can reject everything else: religion, ideology, all received wisdom but we cannot escape the necessity of love and compassion.

Grief as means to love and compassion

Actually, all human beings are connected in invisible way which is, in fact, beyond human's comprehension. We are only a part of the Universe, a part just limited in time and space. Moreover, each of our thought is released by our mind, and resonates in the Universe in the form of energy, and their vibrations are picked up by other sentient beings irrespective to distance. Thus, all those who picked up these vibrations are affected by our thought. However, if our positive thought can heal us, it can also heal others.

Those who have hurt their feet by wearing the tight shoes know better where the shoes are punching. Mean to say, those who have suffer themselves in their lives can feel better the agony of other people. No doubt that suffering is very painful but it can be a crucial part of compassion. Without suffering ourselves, we won't be able to understand the pain of others. Actually, compassion requires that we get in touch with what hurts. Thus it is the pain, the suffering itself that invites the compassion to manifest.

Thus, those who had themselves suffered deeply can remove the suffering of others and become the source of love and compassion. Therefore, you have suffered in your life because it is wish of God that you become source of love and compassion and free all others from suffering. Moreover, as much as you help others in removing their suffering as much your compassion grow.

Thus, have love and compassion to all human beings as much as you can. You are the means to help others who are grappling in the dark. You are the torch of God who can show the path. As you have already complete your journey of grief through this path, you are better guide for others who are on the way and yet to complete this journey. You have seen the Divine light after crossing this dark and terrible tunnel. Therefore, you can show the path of that Divine light to other sufferers better than those who have not yet experienced the grief.

Actually, on helping others you are not only frees them from suffering but you will also become big source of love and compassion. Thus by using of your own experience of suffering, you can deeply feel the unbearable pain of many other people and free them from their suffering by your love and compassion. Additionally, by doing so you can not only be able to live blissfully yourselves but you can also fulfill the real purpose of becoming human being.

Lama Zopa Rinpoche, who was once himself hospitalized for tuberculosis and badly suffer in Buxa DuarTibetan refugee camp after leaving the Tibet, wrote in his book *'Transforming Problems into Happiness,'* "Every living being is the source of all my past, present and future happiness. Therefore, sentient being is the most precious thing in my life. Anything other than working for living beings is totally meaningless and useless because my life isn't benefitting others, and leading such a life would be empty".

Thus he prefers the service of human being over all other things such as health, wealth, friends, relatives, reputation, popularity etc. As he himself suffered very much in his life, he used his experience of suffering to developed love and compassion. Thus he searched a real purpose of life through making his suffering beneficial for others.

In this way, his suffering from disease becomes the cause of happiness of others—just like using snake venom to produce its own anti-venom. Thus make your own suffering the source of love and compassion, and help other sufferers like Lama

Zopa Rinpoche so that they can also become capable to bear their suffering.

How do love and compassion transcend us?

Love and compassion are the essence of spiritual life, and lead us towards enlightenment. Buddha gives *Dharma* teaching inspired by compassion. All Buddha's are also born out of compassion. So, it can be said that compassion is the base of Nirvana. The Dalai Lama said that the practical and realistic aim of human being is a warm heart, serving other people, helping others, respecting others and being less selfish. Thus by practicing these, you can gain benefit and happiness that remain longer.

The Dalai Lama further said, "We usually believe that compassion benefits others, may be at our own expense. That is not correct. When we are compassionate, we are the chief beneficiaries. Our minds are happier and more relaxed. Our lives become more meaningful, and we feel more connected to others. Others may or may not benefit from our compassionate actions. It is depends on their receptivity, and we cannot control that. But for sure, we benefit from having compassion for them".

Thus by developing a good heart, compassion and love, your whole life will become useful and meaningful even your each moment will become a blissful moment. Therefore, it can be said that a mind full of love and compassion is not only helpful for others but also supports your own happiness and well-being. Therefore, in order to attain bliss, be source of love and compassion.

Compassion enables us to know the suffering through intimacy. When we know it intimately, we get rid of the illusion of 'I and others'. Actually, when we shift our point of view from separateness to connectedness, we can feel the harmony, and we start to recognize ourselves to be part of this web of mutuality. Thus we realize that small bounded sense of separateness is nothing than our ignorance or ego. However, when separation falls away, we realize that we are part of whole. Moreover, as and when we recognize ourselves as part of whole, we, in fact, realize that—we are everything.

A Buddhist Scholar John Markransky said that compassion is viewed as a power for purifying the mind of confusion, for inner healing and for protection of self and others. Thus according to Buddhism, love and compassion are such attitudes which consist of wishing all human beings to be happy and find the true causes of happiness. It can be said that love and compassion lead us toward happiness, joy and peace.

Though the literal meaning of compassion is to suffer with, it experiences as delightful rather than miserable. Those who cultivate love and compassion for sufferers and free them from their suffering, they themselves experience great joy. For them, whole world becomes so attractive that each and every thing please them even a blade of grass seems very beautiful. Difference between friends and enemy; relatives and strangers; human beings and flora & fauna is almost eliminated for compassionate people.

Means to say, they love all human beings and other creatures equally without any bias. So those who are source of love and compassion never feel aloneness and deprived from any need due to their nature of 'giving'. Therefore, when we will ourselves become source of love and compassion and free others from their suffering, we will ourselves enter in the blissful state and feel sense of eternity.

Then not only love and compassion reduce the suffering of others but it transcends us also in a trance state. It transcends us in such a blissful state where we feel ecstasy. Thus in such a state of ecstasy, we not only forget the worldly affairs but ourselves also. Mean to say, we are transcends at such height of spirituality where we do not bother about trivial things. Then we become able to enter in the realm of God. Mean to say, the way of the realm of God goes only through love, affection and compassion .So, without possessing these positive emotions, we cannot enter in that realm.

Chapter 17

Live a purposeful life

Whatever we have done with our lives make us what we are when we die. And everything, absolutely everything counts."- Sogyal Rinpoche

We always want to achieve something big; want to accomplish some big project; want a big success and seek some big purpose. However, this wanting, seeking and searching remain continue. Actually, you can search an oasis in desert but you cannot fulfill your desire of wanting more and more. Anyhow, we spent whole life in this searching without accomplishing any good deed. However, we could accomplish some small deeds, if we would not hanker after something big. It is like ignoring the scenic beauty of the way in order to reach at the destination. However, if we enjoy the journey, destination may also be enjoyed.

Mean to say, in the desire of seeking something big achievement, we are wasting our time unnecessarily.

Therefore, instead of seeking big achievement, we should rediscover happiness in small things and by doing small good deeds. In other words, if we do daily some noble deeds irrespective small or big, our days of old age will be comfortable even our death will be easy. On the contrary, if we avoid the day-to-day noble causes, then not only our days of old age will be hard but our death will also be very painful.

The journey of life itself is a pilgrimage.

The journey of life is a big thrill. Thus, instead of seeking any big purpose in remote, we should seek adventure here and now. We should no longer worry about future achievements. What we have achieved so far is only an accomplishment of the past, and what we are going to achieve is only a plan for future yet to complete. So we have only present moment to do worth. The path of life is one way. Means, in the journey of life, there is neither any U-turn nor any about-turn rather you have to always go ahead.

Thus, if you have left anyone in miserable condition on the path, there is no option to return in order to help him or her throughout life. Mean to say, whatsoever you want to do, do here and now. Don't wait for any auspicious time. If there is any auspicious time, that is the 'this moment' only. In other words, yesterday which has gone without doing some noble cause, has been gone forever, and tomorrow never comes however today is still in your hand. So don't let any single moment pass over if it requires your attention for doing something noble. Otherwise you will get only regret.

Anyhow, effect of wrong doing which is known as 'sin' in Christianity cannot be reduced by doing some 'good deeds'. In other words, you cannot reduce effect of those wrong deeds which you have already done in past, by performing good deeds now or in future. For example, if anyone murders one person, but save two or more persons from drowning in water or protect some persons from any fire accident, this act of saving the life of some persons cannot nullify the previous act of murdering of the murderer.

What is the equation between wrong deeds and good deeds according to the scripture is not known to me. However, I believe that the Universe functions on the bases of cause and effect' known as *karmic* theory or law of *karma*. Whatever we are facing today is affected by our own causes created on yesterday while whatever we are doing today becomes the causes which will affect our tomorrow. It is another matter that generally, we forget the causes but remember only event whatever is being happened today is, in fact, the effect of that causes which have been created in the past by us.

Thus, instead of thinking about causes which have been created by us in past, we generally blame some other person or destiny. Actually, our suffering and bliss are emerged from our own *karmic* account (a balance sheet of all our past thoughts and deeds performed by us) of this life only. Thus, we are creating our *karmic* account daily on the basis of day-to-day deeds. Either something is being credited or debited daily in our *karmic* account. If we are doing good deeds, Cosmic Forces lead us towards joy and bliss. On the contrary, if we are doing wrong deeds, Cosmic Forces push us towards suffering. Thus everything is manifested by Cosmic Forces on the bases of our *karmic* account which we have prepared so far.

If we have done wrong deeds (sin) in our life so far, no any pilgrims can eliminate the causes of those sins. How much rituals we do; how much worship we perform; how many days we do fasting; how many religious places we visit; how many holy scripture we recite; etc. Make no difference regarding changing the effects of that causes which have been already created by us in the past. Thus no one can help us in escaping from the effects/consequences of those wrong deeds. Even

God is bound not to change because everything is determined in the Cosmos according to cosmic law. Thus, no any pilgrim can eliminate the causes, and the effects of those causes whatever they may be have to be faced.

On the other hand, if we have done good deeds so far then no need of any pilgrimage. In other words, no any pilgrimage is better than our own good deeds. Moreover, this pilgrimage can be performed only along with doing our day-to-day duty. Thus there is no any pilgrimage is bigger than the noble deeds accomplished by us during performing the day-to-day activities.

In this context, I want to share a story of a Hindi telefilm *'Theerth Yatra'* (pilgrimage).

The story starts from a farewell party, when a general manager of a big firm retires from his post. He feels very proud of himself on hearing much praise about himself on the eve of his retirement party. Anyhow, after retirement, he spent some time very happily on the pretext of being his 'goodness' whatever he heard in the function of his retirement. However, as the time passes, he starts to feel restlessness, and soon he became so restless that his restlessness starts reflecting by his body language.

On observing his restlessness, his son and daughter-in-law tried very hard to eliminate it but they could not success in their efforts. Even they could not find out the cause of his restlessness. Then his son and daughter-in-law suggested him to visit to holy places as a pilgrimage so that his restlessness may be comes to end.

Then he set out for pilgrimages. He visited all four *Dhaams* (most religious places) Bhadrinath in North, Ramesweram in South, Puri in East and Dwarka in west. He also visited all big temples and performed worship there. He dipped in holy water of trivani the merging point of Ganga, Yamuna and Sarsvati holy rivers in Allahabad. He visited Varanasi known as holy city, and he also performed all rituals in other religious places.

Mean to say, he did not spare a single holy place in India to visit, thus he left no stone unturned in order to stop his restlessness and to attain peace. Anyhow, he returned home without eliminating the restlessness. However, his restlessness remains continue.

However, after few days, one day his own conscience appeared and told him to accompany with Him (Conscience) for true *Theerth Yatra*. His conscience brought him in his own office where he had been working as a general manager for a long period. Then his conscience asked him to sit on the chair where many crucial decisions regarding the firm had been taken by him. He argued with his conscience that it was not a pilgrimage rather it was his own ex- office. Anyhow, the conscience conveyed him that it was really a holy place where he might be attained peace.

Then his consciences asked him to open an old file. After opening the file, he found in the file that instead of earning huge profit, he refused to give bonus to the firm workers. Even he showed duplicate statements of account to the workers in which loss was registered in lieu of profit. Then his conscience told him that if he would sanction bonus to the workers in proportion to the profit had been earned by the firm. By doing so, he could bring smile on the faces of the workers as well as their families. Then it would have been his true *Theerth Yatra.*

Then his conscience asked him to open another file. Though he did not want to open the file, he opened it reluctantly. After opening the file, he saw in the file that a worker who had died on duty hours but his dependents got nothing as compensation. Means, neither anyone member of the family was given employment nor any type of family pension was sanctioned by him. Even after requesting again and again by the wife of deceased, he was continuously postponing the matter and eventually closed the file. In the meantime the whole family of deceased suffered a lot.

Then his conscience told him if he would give due amount of compensation to the family and would give employment to the dependent of deceased then he might not only help the family but he himself get satisfaction for performing his duty sincerely. Thus by performing his duty in compassionate manner, he would have completed his true *Theerth Yatra* too.

Then on opening of one more file as his consciences directed him, he saw that a lady employee asked him for maternity leave. Even the lady has prepared her colleague to do extra work in lieu of her during her maternity leave. But, instead of giving her maternity leave he told the lady if her friend is ready to work in lieu of her then only one employee is enough in the office forever. Then instead of sanctioning the maternity leave, he terminated the service of pregnant employee on the pretext that there is no need of two employees in the office.

Then his conscience told him if he would give maternity leave to lady employee along with three months advance salary for her delivery then she could bring up her newly born child without any financial difficulty. Even this good deed can reduce the mental stress of her pregnant employee to some extent. In that case, it would have been his real *Theerth Yatra.* Anyhow, now the retired general manager realized that throughout his whole service he was busy to please his chairman even on the cost of humanity.

Then his conscience asked him to open another file but he could not dare to open other files due to overwhelm. However, he starts crying, and said that he wanted to live his life again but his conscience replied that no one can live this life again. Therefore, in the journey of the life there is no retake, no rehearsal, and no turnabout. Whatever has been done, done forever let it be wrong deeds or good deeds.

Therefore, the restlessness we feel in our old age is only due to our regret whatever we have done throughout our life. Actually, when we decide to do something against our conscience, we are warned then and there by our inner voice but generally we ignore it either due to our selfishness or any authentic presser. However, we should not compromise at any cost with our conscience otherwise it becomes the cause of our suffering any time in future. Thus it is better to live our life purposefully so that we may be escaped from such restlessness in our old age.

Though we do not accept consciously that we have done something wrong in the past, our unconscious mind is always punching us from inside for the wrong deeds done in the past like the general manager who had hurt his employees and gave much pain to them in order to please his boss. Thus his restlessness was only due to hurting of his employees which was somewhere lies very deep in his unconscious mind. Therefore, sin does not leave you till your death.

Thus, the journey of life is itself a pilgrimage and it can be visited only during performing the day-to-day activities rather than wandering at religious places. In other words, good acts of life are only true pilgrimages.

Happiness lies in small noble deeds

Actually, happiness is disguised in day-to-day acts which are being done for the benefit and welfare of others. Our purpose to get biggest achievement may be unfulfilled then we will get depress and invite more sufferings. Thus, instead of seeking very big and remote purpose, do whatever is in front of you right now worth to do. We have possessed so much which can be given to this world. We have a kind heart which is full of positive emotions. Even a little smile towards someone affects his or her life as well as our own life. Thus, seek a purpose to give something to someone in need on daily basis irrespective to big or small.

An attitude of serving higher purpose keeps us cheerful and happy. Therefore, all our actions should be for some noble purpose rather than for our own interest. Actually, selfish actions are fertile ground of stress because they are based upon our own personal gain and satisfaction. So such selfishness breeds further selfish actions and this vicious circle is going on….Means, our greediness is increased by getting short-term gain which gives us only temporarily satisfaction and eventually this temptation pushes us towards suffering.

On the contrary, selfless actions are based upon the benefit of the society and welfare of needy. So such actions lead us towards joy and happiness, and this positive feedback is also going on….In this context Bodhisattva Shanti deva said, "If you want to be happy you should never seek to please yourself, instead you should seek please others.

Here, I would like to share a study which was conducted in University of Zurich Switzerland.

Philippe Tobler associate professor of neuroeconomics and social neuroscience Department of Economics at the University of Zurich investigated how brain areas communicate to produce the feelings. The result provides insight into the interplay between altruism and happiness. They performed functional MRI scans to measure activities in three regions of the brain. First one is the temporoparietal junction where prosaically behavior and generosity processed, second one is the ventral striatum which is associated with happiness and third one is the orbitofrontal cortex where we weigh the pros and cons during decision making process.

The study participants were asked about their happiness before and after the experiment. Then, before the experiment started, some of the participants had verbally commented to behaving generously towards other people. This group was willing to accept higher costs in order to do something nice for someone else while other group had commented to behave generously towards themselves. While the participants of both groups were making their decisions, activities in brain regions were being measured by MRI scan.

The researchers found that the group who made decision behaving generously towards others is happier than the other group. "It is remarkable that intent alone generates a neural change before the action is actually implemented so merely promising to be more generous is enough to trigger a change in our brains that make us happier," says Tobler. Thus doing something nice for another person gives many people a pleasant feeling that behavioral economists call a 'warm glow.'

Thus, it is concluded after analyzing the study of researchers that the people concerned about the well-being of others are happier than those who focus only on their own interest. Therefore, happiness lies in small noble causes, it lies only in giving rather than in having or in getting. So reach out, share, smile, and hug, and do whatever you can do to make smile someone.

What goes around comes around

When you do something good for someone, may be you do not get response positively from that person. Anyway, no need to be bothered, sad or depressed. Rather continue doing your good deeds and after doing them forget. However, a time will definitely come when you will get your reward. Sooner or later; in one form or another; in one way or another, whatever has been done by you, return back to you with interest. It is exact like echo of voices. If you cry, cry will come back but if you laugh, laughing will come back. Means, if you abuse or harm someone, you will get same from nowhere, and if you give happiness to others, you will definitely obtain joy and happiness too.

When you help someone, he or she may help some another needy, and that person helps any third one and so on......Thus, this chain of positive acts is going on continuously till it come back to you. Sometimes this circle completes very soon while sometimes it takes time. However, it is definite that this phenomenon goes around and comes back to you certainly. How much may be the gap but this law of attraction never fails. It can also be said that the Cosmos is a huge Xerox machine.

Here, I would like to illustrate this theory with the help of a true story.

One day a man saw an old lady stranded on the side of the road. Even in the dim light of day, he noticed that she needed help. So he pulled up in front of her Mercedes and got out. He is still sputtering when he approached her.

Even with the smile on her face, she was worried. No one has stopped to help for the last hour or so. Was he going to hurt her? He did not look safe; he looked poor and hungry.

He could see that she was frightened, standing out there in the cold. He knew how she felt. It was those chills which only fear can put in you.

He said, "Here I am help you madam. Why don't you wait in the car where it is warm? By the way my name is Bryan Anderson."

Well, all she had was a flat tire, but for an old lady, that was bad enough.

Bryan crawled under the car looking for a place to put the jack, skinning his knuckles a time or two. Soon he was able to change the tire. But he had to get dirty and his hands hurt.

As he was tightening up the lug nuts, she rolled down the window and began to talk to him. She told him that she was from St. Louis and was only just passing through. She couldn't thank him enough for coming to her aid.

Bryan just smiled as he closed his trunk. The lady asked how much owed him.

Any amount would have been all right for her. She already imagined all the awful things that could have happened had he not stopped.

Bryan never thought twice about being paid. This was not a job to him. This was helping someone in need, and God knows there were plenty, who had given him a hand in the past. He had lived his whole life that way. And it never occurred to him to act any other way.

He told her that if she really wanted to pay him back, the next time she saw someone who needed help, she could give that person the assistance they needed, and Bryan added, "And think of me".

He waited until she started her car and drove off. It had been a cold and depressing day, but he felt good as he headed for home, disappearing into the twilight.

A few miles down the road the lady saw a small cafe. She went into grab a bite to eat, and take the chill off before she made the last leg of her trip home. It was a dingy looking restaurant. Outside were two old gas pumps.

The whole scene was unfamiliar to her. The waitress came over and brought a clean towel to wipe her wet hair.

She had a sweet smile, one that even being on her feet for the whole day couldn't erase. The lady noticed the waitress was nearly eight months pregnant, but so never let the strain and aches change her attitude.

The old lady wondered how someone who had so little could be so giving to a stranger. Then she remembered Bryan.

After the lady finished her meal, she paid with a hundred dollar bill. The waitress quickly went to get change for her hundred dollar bill, but the old lady had slipped right out the door.

She was gone by the time the waitress came back. The waitress wondered where the lady could be. Then she noticed something written on the napkin.

There were tears in her eyes when she read what the lady wrote, "You don't owe me anything. I have been there too. Somebody helped me out, the way I am helping you. If you really want to pay me back, here is what you do; don't let this chain of love end with you."

Under the napkin were four more dollar hundred bills.

Well, there were tables to clear, sugar bowls to fill, but the waitress made it through another day. That night when she got home from work and climbed into bed, she was thinking about the money and what the lady had written. How could the lady have known how much she and her husband needed it? With the baby due next month, it was going to be hard.

She knew how worried her husband was, and as he lay sleeping next to her, she gave him a soft kiss and whispered soft and low, "Everything is going to be all right. I love you Bryan Anderson."

In this story the circle of selfless act has been completed very soon even on same day through his wife when Bryan Anderson gave selfless service to old lady. Bryan did not accept any money because it was not suitable with his nature. He always believed in goodness and helped others without desiring the fruit of his deeds. Though he was himself a needy person, he never chased his service whatever he had done.

The old lady helped the waitress considering her needy at that moment without knowing her. Moreover, problem of money of Bryan Anderson solved through this chain of love. Thus Bryan Anderson got back within no time via his wife whatever he had done to needy lady. Here it is correct to say, "What goes around comes around." Thus, we should work in this world to make people happy, and the happiness will come back to us spontaneously. Moreover that happiness will be true happiness.

Those who take care of others; God takes care of them

According to Buddhist prescription about happiness, if you wish to be protected, you should constantly protect others. So forget yourself, and love others. Here, forgetting means dedicate yourself in the welfare of others. When we help others, we take our minds off ourselves, and in mindless state, we not only forget our own sorrow but also feel great satisfaction in the act of helping.

Thus reaching out to serve others with a selfless purpose, you can transform your smaller self into a higher self. Thus by doing so, you raise yourself at such a higher state where you feel only happiness and joy.

Actually, we suffer till we live in a lower self. As and when we enter in 'higher self', our suffering ceases spontaneously. Therefore, we should seek happiness in the welfare of other people. Happiness is like a scent of flowers which spread with the movement of wind. If we always ready to solve others problem, and always try to make them happy, our problems will be solved automatically.

Even some problems will solve before they occur. However, if you have no any your own problem to solve, you can spare more time to solve others' problems. When you take care of other people around you, some Invisible Power takes care of you; when you free others from their grievances, Higher Power frees you from your grievances; when you favor others, Cosmic Forces favor you. It can also be said that when you are always busy to serve others, Divine Power always remains near to you so that you may not feel difficulties. Even our intention to do something good is enough to attract the chain of service towards our side.

Thus, instead of thinking about yourself, dedicate yourself for others. Some Invisible Power which is omnipotent and omnipresent is remained present in support of you. As and when you start thinking about the welfare of others, your positive thoughts start releasing in the Universe. The thinking process and transmitting of the thoughts in the form of energy wave are going on simultaneously. The resonation of these vibrations spread in whole Universe within no time, and Cosmic Forces start to work in favor of you in order to accomplish your noble intention.

Therefore, don't waste your more time. There is lot to do even your kindness gesture can relieve someone's stress. A little affection of yours can change the day of any gloomy person. Even touching the shoulder of anyone with a tender hand can relax him or her from the burden of the sorrow. Thus the kind gestures and loving emotions are real treasure you can give with your heart.

According to a Japanese proverb, "One kind word can warm three winter months." Thus there are so many ways to give. Even your contribution of little time to someone in need has much importance to needy and your warm hug is sufficient to mend the hurt of a sufferer.

Therefore, don't be miser to give someone your love and kindness which, in fact, do not cost any single penny. Instead, you may be able to sleep soundly in the night because the guards of God remain present on duty when you are in your bed. Thus take care of others; God will take care of you.

Service is the gate-way of bliss

The Bhagwad Gita advised us to become a yogi or the happiest person. If you are useful to those around you, you automatically become yogi. Swami Vivekananda said in this context that they only live who live for others, the rest are more dead than alive and thus, happiness comes when your works and words are benefit for others. Jesus also said that it is more blessed to give than to receive. This is because you feel happier sharing with others.

Helen Keller said that many persons have wrong idea of what constitutes true happiness. It is not attained through self-gratification but through fidelity to a worthy purpose. Thus doing something good for others leads us towards happiness while self-centered pleasure pushes us towards sorrow.

Therefore, instead of self-centered person, we should engage in those activities which uplifts and unites all around us. Such types of activities are known as 'service'. Means, the deeds which have been done for society selflessly are considered as service. The service not only frees the people of their traumatic past but it also holds out hope for them in future. Thus service is the life-line of the society.

Matthieu Ricard a French origin Tibetan Buddhist participated in 12 years brain study on meditation and compassion led by neuroscientist from the University of Wisconsin Richard Davidson. Davidson hooked up Matthieu Richard's head to 256 sensors found that when he was meditating on compassion was unusually light. Thus this Tibetan Buddhist monk declared "The happiest man of the world".

When the reason of such great happiness was asked from Ricard, he linked it with altruism. If you want to be happy, Ricard says, you should strive to be 'benevolent', which will not only make others better, but it will also make you better. "If your mind is filled with benevolence, you know—the passion and the solidarity …..This is very healthy state of mind that is conducive to flourishing", Ricard says further.

Therefore, if we seek happiness in the happiness of others and make them happy, we ourselves experience instant joy. Actually, when you give, you shift the focus from you to others. When that focus does shift, a real transformation occurs. This transformation allows you to be happier, more at peace with yourselves. Thus, the process of altruism fills your whole heart with joy and happiness by positive feedback.

However, the more you give the more feedback you receive in the form of joy. When you have collected lot of happiness, you become a big source of happiness. Then you become able to distribute it and share it to more people.

Thus by doing so, the circumference of happiness starts increasing day by day, and along with others you also feel happiness and joy. In the words of Og Mandino, "Happiness is a perfume you cannot pour on others without getting a few drops on yourself."

The personalities like Matthieu Ricard are always dwelling in the state of bliss because such persons dedicated their lives to serve others. They are big source of love, compassion and bliss. So the circumference of their joy and happiness is unlimited. Thus if we want to enter in the state of bliss, we must have a noble purpose to serve the others. So we should serve the people as much as we can in order to experience bliss. In other words, the way of bliss goes through the service.

Chapter 18

Enhance your intuitive ability

"The intellect has little to do on the road of discovery. There comes a leap in consciousness, call it intuition or what you will, and the solution comes to you and you don't know why or how"—Albert Einstein.

We have to take many decisions daily. However, in critical situation, many of us cannot take right decision due to confusion. Actually, it is very difficult to decide that whichever is the right way and whichever is the wrong one. If we choose right direction then the results will also beneficial. However, unfortunately, if our choice is wrong then the results may be destructive. And taking decision timely is equally important because the state of indecision creates tension.

However, at the time of indecision, many times and many of us take help of other people for taking decision, such as—family members, friends, elderly people, wise people and experts of the field. Actually, it is very difficult to recognize the worth of such people. All that glitters is not gold. Anyhow, on believing on them, a layman usually follows their advice. Moreover, the situation becomes more critical if their advice does not work and many times it does not work.

Then the situation becomes grimmer and a sufferer compels to wander from one door to another in order to find out the solution. Thus he/she run every pillar to post but everything proves futile. In spite of taking advice from everywhere, sufferer remains unable to get rid of the situation. Actually, we believe more on others 'wisdom rather than our own. So instead of seeking outside help, we should turn toward our own wisdom especially wisdom within us. In other words, we should trust on our intuition.

What is Intuition?

Generally, we take our decisions with our intellect. Our conscious mind is remained active, and we decide everything on the bases of pros and cons of the issue. We think logically and analyses the issue thoroughly before reaching at some final decision. In short, we are master in rationalization. However, we forget the fact that the conscious mind which thinks logically is contributing only twenty percent of our brain. Whilst, eighty percent of the brain's gray matter is dedicated to unconscious mind which is usually ignored at the time of taking decisions.

Anyhow, some psychologists believe that conscious mind is hallucination rather than real 'you' while real 'you' is your unconscious mind. Therefore, it is necessary to include the unconscious mind at the time of making crucial decisions. Though conscious mind is expert in logic, its logical analysis fails many times. Thus, decisions taken by intellect may be wrong so it cannot be a reliable faculty for taking the crucial decisions.

On the contrary, the unconscious mind reaches at any conclusion through the past experiences and connects with our conscious mind through signals such as through dreams, feelings, instincts, hunches, visions and gut feelings. Therefore, unconscious mind is more reliable than conscious one.

In addition, we also get external guidance from Universe in the form of synchronicities, unexpected meetings, unexpected occurrence, recurring experiences and miracles. Therefore, we should recognize these messages timely and follow them whether we get them from external source or internal source. Actually, the Universal Intelligence / Collective Unconscious always tries to show us easiest path, but if we ignore its guidance, we may push ourselves towards difficulties.

However, these messages from Universal Intelligence are remained continue in one form or another because it wants to convey us that we are not alone rather we are always supported by Invisible Power. Anyway, the way of receiving these messages is known as 'intuition'.

Actually, the word intuition is derived from the Latin word intueri, the meaning of which is 'to look within. 'Therefore, what we need to know, we can know without reasoning and analyzing only through peeping within our deep seated unconscious.

Francis P Cholle Author of *'The Intuitive Compass'* described, "Unconscious does not follow the logic of analytic reason yet new ideas stem from your unconscious termed 'intuition' which becomes your compass, a navigating device that enhances your flexibility, adjusting your course based on internal wisdom as well as the external circumstances of your life".

Albert Einstein linked the intuition with our earlier experiences which we have experienced so far. According to him, a new idea comes suddenly and in a rather intuitive way, but intuition is nothing but the outcome of earlier intellectual experience. Mean to say, the more experiences we have in our life, the more power of intuition we have.

Thus, intuition is the ability to understand instinctively without the need of conscious reasoning. In other words, intuition is a process that gives us the ability to know directly without analytic reasoning bridging the gap between our conscious and unconscious as well as between instinct and reason.

Though there is no evidence how the knowledge was acquired, it is sudden outcome from nowhere without thinking and conscious reasoning especially when we are in the state of tranquility. In other words, intuition is—knowing within blink of eye without thought, reasoning or efforts, even it does not guide you based upon worldly rules. Thus it is the ability to understand something without conscious analyses.

Above definitions of intuition indicate that intuition is an immediate kind of knowledge which does not require any intellect effort. However, it seems that knowledge stored in our memory bank and past experiences which have been encoded in our subconscious since our childhood are main sources from this processing and syntheses information we gain instantly. Thus it is the ability of conscious brain picking relevant conclusion from unconscious which we get through various ways.

Anyhow, it may be voice of our own soul, Divine's voice, ability of our brain, signal from our unconscious or Universal Intelligence, whatever it may be but it is sure that this voice is trust-worthy. Therefore, we should not ignore intuitions. Instead we should follow them because they are our best guide, and always lead us towards correct decisions.

Psychological aspects of Intuition

Intuition, in psychological term, is refers to subconscious knowing, which is the result of the processing of a range of experiences and past knowledge. Carl Jung referred intuition as a perception via the unconscious, highlighting the idea that intuition is often seen as beliefs which are known without understanding how they are known.

Whilst Hope College Social Psychologist David Myers, Ph. D, explains that intuitive right brain is almost always reading your surroundings, even when your conscious left brain is engaged in otherwise. The body can register this information while the conscious mind remains blissfully unaware what's going on.

Another theory suggests you can 'feel' approaching events specifically because of your dopamine neurons. In this context, Jonah Lehrer Editor in *'How We Decide'* describes, "Jitters of dopamine help keep track of reality, altering us to those subtle patterns that we can't consciously detect. If something in environment is slightly irregular—the speed of an approaching track, the slightly unusual behavior of someone at party—your brain squirts dopamine and you get that 'weird' feeling". Actually, listing intuition entirely depends on your awareness so whether you pay attention or not can make all the difference.

Some modern psychologists consider the intuition a psychological phenomenon of processing the information on the level of subconscious which yet to understand fully. According to team researchers at the center for organizational Strategy, Learning and Change at Leeds University Business School, "Intuition is the result of the way our brain store, process and retrieve information on the subconscious level and so is a real psychological phenomenon which needs further study to harness its potential".

The best psychological explanation now offer is that intuition is a mental matching game. The brain takes in a situation, does a very quick search of its existing files, and then finds its best analogue among the stored sprawl of memories and knowledge. On the based on that analogue, you ascribe the meaning to the situation in front of you so that suitable solution of the current problem can be retrieved on the basis of the experiences of previous solutions.

Actually, experience is encoded in our brains as a web of fact and feelings. When a new experience calls up a similar pattern, it not only unleashes stored knowledge but also an emotional state of mind and predisposition to respond in a certain way. Thus our subconscious chooses best suitable data from the knowledge bank and encoded experiences according to current situation and rejects excess information so that it can respond efficiently within a split of seconds. Thus brain reaches straight to the objective without informing our conscious mind how it got there. Therefore, our earlier knowledge and experiences have great role in the intuition.

However, psychologists also have concluded from various studies that roll of experiences are more in emerging the intuitions than knowledge because those experiences have been encoded in our brain since our infancy. Though our conscious mind does not remember any memory associated which had been happened in infancy, our subconscious picks the relevant data from encoded experience created by that particular happening in solving current problem. In other words, the experiences which are not remembered due experienced in the state of our infancy also play their role in emerging the intuition.

Thus all our experiences are equally important in the context of intuition.

You have noticed that critical problems which are remained unsolved even after our full efforts then generally we sleep in the night without finding any solution. However, solutions of such problems occur in our dreams in form of some meaningful hints. Sometimes as we wake up early in the morning, solutions arise suddenly in our mind in one form or another. Anyhow, it is not a coincidence rather these hints are intuitions. Actually, during sleep our conscious mind dips into the unconscious while our subconscious constantly ponders on that particular problem and we are not aware of it.

However, the positive aspect of this process is that in the subconscious, rationality does not censor unusual or irrational ideas. Thus ideas that would be rejected by logical mind as too weird are also given a chance to grow because cognition process is limited up to conscious mind. Therefore, our conscious mind follows whatever rules we have learned; our thoughts are linear and trapped on familiar and predictable lines. In the subconscious mind bizarre ideas can be explored and might lead to special solutions.

Sonia Choquette, Ph. D, intuitive and best-selling Author of *'Trust your Vibes'* describes, "That birds have radar, whales have sonar and we have our vibes". In other words we have hardwired for intuition. Choquette also encourages individuals to think about how our sixth sense should be our first sense due to its importance and value in our lives.

Spiritual aspects of Intuition

Spiritual people consider the intuition as voice of God. All of us have this ability to hear this Divine's voice but generally we ignore it. In other words, we are unable to pay attention on this call of divine due to engagement in activities; external disturbances; internal chattering or lack of tranquility.

In this context, Dr. Judith Orloff Author of '*Second Sight* 'describes intuition as "accessible to us all; it is a still small voice inside—an unflinching truth-teller committed to our well-being."

Whilst, according to Micara Link an Intuitive Soul coach and Reiki master, it is an inner voice or feeling that directs you toward greater love, truth and healing. It is an energy that communicates to you from a place of spiritual and unlimited potential. When you follow the guidance of your soul, you live a divinely inspired life, a life that is infused with purpose, synchronicity, ease and grace. Therefore, intuition is such sacred navigator which guides you towards self-realization.

Advaita Vedanta in Hindu philosophy referred the intuition as a glimpse of higher and wider self-knowledge. Connecting with our intuition is an experience of coming into contact with *Brahman,* the ultimate reality in the Universe; the Eternal Truth or Spiritual Bliss we had not realized so far because we are lacking the internal connection with ourselves. Means, we are unable to recognize our intuition being very silent voice blocked by loudness of external noise.

According to Buddhist prospective, getting an intuition means connecting with Collective Unconscious. Thus in Buddhism, emphasis is given on interconnectedness of all sentient beings. Mean to say, humans are infinitely creative beings that is interconnectedness with all that exists. Moreover, Collective Unconscious plays a role in understanding and defining intuition on shared and personal level. Thus intuition is a way to connect with and experiencing God.

According to Christel Nani a Medical intuitive and Author of *'Sacred Choices',* when you are touch with your intuition, you are in a place of profound power aligned with your spirit and, communication with Divine. Thus listening to your intuition will raise your vibration, as your spirit provides you with the necessary information to evolve to an easier and joyous life.

However, I believe that intuition is not from any outer space rather it is from our inner space. It is the wisdom obtained by experiences which is hidden very deep within us. Mean to say, intuition emerges from inner core of our unconscious.

Thus, on recognizing and following the intuition, we can make correct decisions, and escape from wrong doing. It is the means by which our conscience communicates with us, motivates, inspires and guides us. Actually, it is the way of attaining joy and bliss. We can experience the Eternal Truth and feel the presence of Higher Power, if we remain touch with our intuition.

Link between Gut feeling and intuition

As our gut feeling is not without any reason, many experts relate the intuition with gut feelings such as tight gripped or clinched. They may be signals of some kind of stress.

Michael Gershon, Author of the *'Second Brain'* and a professor at Columbia University says, "The gut itself literally feeds gut feelings; think of butterflies in the stomach when a decision is pending. The gut has millions of nerve cells and through them, a 'mind of its own', still gut feelings do not originate there but signals from brain".

Marcia Reynolds Psy. D also has same view about intuition. She says, "There are hundred million neurons and every class of neurotransmitter in your gut used to process external stimuli and send signals to your brain. Your heart also receives input and send out signals. The brain translates these signals so we can make decisions and act. It also edits, censors, and rejects some of the data it receives especially if emotions are triggered".

Judith Orloff PhD, a Los Angeles based intuitive psychiatrist and Author of '*Guide to Intuitive Healing*' explains, "Your body is a powerful communicator. Intuition allows you to get the first warning signs through your gut feelings." Anyway, we use so many words to describe this gut feeling such as— knot in the stomach, gut wrenching, butterflies etc. Actually, gut is lined of billions of neurons which make up the enteric nervous system.

It can also be said that the vagus nerve which runs from the brain stem all the way into abdomen act as a sort of intercom system that delivers messages back and forth from the gut to brain. Thus due to this communication system, our brain receives the information from the gut. Therefore, the gut which was previously considered only for the purpose of digestion, excretion etc., but now the gut has been proved as a 'second brain' also. So hunch and gut feeling are also a way of intuition which should not be ignored.

How to recognize and follow the intuitions

Intuitions appear in many forms such as—dream, insight, hunch, gut feeling, quick flash, vision, vibes, coincidence and synchronicity but generally we fail to attend them. Actually, intuitions come suddenly when we are busy in thinking. So due to lack of our inner silence, we cannot recognize them thus they pass through us unattended. Often we cannot recognize them and sometimes we ignore them even after recognition. However, not only we have to recognize them but also we should follow the message of intuitions so that we may take correct decisions and lead towards happy and blissful life.

We get intuition through gut feelings also so it is necessary to recognize that gut feeling which is associated with intuition. Actually, it is very difficult to choose that which gut feeling to be trusted. In this context, Judith Orloff describes, "Intuition allows you to get the first warning signs when anything is off your body so that you can address it. If you have a gut feeling about your body—that something is toxic, weak or off—listen to it".

If you are around somebody and your energy goes down, that is an intuition which should not be ignored. Thus sudden drowsiness can mean that you are in presence of an energy-draining person or circumstance; it can be your body's way of communicating that these conditions are taking more energy than they give. If you stay in that situation that makes you feel intensely depleted, it can easily lead to a situation where you become depressed, anxious and even stuck.

David Myers a professor of psychology at Hope College in Michigan, U S believes that the feeling you get about a person in the first ten seconds express 'ancient biological wisdom'. Early humans, who can speedily detect whether a stranger was friend or foe, were more likely to survive, he says, and they would create descendants who were able to read emotional signal in another person's face almost instantly. Thus first impression of any stranger should also be considered.

However, I believe that there is a transmitter and a receiver in our brains and we transmit and receive the thoughts in the form of energy wave. Whatever thought the stranger transmits, we receive then and there. That's why attraction or repulsion occurs towards any stranger. If thoughts of stranger are matched with ours, we feel attraction otherwise in the case of mismatch, we feel repulsion. Thus our brain works as radio-set also. Therefore, if we remain mindful, we can recognize the vibration of thoughts in the blink of eye whether the thoughts of anyone is pure or malicious.

Whatever the way you use to recognize the intuition but recognition is useful in our day-to-day decisions. Here, I would like to share my personal experiences how I recognize the intuitions. Generally, I get intuitions through flashes. During meditation, I get perception of visual images which appear like a moving reel. Actually, whatever appears in my mental image, the same happens in my life in future very soon. This phenomenon of visual image has never failed so far. Therefore, I trust fully in these quick flashes. Additionally, often, my dreams are also proved true.

However, when I notice intuition through gut feelings and vibes, I do not decide them blindly. Means, I engage my rational mind also for taking decision along with my intuitions. Generally, I take most of my decisions next day as and when I wake up in the morning. After taking the decision, if I feel euphoria, easiness, comfortable and profound peace, I sustain my decisions.

On the contrary, if I feel boredom, restlessness or uncomfortable on taking the decision, I reanalysis. I analyses the situation again and again to change my decision till I feel easiness and calm after confirming the decision. Even sometimes this process takes some days but this is sure and certain way of taking final decisions.

Though the body is a powerful intuitive communicator, listening to our body's subtle signals is a critical part of exercising our intuitive sense. Therefore, hurry in recognizing the body's signals may lead towards wrong direction. Thus it is better to take some more time to make final decisions. That's why the intuition noticed through gut feeling; vibes and other body's feeling; I do not follow them immediately. Therefore, I decide everything after balancing between intuitions and rational mind.

However, the concept of balancing is not due to mistrust on my intuitions but I want to confirm them. So an analysis with rational mind is only for confirmation of the intuitions. Actually, sometimes gut feelings and body's uneasiness may be due to some other physical disturbances thus confusion may be arisen. So to rectify this confusion, it is necessary to think logically simultaneously along with intuition. Thus, after balancing of both the intuition and rational mind, the decision will be correct naturally.

Francis Cholle also says that we do not have to reject scientific knowledge in order to benefit from instinct, and by making this balance all resources of brain can be brought under action.

Therefore, next time when you get positive vibes such as—a sense of warmth, ability to breath easily, a wave of goose bumps, fluttery sensation etc. need not be worry. Rather these symptoms of your body are sign of good happening in future.

On the contrary, if you feel negative vibes such as—icy cold hand or feet, clinching pain in gut or chest, fatigue or dizziness, nausea or headache etc. are sign of some problem approaching towards you. So instead of ignoring them, pay attention on them. However, you may also analysis them for confirmation but it is very necessary to recognize the intuition timely in order to avoid the critical situation before approaching it.

In addition, coincidences can also be tested through rationally whether any coincidence is mere a coincidence or signal of God. I believe that there is nothing happens as coincidence in the Universe. Rather whatever happens happens according to cosmic plan however human cannot understand it. Therefore, coincidences and synchronizations are only Divine's message for us to convey something. Thus, when coincidences and synchronizations increase in your life, try to find out the meaning of such occurrences.

How to enhance the intuitive ability

It is said that sincere asking is the key to real answer. When we intent to know something, it reveal one way or another. So we must always be attentive and mindfulness. Answers are revolved around us in many forms. It may be found—in any stanza of the lyrics; dialogue of movie; column of newspaper; sentence of a book which is currently being read; statement of any person; from the mouth of any innocent child etc. It can also be said that we can find solution of the issue by any means throughout day if we live in full awareness. Thus, due to lack of mindfulness, we generally ignore many intuitions unknowingly.

When we pay more attention to the intuition, it will get stronger. So by inviting intuition into our daily life, it will appear itself in one way or another. Thus in order to enhance our intuitive abilities, we have to pay attention what is going on around us. The more data and information we absorb from our environment, the more our subconscious mind has to work at the occasion of decision making. In addition to our experiences, our unconscious mind uses the information gathered by conscious mind also for creating the intuitions. Thus we get the solution according to the proportion of information. Means, the more the information available in our subconscious mind, the better will be the solution.

Generally, we are always surrounded with noisy environment. In addition, our own incessant thinking also adds in this noisy environment. Therefore due to these both type of noises outer as well as inner, we have no time for silence and peace of mind. Thus, in order to get silence, we have to seek a lonely place and have to cease our internal dialogue. Actually, we become more receptive to insights, when we live in solitude and remain mindful. Therefore, to enhance our capacity for intuition, it is necessary to maintain our silence and be away from noisy environment.

In this context, Sophy Burnham Author of '*The Art of Intuition*' describes, "If you want to touch with the intuition, a little time alone may be the most effective way. Solitude connects to our deepest inner wisdom so spare a little bit time for solitude and silence. In the middle of craziness—you can't recognize intuition in the noises of everyday life". Mean to say; if we remain silence for some period and spend some time in solitude, our capacity for intuitions can be increased manifold.

In addition, living close with the Nature also enhances the intuitive ability. Actually, when we make keen relationship with Nature, not only concentration of our conscious mind increases but signal of unconscious can also be recognized clearly. Actually, spending time in Nature improves our sleep, and vitamin D level in our body which increases the level of serotonin hormone and decreases the level of stress hormone cortisol. Naturally, in such peaceful state of mind, we get more intuitions than disturbed state.

Therefore, we should try to spend some days with Nature such as—on mountains or hilly regions; in forests or any other wooded area; on beaches or sea shore, on the bank of rivers, under the star strewn sky etc. In addition, some outdoor activities should also be added in our daily-routine such as—gardening or some other activities related to soil; walking or jogging in parks; some outdoor play etc. so that our intuitive ability may be enhanced.

Meditation is the best method to access to the subconscious and awaken the intuition. Mental stability which is very essential for intuition can be increased through meditation. It also helps to cease the thinking process which resulting in quiet the mind. Suppressed emotions are also released during meditation. Thus, the state of calm mind and mindfulness give our intuition space to grow and enhance. Mental imagery flashes can be observed in the state of thoughtlessness which can be created only through meditation.

It has been already mentioned under the sub-heading of psychological aspect of intuition that intuition is mostly about matching patterns based on knowledge and experiences. Thus, your intuition will be more reliable in the fields in which you have more experiences and knowledge. So in order to get more experiences, you must learn new things; leave your comfort zone; explore new fields; initiate any new project; travel to unknown sites and enter in socialization areas. Mean to say, more life experiences you have, better your intuition will be due to having more data to retrieve from your subconscious.

Massimo Pigliucci professor of philosophy at CUNY—city college and Author of '*Answer for Aristotle: How Science and Philosophy can lead us to a more Meaningful Life*' cites some of the recent research on intuition and how it can be improved: "Intuitions enhance with practice because intuitions are about the brain's ability to pick up on certain recurring patterns; more we expose to particular domain of activity, more familiar we become with relevant patterns and faster our brain generates heuristic solutions to the problem going to be happened within that domain". Thus intuition is a dynamic, powerful and highly valuable skill to develop.

Preparing the mind before going to sleep also helps in improving the intuition. Means, if we focus on all alternative of solution just before climb on the bed, the solution will reveal by one means or another. Probably you will get answer in your dream, otherwise pay attention on first thought or idea as and when you wake up early in the morning. I always follow my first thought when I wake up in the morning and it has never betrayed me so far.

Actually, in the morning there is much clarity in our mind as well cleanness in Cosmos due to less thought pollution because many people are in sleeping state at that time. Thus these both conditions are favorable to connect our 'Self' to the Universal Intellect. And our own self connects directly to Universal Intellect/God which makes enable our unconscious regarding solution of the issue in question. Thus, it can also be said that our first thought after waking in the morning is the voice of God. Thus first thought or idea should not be ignored.

Physical work also helps in enhancing the intuitive ability. So keeps your energy in movement with the help of activities such as—yoga, aerobic exercises, jogging, walking, cycling, gardening etc. Acknowledgements also increase your intuitive capacity. Thus honor your intuitions and pay gratitude to Nature and God for intuitions you get. The more you acknowledge your intuition, the more accurate and stronger it gets connecting with your inner source. In addition, curiousness and creativity also improve the intuition. Therefore, your curiosity and creativity should not come to end.

In addition, noticing and feeling of feelings are also helpful in enhancing the intuitive ability. So it is very important to be open to feelings and to be able to discern what you feel. The more you open yourselves to feelings, the more powerful your intuitive ability will become. Thus don't hide your feelings rather observe them and feel them, even bear the pain of feelings. In doing so, you will become free from mental pressure and feel very light then you can recognize the signal of intuition clearly.

Thus as a last but not least step, to follow your intuition is essential measure to enhance intuitive ability. Moreover, all of us have this ability and we can enhance it up to unlimited level despite our background and circumstances. Therefore, only recognition of intuition is not enough rather it should be followed in order to enhance intuitive ability in future.

Importance of Intuition

We are taking many decisions daily out of them some are very crucial. Thus a correct decision may lead us in heaven while only a single wrong decision may push us in hell. Actually, in the world, the top killer is not any chronicle disease or any calamities rather the main killer is our inability to make correct choices. Thus, inability for making correct decisions ultimately leads us to engage in self-destructive behavior.

Sometimes we believe that our decision is right and we need to go ahead. In the meantime, our ideas and goals change and Cosmic Forces assist us by adjusting our path. However, the message we receive from Universe seems contradictory but we should not ignore this message. As the ways of God to send us hints of warning are innumerable which remain mysterious, we should recognize the hints, in fact, these hints to be considered as intuitions. Thus in such critical confusion, only our intuition can show us correct direction.

In this context, Frances Cholle describes, "Even when you are tune, there will be times in your life that are chaotic—when you will have doubts and feel confused. This is usually the times for internal and external change. Change often occurs on the border between order and chaos; clarity and confusion; reality and fantasy; pain and pleasure". Thus life often challenges your flexibility, depth and ability to adapt to these possibilities.

It can also be said that at such critical situation only intuitions can guide us towards right direction. Thus we can adjust our course based on our internal wisdom as well as external circumstances. Thus our intuitions enhance our flexibility also. Therefore, intuition plays very important role in such critical situations when we are running on the edges.

Duke University's Ralph Keeney Author of 'Smart *Choices a practical Guide to make better Decision* 'found in a research that each year more than a million people needlessly die in the U S alone because of their own personal decisions. Thus taking correct decision at correct time has very much importance in our life but most of us cannot take correct decision at right time.

In addition, state of confusion in taking decision makes the situation more critical. Thus neither taking right decision nor taking wrong decision at suitable time resulting in the mental tension because not taking any decision at right time is worse than taking wrong decision. Thus indecision is the worst scenario and ultimately the person who is unable to take any decision for long time entangle in depression and leads to the state of sorrow. It can also be said that indecision is a main reason for mental stress.

Therefore, it is necessary to avoid the situation of indecision as well as to escape from wrong decisions. Then question arises, how can we take correct decisions? Thus, I believe that the correct decision can be taken neither by heart nor by mind.

Mean to say, the decisions taking emotionally generally are proved wrong while decisions taken by rationally may also fail. However, the third option for taking correct decisions is utilizing the intuitive guidance over the logic. Mean to say, in order to take correct decisions; listen your inner voice.

According to Albert Einstein, the intuitive mind is sacred gift and the rational mind is a faithful servant. We have created a society that honor the servant and has forgotten the gift. Intuitive is a signal sent by God which we often fail to notice. Actually, the conscious mind is limited in its ability to comprehend only systematic working of Cosmos while unconscious mind comprehend beyond the law of physics.

Malcolm Gladwell the Author of '*Blink: The Power of Thinking without Thinking*' describes, "If we are to learn to improve the quality of the decisions we make, we need to accept the mysterious nature of our snap judgment". Actually, the importance of intuition is not limited up to problem solving and decision making rather it is also very essential to live a happy life.

Judith Orloff believes the benefit of listening to your instinct go far beyond making good on life-or-death decisions. She says, "Living more intuitively demands that you are in the moment, and that makes for more passionate life". Thus, ignoring the intuitions push you towards fatigued, feeling of restless, dissatisfied and depression which resulting in loss of passion and unhappiness.

Christel Nane Medical Intuitive also says, "Actually, intuition is a Divine directive. Longer you ignore it, more out of balance you become. Nothing really excites you anymore; your life becomes uneventful and you lose your passion. Then initial whisper becomes so loud, you must cover your ears to avoid it; this requires a tremendous outpouring of energy".

Every one of us has noticed that when our life becomes steady without any further activities, we feel boring. Or it can also be said that this loss of energy leads to feeling us unhappy, trapped, bored, and depressed. Sometimes we feel physical symptoms also like headache or dizziness. Thus a state of energetic stagnation appears where minimal energy flow through the *chakra* system. The state of energetic stagnation is termed 'energetic suicide' by psychologists. People in energetic suicide feel exhausted, lost and empty; have lost their passion and drive. Thus, to avoid these serious physical, mental and spiritual crises, we must always touch with our intuitions.

On the contrary, on following the intuition, we lead towards great joy and bliss. It is, in fact, our inner wisdom, and implication of this wisdom is the best and quickest way to achieve long-lasting happiness in life. Therefore, in order to reduce the mental stress; to deal with the problems effectively; to make the correct decisions at right time; to prevent for developing of negative thinking; to release suppressed emotions and to retain overall well-being, it is necessary to enhance the intuitive ability and intuitions must be followed.

Chapter 19

Live in present moment

"The secret of health for both mind and body is not to mourn for the past, worry about the future or anticipate troubles but to live in the present moment wisely and earnestly"—Buddha

We cannot escape from ups and downs of the life's journey. Along with spending joyous moment, we have to bear the consequences of adversities and have to face the challenges and problems in our life. However, overcoming of these obstacles require lot of effort, energy and will power. Thus we should routinize our day-to-day life accordingly with the situations. There is no doubt that there may be some very bitter experiences in our lives which are very difficult to forget even seem impossible to forget. Instead of trying very hard, they are recreated again and again on our mental screen. Therefore, it is really hard to forget the past and we generally remain thinking about those past painful experiences. In other words, our thoughts about those memories are going on incessantly. Actually, thoughts are noting but recurring memories.

In addition, we are worrying and anxious about future which is unknown and unpredictable. It can also be said that either we live in past or in future. On other bright side of life between past and future there is present also and generally that present is ignored. In fact, present moment is actual moment worth to live. However, by ignoring the present, we really miss the charm of life. Actually, whatever is happened always happens in the present. Everything that ever happened and will be happen, in fact, happens in the present moment. Mean to say, whenever any event happens irrespective to past, present and future, that happening time is always running in the present moment. Therefore, past and future do not exist rather they are just mental concept of our brain.

Therefore, everything exists here and now. Present moment is the only a moment where there is no time. It is the exact point between past and future where life actual flourishes. Nothing can thrive in past and future because past is the thinking of memories while future is the projection ahead. In fact, this moment is all there ever is—everything else is just an illusion of mind, bundle of thoughts and imagination of future. According to Buddha, "Things are as they are and this is the 'isness' of the present moment". Thus in order to attain peace of mind, we have to align with the present moment.

Actually, past cannot be changed because it has been happened forever and future cannot be predicted because it is still in the womb of cosmos while present moment is still in our hand. So instead of living in past and future, we should live in present moment. Cartoonist Bill Keane said that yesterday is history and tomorrow is mystery only today is gift that's why the gift is also called the present. I think now there is no need to describe that why the term 'present' is used for gift. Thus, if we start living fully in present, we can create whatever we will. Then miracles will begin to happen and these miracles will be the best gift for us given by Cosmic Forces.

Meaning of living in the present moment

Generally, living in present and mindfulness both are used interchangeably. However, some Buddhist monks consider mindfulness as a kind of meditation. According to them mindfulness is a method of shifting one's attention inward to observe one's thoughts and emotions without interpretation and judgment while living in present moment means to aware about one's surroundings. It means mindfulness is about awareness of our thoughts and feelings while living in present stands for awareness about what is happening all around us. In other words, mindfulness is seeing inside while living in present moment is seeing outside.

Actually, due to subtle difference in mindfulness and living in present, it is really difficult to differentiate between both. Anyhow, living in present refers to 'being fully present in each moment'. When we give full attention on our each activity even on simplest task and notice each scenery and beauty around us that is true living in present moment. Thus, living in present moment is when we actually conscious fully at present what is going on around us. This is real meaning of 'being in present 'rather than focusing on particular present event. In other words, it is living with awareness moment to moment.

It can also be said that living in the present moment means conscious, aware and present with all senses rather than dwelling on the past or being worried about future. It means when we listen something, listen it attentively; when talk something, speak it with the harmony of mind and heart; when touch anything, touch with its texture; when eat and drink anything, consume them with full savor; when walk, observe each step and when do some activity, absorb fully in it. Actually, everything that exists exists only here and now. We do neither smell, feel, touch, watch, hear and see anything in past nor in future. Everything is happening here and now at this moment only.

Thus when we do anything wholeheartedly, we have no moment to think about past and anxious about future. So such type of living, in fact, is living in the present moment, the true reference point of time. By living such way, we experience the feeling of presence; being here in this body and mind and seeing the world through these eyes. This reference point of time is known as 'existence'. When we start living in this existence, then not only our awareness increases but we may also escape to become victim of time.

It is also said in Bhagwad Gita that concentrates on your work and does not think about its fruition. It is not in the sense that you have no right of fruition. However, it means, that if you are continuously thinking about the fruition while you are doing your activity, you may distract from your work which is occurring in present moment. Thus Bhagwad Gita only wants to convey the message that live fully in the present moment is much more important than looking towards future. In other words, when we do something with full awareness, results will spontaneously fruitful.

Thus living in the present moment means that your awareness is completely centered on the here and now. You are not worrying about future and not thinking about the past. You are noticing even very smallest change around you. You are living where life is flourishing and events are happening. You are tuned with each and every sight and sound and fully aware to your senses to the world around you.

Why is living in the present moment so hard?

Living in the present moment is not only difficult but according to psychological aspect, it is almost impossible also. However, Sufi-saints, Buddhist monks, sages and some other spiritualists make it accessible to some extent. How much efforts, practice and patience it requires to stay in the present moment is another matter. Here the big question arises why psychologists consider technically impossible to live in the present moment.

In this context, Gary L. Wenk, Ph. D a professor of Psychology Neuroscience, Molecular -virology, Immunology and Medical Genetics at the Ohio State University gives following logic:-

Actually, our brain did not evolve in a world that rewarded us for being still while ignoring our external environment. Our brain requires stimulation for its satisfaction such as coffee, coke etc. When we do not provide our brains with input from external world such as TV, music and other entertainments, our brain disengages and goes in to what neuroscientists call 'default mode'. The rest of us call this state 'daydreaming'.

Our brain evolved in a sensory rich world and rewards us exposing it ever more complex sensory experiences. Every time we experience something new our brain releases a jolt of dopamine in the frontal lobe; dopamine is the major reward neurotransmitter in the brain. We can artificially stimulate the release of dopamine by ingesting coffee, cocaine or by listening music, communicate to someone else etc. The brain rewards us for obtaining new information and having lots of thoughts because doing so might have survived value.

Thus we are all burdened with a brain that demands constant entertainment that powerfully rewards us for providing it. When we do not provide adequate amusement, our brain goes into default mode or daydreaming i.e. it generates its own entertainment. Clearly mindfulness and remains in awareness forever although wonderfully peaceful and restorative for the body and mind is not something that our brain evolved to accomplish.

Therefore, due to this above logic of professor Wenk, it is very difficult to cease daydreaming. In addition, our attachments and desires enhance this daydreaming.   We feel pleasure in doing so. We remember our first experience of any pleasure moment and thinking to resume it again and again. Moreover, often we think, "Would that life were in another way! Would that I were powerful! Would that I were so and so! This thinking is like a dog that chews bone incessantly and relish of its own blood on the pretext of the bone.

However, our desires and ambitions do not fulfill almost throughout our whole life. When one desire fulfills, another one appears from nowhere which is main reason of worrying, anxiety and projection of future. Thus in order to fulfill the pleasure of accomplishment of these desires and ambitions, our daydreaming are going on constantly. Means, we feel pleasure on our mental screen through thinking of past pleasurable thought or future projection. Anyhow, we stimulate our brain artificially by daydreaming so that we feel pleasures by releasing the dopamine in our brain. So it is very difficult to remain in present moment.

Eyal Winter Ph.D. Professor of Economics at the Hebrew University, Author of *'Feeling Smart: Why our emotions are More Rational than We Think'* also describes that why it is technically impossible to live in present moment. According to him, "Human psychology is evolutionary hard-wired to live in past and future and human survival relies very much on learning and planning".

Thus it is almost impossible to learn something without living in the past, and this fact is also true that we cannot plan without living in the future. In other words, most of things we learn from our mistakes done in the past because we do not want to repeat them while whatever we are planning now will be implicated in future.

He also explains one more reason in this context, "Our mind views time as a continuous and linear process. Because it is continuous, any millisecond before the present moment is already past and any millisecond later is already a future". Naturally, our intelligent cognition cannot accept this existence because counting of every millisecond is impossible in context to live in present moment. However, research evidence does also show that people who are capable of discarding thoughts about the past and the future are generally happier. This is the reason that Buddhist Monks, who have attained the state of thoughtlessness, are happier than normal people.

Mr. Sarmang a Japanese spiritual seeker has also similar view. According to him, the question of living in the present is very complicated issue: living in this state is quite impossible because it changes constantly; every moment is unique and lasts for millisecond to leave the place to another moment and maintaining such rhythm. Thus present moment is a flash, and is followed by another and another and another…..and we are not able to stay there. However, he also illustrates a Japanese kendo practice which makes accessible to live in the present moment. (Describes under next sub-heading)

Thus it seems really very difficult to live in the present moment because it is millisecond even nanosecond that spots between the past and future. St Augustine described, "Now is neither in time nor out of time". Thus the elusive present moment is not measured by the tick tock time of clock nor is it separate from past or future. However there is no time line as we think rather each moment is fleeting and we are continually being shaped by it. Therefore, present moment could best be described as the 'flow of life'.

Anyhow, live in awareness fully here and now increases our happiness manifold so don't miss this moment in waiting for the next moment. Famous film Director and Song writer Gulzardescribed how to enjoy 'the present moment' in very beautiful way in the song of film Gol Mal:-

"Aane wala paljaane wala hae

Ho sake to iss mae zindagi bitaa do

Paljo yeh jaane wala hae."

Means, every moment is fleeting moment so enjoy each and every moment with wholeheartedly otherwise this moment will also pass.

How to live in the present Moment

Actually, we always in hurry therefore we miss many things which are being happened around us at present. The life is only here and now. Therefore, in order to enjoy it, we should not be in hurry. There is no destination in the journey of life rather here and now is itself destination. If we start to live slowly, we may catch and enjoy the experience of each moment. In this context, I want to share a poem of unknown poet.

Have you ever watched kids on a marry go-round?

Or listened to the rain slapping on the ground?

Ever followed a butterfly erratic flight?

Or gazed at the Sun into the fading night?

You better slow down. Don't dance so fast.

Time is short. The music won't last.

When you run so fast to get somewhere,

You miss half the fun of getting there.

When you worry and hurry through your day,

It is like unopened gift through way.

Life is not a race. Do take it slower.

Here the music before the song is over.

Thus, going slow with life is the best technique to live in the present moment. Moreover, as and when we start doing everything slowly, we start enjoying the beauty of Nature such as rain, dew on grass and leaves, drizzling, sunshine, flacks of snowfall, whistling of wind, chirping of birds etc. And we relish our food by eating it slowly. Tea or coffee can give more enjoyment by drinking them sip by sip. Thus, in order to enjoy the present time moment to moment, we have to slow the speed of our lives in all day-to-day activities. Even we should spare some time daily to sit silently without doing anything. If we will do each activity with full awareness, the thinking about the past and daydreaming for the future may be minimized to some extent.

According to a Japanese Kendo practice known as Zanshin or spiritual austere suggested by Mr. Sarmang, the spirit that remains aware, who can act without remaining attached to anything happened in determined moment. Zanshin means, taking care of every action we perform and remain attentive of what could happen a moment before. Mean to say, remain intense aware at the time of doing each and every act. In fact, in order to remain aware, we need to be more or less in the determined moment in that present not elsewhere.

Thus focused in such a way our senses are able to catch every infinitesimal changing, almost with the same speed of the same changing. We need an empty mind, without 'before' or 'after'. We need to be receptive. And this might become the natural state in our everyday life: this is particular way to grasp an object, a glass, a spoon, a pen, a tool, to do other work etc. We grasp an object with care and wait a moment before taking a mouthful. When walking, pay maximum attention on the feet as they touch the ground etc.

In such state, the time really expands, it becomes graspable. The milliseconds become longer, we start to perceive the situation in expanded way—just as we watch a movie's scene in slow motion. So we will able to anticipate the speed of pre instant, and always be there, perceiving the change that happens at lightning speed but perceiving it elegant short of reality.

In addition to this kendo practice and living slowly, some other ways also can be adapted such as—by noticing activities around you; listening the chirping of birds; smelling the fragrance of flowers; noticing the dew on grass or new shoots of plants in morning time and by noticing new things. By acquiring the habit of noticing new things, we recognize that the world is changing constantly. Once this noticing practice becomes habit, you will find it adventures—and the more you notice, the more you excite. Thus, the adventures and excitements are the real motivators to retain you in present moment.

Additionally, enjoy your waiting rather than irritation. You can make your waiting time interesting by observing the scenery of surroundings; by watching people's behaviors, moods and activities; smiling faces of children; etc. around you. By availing this practice, you may replace waiting place into enjoyable place. Therefore, enjoy the waiting time rather than become bore then hours may be passed in blink of eye without feel boredom due to your living in the present moment.

There are some other ways also for practicing such as—change your schedule; rout of morning walk; path of going office; accept new challenges; do only one thing at a time and do such more things you have never done before. Mean to say; try to seek such adventurous activities which generate excitement and enhance your experiences. Actually, when we experience something new, our brain makes new connections and builds brand new pathways. In other words, when we have to respond to something we have been never faced with before, it is almost impossible to put ourselves on autopilot mode. Thus, when we are not on autopilot mode, we have to live in present moment because the activities out of routine require our full attention. Naturally, we cannot give our full attention on any activity until we live in present moment.

Thus, next way to remain in present moment is absorbing in the actions what you are doing now. The state of total absorption is termed 'flow' in psychology. Actually, flow occurs when you are so engrossed in a task that you lose track of everything around you. The depth of engagement absorb you powerfully, keeping attention so focused that distraction cannot be penetrated. Thus in this state of absorption, you focus so intensely on what you are doing that you are unaware of the passage of time even you forget about your hunger and thirst when you absorb fully to complete your task. Mean to say, do wholeheartedly whatever you do. This flow will not only keep you in the present moment but the results of that task will also be fruitful.

However, you can remain in present moment at the time of listening the song. Mean to say, emphases on each and every phrase and sentence of the lyrics of the song. When you will listen anything intensively, your concentration from present moment will not distract. Thus in order to live in present moment, listen the radio and watch the TV intensively.

It is nature of mind to wander and busy in daydreaming. So we can remind ourselves to return at present moment by using any reminder such as by tying string on the wrist, posting flaps on furniture of the rooms, on gadgets in the kitchen and on other household items etc. Anyway bring the mind back by one way or another whenever it wanders. Bringing back the mind again and again at present moment, you not only become capable to live in the present moment but you may increase your concentration also.

Importance of living in present moment

When we enjoy the present moment without regretting of the past and fears of future, we become centered on a blissful experience. On the contrary, if we live in past, we live our old lives over and over in our memories. The life shattering experiences are clung with us like chain. This chain resists us to move forward. Therefore, in order to move ahead, we have to break the chain of painful happenings. If we remain clinging to the past, it will not give the space for new yet to come.

Motivational speaker Joyce Meyer says, "God's mercy is fresh and new every morning".

Thus when we start living in the present moment, every moment brings something new. When we live moment to moment, our each moment becomes bright and beautiful. Naturally, our next moment will also full of wonder. However, by chance if we have to face any tragic event in the future, till then we have accumulated so much strength and energy by living in present moment that we can face the tragedy with patience and tranquility. Thus living in present moment helps us to get rid of the consequences of any type of tragedy, and leads us towards blissful state.

Ellen Hanger Harvard psychologist says, "The more mindful we are, the more we can create the contexts we are in. When we create the context, we are more likely to be authentic. Thus our intense awareness lets us see things in a new light and believe in the possibility of change". Actually, awareness creates that contextual field where favorable condition appears automatically to prepare circumstances for happening something. Thus living in present moment is the key factor to fulfill our will or whatever we want.

In the context of spiritual aspect, it can be said that when we live in present moment, we are connected with God because He Himself live in present moment. He is always busy in creation. He is creating something each and every moment. Thus coincidence, synchronicity and miracle happen in our daily life when we live in the present moment. All these happen because our intense awareness helps our intention to merge with the intention of God which creates contextual field.

Living in the present moment reduces the stress and make us capable to get rid of grief. Actually, when we live in present moment and encounter to grief with full awareness, our thoughts become ineffective to make it more severe. Mean to say, thoughts work as feedback to increase the grief which can be minimized by living in present moment. However, my personal experience is that living in present moment with full awareness is the best way for recovering from the grief. Actually, our negative thoughts are main culprit to hold us in grieving state. However, when we become success to cease these thoughts by one way or another, our grief heals spontaneously and, living in present moment is more than enough to cease the flow of thoughts.

Some psychologists believe that living in full awareness calm the amygdule a part of the brain which trigger the brain for anger, anxiety and similar other disruptive emotions. The more you practice, the less reactive your amygdale becomes while some others have another views and they related the awareness with the prefrontal cortex part of the brain. According to them, living in present moment with full awareness shrinks the right frontal cortex which is responsible for many destructive emotions like fear, unhappiness, anger etc. Whatever the reason may be but it is sure that living in present moment reduces the suffering.

When we aware fully what we are eating and drinking, awareness increase our taste of edible things. We not only feel more taste in food but we also satisfy sooner with less food. Sonja Lyubomirsky professor in Department of Psychology at the University of California Riverside and Author of '*How of Happiness: A New Approach to Getting the Life You Want*' expands on the concept of savoring —involving your senses in whatever you are doing in the present moment. Savoring forces you in to the present —so you can't worry about things that aren't there.

When her research subjects took a few minutes each day to savor something they usually hurried through eating a meal, drinking tea etc.—they began experiencing more joy and other positive emotions and fewer depressive symptoms. Thus research has shown that anchoring awareness in the here and now reduces the kind of impulsive actions that underlie depression problems.

Other benefits related to living in the present moment are—when you live in present moment, you get a feel for the other person's humanness above their social positions thus it increases the empathy and compassion; it boosts concentration, memory, and increases the emotional intelligence and sense of well-being by increasing immune system. In addition, when you remain in the present moment during day time, you sleep better during night which resulting in enhance the work efficiency that ceases the wastage of energy and you always feel fresh and cheerful.

I would like to close this chapter with few lines of popular Buddhist monk and prominent Author Thich Nhat Hanh which he has mentioned in the book *'Twenty Four Brand New Hours'*, "Peace is present right here and now, in ourselves and in everything we do and see—the question is that whether or not we are touch with it. We don't have to travel far away to enjoy the Nature. We need only to be awake, alive in the present moment".

Chapter Twenty

Practice meditation

"Meditation is not a means to an end. It is both the means and end"—J Krishnamurti.

We are living in the age of information. We hear the News from many various sources, surf the internet and read many other printed materials. It can be said that our mind is full of all type of stuffs. Additionally, there are lots of outside disturbances and stresses of day-to-day chores. Mean to say, noise pollution of internal as well as external dominates us in such a way that we have lost the tranquility. Actually, our conscious as well as our subconscious mind has become a warehouse of such information.

In addition, there may be some negative emotions and hurtful memories in our lives which have been suppressed since our childhood. Anyhow, neither we are aware of our unconscious stuff which is main obstacle in our peaceful living nor we are able to get rid of current disturbances. Thus, in order to get rid of unconscious stuff, many kinds of remedies are being used throughout the world such as—psychotherapy, self- hypnosis, Tai Chi, yoga, meditation etc. However, these therapies require experts of the concerned field which are, in fact, very difficult to find out. So due to lack of trained master of the field, some novices have entered in the field of meditation and yoga, and they became so-called professional *guru*.

Therefore, yoga and meditation have become fashionable terms in the modern world. Thus, much confusion arises among common people regarding yoga and meditation. Though the techniques of meditation are very simple, the so- called masters make them complicated deliberately so that laymen remain in ignorance, and the profession of so-called masters may flourishing. This is the reason I have tried much to define the term of meditation and explained its practice's procedure according to my own practices and experiences along with the views, opinions, techniques and researches of some experts so that all readers may know better about meditation and they may practice it.

What is Meditation?

Actually, the origin place of meditation is India and its time was about three thousand years ago during Vedic period. So this term meditation is linked with the Indian culture. However, now it is being practiced throughout the world in various forms. Anyway, Ashtanga yoga Sutra which was composed by sage Patanjli known as father of yoga about two thousand years ago refers the mediation to the seventh of the eighth limb of Yoga, a step called *'dhyana'* in Sanskrit.

In meditative term, the meaning of *dhyana* is a state of being keenly aware without focus. It can also be said that the term meditation is primarily associated with awareness. The meaning of awareness in Buddhism is, "A person remains true oneself into a certain mental objects and also to a sense of being thoroughly and without any distraction."

In Zen, *dhyana* is equivalent of a sense of meditative absorption without anything in your mind at all to grasp into. Therefore, definition of meditation here is the ability to be as you are without further contrivances to make yourself comfortable. Thus definition of meditation is just a sense of being, a sense of isness that happening.

Many practitioners are confused that concentration on any object is meditation. That's why they use object for concentration such as gazing on candle's flame, any particular star in clear sky, a specific energetic center in the body, an image of deity etc. However, these practices also slow down the thinking process by concentrating on a single mental object. But such concentration is the sixth of the eighth limb of the Yoga Sutra a step called '*dharana*'; that is prior stage of the mediation. Though both processes are appeared to be one and same, a fine line of distinction exists between these of two. As mentioned above, dharana emphasis on concentration by using any object while *dhyana* emphasis on awareness.

Thus, whatever you do with awareness is meditation. For example, watching the breath with awareness is meditation; aware about your thoughts and emotions is meditation; listen to someone with awareness is meditation; walking with awareness is meditation; even watching the TV with awareness is also one form of meditation. However, in deep sense meditation is awareness of inside. Therefore, awareness of inside such as awareness about your thoughts, emotions and feelings is core factor of meditation. Or it can be said that to be aware regarding your thoughts and feelings is real meditation. Thus, as long as you are aware fully without any distortion, you are in meditative state.

Thus, meditation, according to spiritual aspect, is the effective means to remain aware on your thoughts, feelings and emotions so that this 'state of being aware' pushes your awareness inwardly towards subconscious and unconscious till pure awareness is achieved. Then your awareness goes deeper and deeper till you meet with your own 'Self'. In other words, it is the way to know oneself. Thus, meditation is an effective means to realize being awake inside without being aware of anything except awareness itself.

Therefore, in order to achieve this inner awareness, observing the thoughts patterns and watching the mind is key factor of meditation. Whatever thoughts or emotions passes, you have to simply observe them rather than controlling or resisting them. Even you need not to judge them, not to condemn them; rather you have to only watch them without any prejudice. Just remain there and be only being witness. Thoughts come and go, let them come and let them go. Only watch them and follow them.

Then after some practices, you become aware that your thoughts are reducing. As the thoughts reduce as you become aware that less thoughts are passing. The more you aware, the more thoughts reduce, and a gap starts creating between two thoughts and you feel very calm and quiet in this vacuum. Size of vacuum is directly proportion to your awareness. Thus, when you achieve higher state of awareness, the vacuum between thoughts becomes big. This emptiness of mind make you refresh, rejuvenate and tranquil. Actually, the process of creating the emptiness of mind effortlessly is meditation.

Therefore, meditation is a practice to train the mind so that a noisy mind can transfer into self-regulated mind. In other words, it is a means of transforming the mind. Actually, meditation is a process to attain the calmness by ceasing the thoughts and by releasing the suppressed emotions. Moreover, for ceasing the thoughts and attaining the state of tranquility, we require a self-regulated mind rather than a monkey mind. So meditation is very effective tool to transform the mind.

However, as per the Buddhist concept regarding meditation, absorption is the central characteristic in the practice of meditation. Thus Buddhist meditation practices encourage and develop concentration, clarity, emotional positivity, and a calm seeing of true nature of things. By engaging with a particular meditation practice, you learn the patterns and habits of your mind. Thus the practice offers a mean to cultivate new and more positive ways of being. Regular practice and patience create an obedient and self-regulated mind which is profoundly peaceful and energized state of being. Actually, such experiences can have transformative effect and can lead to a new understanding of life.

Therefore, in order to experience such amazing effect, Tibetan Buddhists monks practice with lot of patience even in severe weather conditions. The patience of Buddhist monks can be estimated from an answer given by The Dalai Lama. Once during dialogue between Western Scientists and Buddhist scholars on the benefit of meditation sponsored by 'Mind and Life Institute' a scientist asked the Dalai Lama what he believes is the minimum amount of time a person should spend meditating to gain the benefit. The Dalai Lama replied most sincerely, "A life time."

Thus in Buddhism, meditation is a process to achieve calm and remain in state of bliss that goes throughout life. Actually, Buddhist meditation practice is three-in-one. Means they have combined in their practice of meditation, the practice of *dharana* (concentration*), *dhyana* (meditation*) and *samahdi* (absorption) 6th, 7th and 8th stages as per Patanjli Yoga Sutra. They startpractice from concentration level and reach up to absorption. The goal of their meditation practice is to achieve the Nirvana so that they may live in state of bliss. That's why their practice process is so long, and they practice with patiently.

The meditation practice that Buddha did is described by Lodro Rinzler Author of '*The Buddha Wake up in the Office*' "Practice is about being present to the way things are. This is known as *Shamatha* or calm abiding meditation. The more we can connect with the present in a calm way in our life or work, the more we can be of use to the world around us. Mean to say, Buddha did not meditate to achieve magical power rather his aim was to attain tranquility. Thus, the more we present to the way things are, the more calmness we will attain.

Roger Walsh, Department of Psychiatry and Human Behavior, University of California College of Medicine and Shauna LShapiro Department of counseling psychology, Santa Clara University have given the definition of meditation in the meeting of Meditative Disciplines and western Psychology in 2006. They refer the meditation to a family of self-regulation practices that focus on training attention and awareness in order to bring mental processes under greater voluntary control and thereby foster general mental well-being and development, and/or specific capacities such as calm, clarity and concentration.

Thus, this definition differentiates meditation from a variety of other therapeutic and self-regulation strategies such as self-hypnosis, visualization and psychotherapies. Generally, the aim of these strategies is primarily to change mental stuff such as thoughts, images and emotions which are only objects of attention and awareness. Whilst, focus of meditation is primarily direct on training attention and awareness.

I am big admirer of philosophy of J Krishnamurti especially about his meditation practices. Actually, I learnt all about meditation from him indirectly, means, by listening his audio clips and by reading his books. Now I have learned many other techniques of meditation even I have practicedsome of them as an experiment but still I preferred the technique of J Krishnamurti. Therefore, I think the definition of meditation cannot be completed without describing the views of J Krishnamurti on meditation.

According to him, meditation is not to sit in a corner in crossed or folded legs and close the eyes and concentrate, like school boys trying to concentrate on a book. Additionally, meditation is related to mind rather than body posture. In fact, Meditation is neither about seeking the God nor about achieving *moskha* or *mukti* etc. Rather meditation is all about to become quiet and still through releasing the repress emotions. Thus watching the thought and feeling without any condemnation, correction, judging or justification is the core point of the meditation of J Krishnamurti so that mind can be freed and purified from all its stuffs.

Therefore, on the bases of meditation practice for long time whatever I observed and concluded is that in the process of watching of thoughts and feelings, when we go very deep in our subconscious, we start to release buried emotions one by one. Then every hidden thought and every buried feeling comes on surface and disperses. However, slowly and slowly our mind becomes empty and we become almost thoughtless. Then not only our mind but our whole being becomes quiet and still and this whole process is meditation.

Thus, it can also be said that the aim of this process of understanding the nature of thought is to be free from all thoughts and feelings so that your mind, whole being becomes very quiet. In other words, meditation is means to emptying the mind completely. Actually, emptying the mind is not an intellectual process rather complete awareness empties the mind spontaneously. Thus meditation is very effective means to train the mind to be habitual in an adaptive way.

Meditation is more effective and easier than yoga and Tai Chi because these practices require additional elements. For example— controlled breathing and body posture is essential in yoga while body movement and supposed energy manipulation is the main element of Tai Chi which is a complicated process. On the contrary, meditation is a simpler way to visit your subconscious even up to unconscious level in order to dig out and clean the buried emotions, and provide you a calm and quiet state of mind.

How to Practice Meditation

There are innumerable procedures of practicing the meditation out of them how many are right and how many are wrong cannot find out. However, some of them are experienced by me and which I found suitable or near to suitable I am going to mention them.

The meditation practice according to J Krishnamurti which is also being practiced by me, meditation is not to sit in a corner repeating a lot of words; or to think of a picture and go into some wild, ecstatic imaginings. Actually, meditation is something extraordinary. First of all, sit very quietly; do not force yourself to sit quietly, but sit or lie down quietly without force of any kind. Then watch your thoughts. Watch what you are thinking about. You find you are thinking about your shopping; your dress; your diet; what you are going to say, the noise of outside; the chirping of the birds and so on…..,Anyway, do not resist these thoughts rather follow them and enquire why each thought arises.

Then instead of trying to change your thinking, see why certain thoughts arise in your mind so that you begin to understand the meaning of every thought and feeling without any enforcement. And when a thought arises, do not condemn it, do not say it is right, it is wrong; it is good, it is bad. Just watch it so that you begin to have a perception, a consciousness which is active in seeing every kind of thought, every kind of feeling. You will know every hidden secret thought, every hidden motive, every feeling without distortion. When you look, when you go into thought very deeply, your mind becomes extraordinary subtle, alive. No part of mind is asleep. The mind is completely awake.

Actually, this process is merely the foundation. Then your mind is very quiet. Your whole being becomes very still. Then go through that stillness, deeper and deeper, further—this whole process, in fact, is meditation. Thus is this whole process of thinking and feeling the feelings, suppressed pain start to release and after some duration of practice mind frees from all thoughts; from all feelings. Thus your mind becomes empty and your whole being becomes pure and very quiet.

Apart from procedure of J Krishnamurti, I like meditation practice of Vietnamese Buddhist Monk Thich Nhat Hahn also and sometimes I practice this technique also. However, there is slightly difference between both of them.

Thich Nhat classifies the meditation into two categories. First one is sitting meditation and second one is mindfulness meditation. Mindfulness meditation can be done at anywhere and at any time, sitting, walking, cleaning the dish, doing gardening etc. However, sitting meditation requires a certain procedure. It is most intensive exercise because it allows the practitioners to attain the highest state of absorption. So it is most effective. Like J Krishnamurti, Thich Nhat Hanh also does not give emphasis on body posture in sitting meditation. Rather he gives emphases on breathing.

According to him, first sit in any comfortable posture with eyes closed. Then pay your attention on breathe without changing the breath pattern. Just watch your breath, watch breathing-in and breathing-out. By doing this process, you can bring your full attention easily what is within and around you. You realize you can just be with whatever is within you—your pain, anger, irritation, joy, peace etc. You are with whatever is there without being carried away by it. Let it come, let it stay, and then let it go. No need to push or oppress it, only follow it and come back over and over again on your thought pattern. Thus observe the thoughts and images of mind with an accepting and loving eye.

In this process, if your legs or feet fall asleep or begin to hurt during the sitting, you are free to adjust your position quietly. You can maintain your concentration by following your breathing and slowly and attentively change your posture. Thus, you can be still and calm your mind despite the storms that might arise in you. Thus, in order to increase the duration of meditation, Thich Nhat Hahn ignore the posture of sitting meditation even he advice to change the posture.

Mindfulness meditation became very familiar among most of the Buddhist monks due to Thich Nhat Hanh. Actually, meaning of mindfulness is complete togetherness of mind and body. Mean to say, whatever you do, do with full attention so that your mind does not wander here and there. For this practice—you breathe in and breathe out mindfully, you bring your mind back to your body, and you are there. When your mind is there with your body, you are established in the present moment. Then you can recognize many conditions of happiness that are already present in your lives and around you. Means mindful helps us to recognize that conditions. Thus, mindful meditation is both the quality of being, as well as the practice of keeping yourself alive to the present moment.

So, you don't have to wait it. It is present in every moment of your daily life. In fact, like flourishing any plant mindful is effortless. You have to just allow your breath to take place. Become aware of it. When you breathe in, and you are aware of your in-breath you touch the miracle of being alive. That's why mindfulness is a source of happiness and joy. Thus, enjoy it effortlessly.

For mindfulness meditation Thich Nhat Hanh prefers walking meditation. Walking meditation is practicing meditation while walking. For its practice, take short steps in complete relaxation; go slowly with smile on your lips. Coordinate your breathing with your steps and walk with dignity, calm and comfort. Consciously make the imprint on the ground as you step. At the time of walking, you should fully awake to the act of lifting, swinging, and placing each foot down and you are aware of thoughts, feelings, or sensations that arise while walking. Live fully in present moment, not reflecting on the past or planning for future.

Mean to say, during walking meditation, you have no purpose or direction in space or time so you may go on stroll. The purpose of walking meditation is walking meditation itself. Going is important, not arriving. Walking meditation is not a means to end rather it is means as well as end. Each step is life; each step is peace and joy. That's why we don't have to hurry. We seem to move forward, but we don't go anywhere. We are not drawn by goal.

During walking, you may stop for a while to look at—tree, flower and other scene such as playing children, grazing cattle, flying birds etc. Means, you are fully aware all around you at the time of walking meditation. Thus, walk so that your foot prints bear only the marks of peaceful joy and you remain in state of elation during walking.

Thus Thich Nhat Hanh gives emphases on breathing in sitting meditation as well as in mindfulness meditation while concept of breathing is completely missed from the practice of J Krishnamurti. However, using the breath-in and breath-out technique in meditation is somewhat easy than the technique of J Krishnamurti but mediation practice of J Krishnamurti is more effective than anyone else. However, not only Thich Nhat Hanh but other Buddhists also emphases on breathing process in meditation practice. Actually, Buddhists emphases on breathing process due to two following reasons.

First one is that breath represents the movement of energy in the body. So proper breathing is the key to self-healing and anxiety control, providing astonishing cares by our mind for our body.

Secondly, breathing seems to have closest link not only with our body but also with the flux of emotions and mental activities. Thus breathing is used as basic crutch. Or we can say that in the process of breathing, conscious touches with the unconscious.

In addition, there is another technique of meditation practice known as transcendental meditation (TM). Maharishi Mahesh Yogi was the founder of TM and he introduced it in US in 1963. Though this meditative technique became very popular there, it is similar to concentration (*dharana*) 6th stage rather than meditation (*dhyana*) 7th stage as described in Patanjli Yoga Sutrabecause a mantra is used as an object to concentrate on while no any object is required in meditation practice. Even, this meditative technique is also similar to self-hypnosis. Actually, TM becomes familiar in US because it appears as meditation, and its procedure is somewhat easier than real meditation (*dhyana*).However, it provides the relaxation to mind and body easily.

Whatever I have learnt about meditation throughout my life and the experiences I have experienced in meditation practice, it can be concluded that there are three main purposes of meditation. First one is providing relaxation and overall well-being; second one is meeting to your own Self is the spiritual purpose of meditation; and third one is bring out the suppressed emotions on the surface from unconscious so that they may be released forever.

Thus, I believe that TM fulfills first two purposes third one is in doubt which is related to suppressed emotions arising on the surface successfully. In TM, your mind needs some mantra to be recited as an object to focus on. So by using the object, your mind engages in reciting mantra thus thoughts do not arise on the surface. Therefore, thoughts are resisted rather than bringing on surface. However, in such condition either thought do not arise in first place or they are pushed back inwards. Means, practitioners deliberately minimize the thought process by engaging their minds in reciting the mantra. Then in such condition, thoughts remain suppressed in unconscious and due to not arising on surface their releasing are impossible. Therefore, thoughts are not free to release in this meditation technique. Then how can the painful stuff of unconscious be cleared?

Anyhow, I am going to describe the procedure of TM also so that interested readers may practice it. For TM practice, sit in a comfortable position with eye closed and start repeating the mantra silently. A mantra is a word or sound that is used to focus your concentration. According to Maharishi Mahesh Yogi, "Mantra is a specific thought or a suitable sound which you receive from a trained teacher of TM." Generally, the sound or word is without any meaning, and is kept secret by practitioners. Mean to say, the practitioners are instructed by their TM teacher not to disclose the mantra of practice to anyone else.

Actually, the mantra is only a means to avoid the distraction of thoughts so the relation which a practitioner experience is not due mantra but due to the effortlessness of the practice. By using the mantra as object, the process of practice becomes easier. As long as you repeat the mantra, there will be no place of thought to be arising in your mind. Actually, any word, sound or object can work and serve your purpose of train the mind. Thus, you can make your own mantra. Some positive word or phrase can be more effective such as—truth is god, love is life, take off hat, thanks, blessing or whatever you want because is mantra is only a tool to slow down your thought. Thus, neither you require any trained teacher nor you have to keep your mantra secret for such self-hypnosis or transcendental meditation.

Like TM practice which use mantra as object, some meditation practices are also being practiced in some other meditation centers. In these meditation centers, practitioners use other objects for concentration and for slowing down the thought process such as—concentrate on their own parts of body one by one; gazing in the sky; gazing on the flame of candle; gazing on image of any deity etc. Even for minimizing the thought process sheep counting method is also being used. In fact, such all techniques including TM are sort cut methods of meditation practice. Thus, if you want instant results, you may practice any one of them.

Actually, we all have a deep layer inside us which is already calm but it is covered with lots of unnecessarily stuff. Thus we require any effective technique of meditation which makes useable to empty our unconscious's stuff. After emptying the unconscious mind, this calm state emerges spontaneously.

Difficulties occur during meditation practice and how to overcome them

Meditation practices are associated with some difficulties also. The more the effective is the technique, the more the difficulties are occur. However, some of the following difficulties and obstacles distract practitioners during meditation practice.

First obstacle is that beginners of meditation experience that thoughts are continuously distracted them during practice. Actually, meditation practice requires lot of effort and patience because ceasing the thought and emptying the mind is slow and lengthy process. So this state of mind is attained only after doing lots of practice. However, many times practitioners lose patience and want to give up. Sometimes it becomes boring and starts annoying you because your thoughts especially negative one distract you continuously. Anyhow, no need to be worrying rather it is good thing because you are becoming more mindful. Actually, thoughts are parts of meditation so don't resist them by using any tool. Simply acknowledge the thoughts, watch them, and observe them.

In fact, meditation is all about observing your thoughts and seeing them what they are. Therefore, there is no need to cease the thought forcefully. Following the thought is, in fact, the way of surfacing the suppressed emotions in the meditation practice so that they may be released. Thus, arising, observing and following the thoughts are the parts of the process of meditation practice. So focus fully on awareness in order to make the meditation process easier.

Then at some point, within the state of boredom, you begin to entertain yourself with all kinds of hidden neuroses. However, they may be painful but accept what you feel during meditation. If you feel angry, embrace that anger; if you feel sad, embrace that sadness and embrace all other sensations even embrace the boredom. As and when you accept your feelings and emotions honestly and label them as anger hate etc., you start feeling ease and calm within no time. Actually, all these things that happen in sitting meditation are related with yourselves, working with yourselves and exposing your all kinds of neuroses.

However, if you continue on your meditation practice in spite of such interruption, you become adaptive after a certain amount of practice. Then you begin to feel that you, in fact, have a real life that you can relate to instead of trying to escape. At this point, you begin to realize the meaning of pain and understand the mystery of ignorance and illusions. In other words, you enter into the realm of light.

Jon Kabat- Zinn founder of Mindfulness- based Stress Reduction says that even boredom is fascinating when we bring our awareness to it. Naturally, this process takes some time so have patience because practice makes everything easier and easier.

Feeling drowsy and sleepy is also a problem associated with sitting meditation. Actually, when we require sleep, we sleep during meditation to fulfill the sleeping requirement. After slowing the thought process, in fact, we feel calm thus calm mind and relaxed body push us toward drowsy which is suitable condition for sleeping. Thus, due to lack of adequate amount of rest and sleep, we sleep during the meditation. So instead of taking it too much seriously, you can start meditation again after waking and becoming fresh and full of energy. However, morning time when you are fresh is the best time for meditation.

When you go very deep within you during sitting meditation, your painful suppressed emotions start surfacing. Mean to say, you have buried your trauma or grief deep inside your unconscious throughout your life. Thus, during deep meditation, these suppressed emotions start releasing and become very intense and painful. Sometimes the pain becomes unbearable especially for those who have been traumatized in their lives. It seems that meditation amplifies the emotional shock. However, bring out the buried emotional hurt to the surface is the real healing of the trauma. Otherwise such trauma remains lying hidden under the surface and the pain will be oozing continuously throughout life and enhance the grief. Therefore, how much unbearable the pain may be, let it be released completely.

Therefore, it is better to bear the pain as much as you can. However, if the pain becomes really unbearable, you may shift your attention to something else. You may remember those persons who really trust you, understand you and love you so that a state of balance may be established. You may remind yourself about surrounding atmosphere even you may open the eyes and listen the sounds. Mean to say, when energy of pain becomes too strong, you may postpone the meditation practice to avoid further pain. This is the reason that after surfacing too much pain on conscious levels, psychotherapists hold the practice of psychotherapy in mid-session. Thus, too much pain may harm you also so remain fully aware during meditation practice.

However, the amount of pain which has been already raised to the surface in meditation process has to bear because there is no other way. Even the pain may remain with you for few days so halt the meditation practice till you become normal. Actually, pain of any particular trauma does not arise on the surface at a time. Mean to say, it is a long process to release the whole pain which require much practice and many sessions of meditation. Thus, you require lot of patience to clear all the suppressed emotions from your unconscious so that the healing process may be completed.

There may be also some other miner difficulties such as lack of time, noisy environment, uncomfortable sitting for a long time, aching of legs etc. However, keeping the usefulness of meditation in mind, these difficulties can also be overcome easily. Once you start the practice of mediation and continue it for some days, it becomes habit. Moreover, if you practice the meditation daily at the same time and same place, it routinizes easily.

Meditation practice improves our personality and overall well-being.

Meditation is beneficial for us in many ways such as—it not only helps to bear the pain but also enhances our physical, mental and emotional health. Additionally, it enhances empathy and compassion; decreases aging process and develops spirituality. Zen meditators believe that practice of meditation reduces the pain by focusing the attention on the part of the body where you feel intense pain.

A research group from the University of Montreal also verified this hypothesis. Researchers exposed 13 Zen masters and 13 comparable non-practitioners to equal degree of painful heat while measuring their brain activity in a functional Magnetic Resonance Imaging (fMRI) scanner. What they discovered is that the Zen meditation practitioners reported less pain. Actually, they reported less pain than their neurological output from their brain may be receiving the same amount of pain input but due to meditation practice, they feel less amount of pain.

In this context, Karine Bell a meditation teacher explains, when we meet grief at the door with mindfulness, the grief allowed its full expression— we experience the emotions just as it is. Our bodies become animated by it; our chest rises and falls, our eyes fill with salty tears. Like a wave it rises and rises, only to fall again. Our ability to work with grief mindfully means to simultaneously meet the powerful force of grief when it arrives, and let it move unimpeded by the thoughts.

According to some other specialists, those who turn the awareness towards the feeling in aching part of body make it much easier to bear. Whilst turning away from a sensation of pain, transfer it into resentment, blame and other kinds of negative feelings. This is what converts the pain into suffering.

Psychotherapist Dr. Ron Alexander reports in his book *"Wise Mind, Open Mind"* that the process of controlling the mind through meditation, increases mental strength, resilience and emotional intelligence. That's why you feel less pain.

In another experiment, EEGs taken of subjects in the meditative state revealed hyper activity in the left prefrontal cortex, an area associated with positive feelings such as joy and liveliness. On the other hand, right prefrontal cortex which is linked to negative feelings such as sadness and depression revealed reduced activity. When EEGs of Buddhist monks were compared with those of people who occasionally practice meditation, the monks showed an increased neural activity two or three time greater than that of occasional practitioners. And there was evidence that their parietal areas were also involved.

These observations suggest that intense mental activity during meditation involves several different parts of the brain at the same time, and after thousands of hours of practice, it produces permanent changes in physiology and cerebral connections.

Magnetic Resonance Imaging (MRI has also shown that the cortex of elderly people who practice several hours of meditation each week is thicker than the cortex of individuals who do not meditate. These conclusions could be of interest in fighting mental aging because thickness of cortex that is layers of neurons—tends to decrease with age. According to same hypotheses meditation might also increase the level of serotonin in the brain, just as some antidepressants do.

Meditation practice provides full relax to our mind and body even it refresh the mind more than sleep. Actually, in our sleep duration our mind is functioning continuously through our dreams while at the time of lying down to rest we are still feeling restless and our muscle remain tense. However, in the practice of meditation we recharge our mind by quieting it. Thus, we experience less anxiety, and experience more peace and happiness. The more we meditate, the less anxiety we have. Actually, anxiety turns out due to loosening the connection of particular neural pathways because meditation helps to loosen that connection.

Meditation practice not only improves the mental health but it improves physical health also. Harvard Medical School used MRI technology on participants to monitor brain activity while they meditated. They found that it activates the sections of brain in-charge of automatic nervous system, which governs the functions in our bodies that we can't control, such as digestion and blood pressure. These are also the functions that are often compromised by stress. It makes sense, then that modulating functions would help to ward off stress-related conditions such as heart disease etc.

Many times I myself measured my own blood pressure before and after meditation and difference was noted every time. I found systolic about eight mmHg lower and diastolic about five mmHg lower just after meditation.

Emotional well-being is the main objective of meditation practice. When you are fully aware of your thoughts, the suppressed emotions start to arise to the surface from your unconscious. Thus, instead of pushing back, embrace them because meditation is about acceptance rather than avoidance. More you accept the arising feelings, the more they reach upwards. And that is the exact moment when real emotional healing begins. Your hidden fear, anger, stress, trauma etc. arise to the surface so that the buried emotions let and run their course and dissipate. Thus you can release your suppressed emotions during meditation and you may free from them forever.

In addition, meditation not only enhances the attention, concentration, memory and insight but empathy, kindness and compassion also. The Buddhists practice loving kindness meditation known as *metta* practice. In this practice, Practitioners focus on developing a sense of benevolence and care towards all living beings. According to a study from Emory University, such experiences effectively boost one's ability to empathize with others by way of reading their facial expression.

Whilst Eileen Luders, an assistant professor at the UCLA Laboratory of Neuron Imaging, and colleagues, have found that long-term meditations have larger amount of gyrification('folding' of the cortex, which may allow the brain to process information faster) than people who do not meditate. Scientists suspect that gyrification is responsible for making the brain better at processing information, making decisions, forming memories and improve attention.

Above all, meditation helps us to achieve spirituality. Meditation is the way to thoughtlessness which is itself a state of bliss. How the thoughtlessness state touch the highest point of spirituality is the content of next chapter.

Chapter Twenty One

Attain the state of thoughtless awareness

"Thought is chasing its own tail all the time but the moment the thought stop chasing its tail, you are full of energy because in that chasing, your energy has been dissipated."—J Krishnamurti.

When we look at someone, often we look with our prejudices which are based on our thoughts. Generally, thoughts are biased so they cannot be pure. Thus thoughts are polluted, and the pollution of thoughts is so subtle that even we are unaware of this kind of pollution. Our mind is continuously transmitting the thoughts in the form of vibration into environment. Thus, not only local environment but whole Universe also fills with these polluted thoughts. Like radio wave, these polluted thoughts are reflected back to us.

Therefore, the world cannot be free from thought pollution until we stop the releasing of such polluted thoughts. Mean to say; when we will start looking at this world without thoughts, any judgment or prejudice, we may able to see it in its real form. Actually prejudices are the main cause of the suffering of human beings. So, there is only one way to remove the suffering and that is seeing the world without thought. Therefore, we have to look at everything without prejudice.

Even we destroy the beauty of Nature, when we look at it with thought. Actually, the thoughts are always impure. So in order to eliminate the suffering of human being and to make the world beautiful, we have to move towards the state of thoughtless awareness.

What is the state of thoughtless awareness?

In the state of thoughtless awareness, the occurring of thoughts comes to end. It can also be said that it is the extension of meditation. In the practice of meditation, a time comes during practice when a gap begins to appear between the two thoughts. As the awareness increases, the gap increases and thoughts start to disappear. However, if the practice is continued for long time, the thoughts disappear completely, and you realize the thoughtlessness. In this state, the mind thinks neither about past nor about future. It remains calm and quiet in the present moment.

Thus thoughtlessness is a state of 'no mind' because mind means bundle of thoughts therefore mind exists only in thoughts. If there is no thought, there is no mind. In other words, the state of thoughtlessness is the state of empty mind. Means when thoughts disappear completely or no longer arise but the practitioner remains aware, this state of mind known as thoughtless awareness. In this state, the mind becomes complete void, calm and still without any thought. That's why it is known as 'Nirvichara Samadhi' in Sanskrit language.

However, thoughtlessness is somewhat different from the term *Samadhi* last stage of the eight elements of the Noble Eightfold Path of Buddha and the eighth and final limb in the Yoga Sutra of Patanjli. Actually, *Samadhi,* according to Patanjli Yoga Sutras and Buddhist Noble Eightfold Path is a meditative absorption or trance, attained by practice of meditation which emphasizes on single point awareness. Mean to say, *samadhi* is a state of being totally aware of the present moment; a one pointedness of mind.

Thus, the *samadhi* is a non-dualistic state of consciousness in which the consciousness of the experiencing subject become one with the experienced object. Means, in meditative absorption, the difference between act of meditation and object of meditation is eliminated completely. Thus it is the oneness with the object of meditation. Actually, the seekers who want to attain spiritual awakening or Nirvana practice such type of *Samadhi*. Mean to say, the seekers who want to seek Supreme Power concentrate on any deity or any other single point practice this eighth stage of Yoga Sutra.

However, I am not talking about such spiritual awakening. Rather I am talking about complete thoughtlessness without concentration on single point or any deity. I am not writing about the attaining enlightenment rather my aim of writing the book is to attain bliss. Though some philosophers use the term enlightenment and bliss interchangeably, I consider bliss somewhat different from enlightenment. I believe that bliss is simply perfect happiness or intense joy. As seeking Supreme Power can be the ultimate goal of spiritual seekers, so enlightenment is the end of all types of practice. Thus, bliss is both means as well as end while enlightenment is end. And *Samadhi* is the means to that end. On the other hand, to attain the bliss, only state of thoughtlessness is required where no need to concentrate on single point or any deity.

However, reaching at the end of any goal means accomplished the work and ceasing of all type of activities or ending of struggles because the goal has been already achieved. No doubt that everyone feels satisfaction on attaining any goal. As enlightenment is considered ultimate goal of life, obviously it will not only provide unprecedented satisfaction but much happiness also. However, after obtaining that superb satisfaction there is full stop and after some duration the happiness level will also diminish and will return at its previous level. As you have already climbed at highest peak of your life, nothing will remain to climb. However, your mind will demand something more to attain. Whilst in absence of any higher goal, your mind will feel emptiness. Then you will be compelled to live in boredom throughout your remaining life.

This is the reason that I prefer means even above the end because means is going on forever while end is termination. In fact, journey is most enjoyable than destination, and life is itself a journey. So bliss makes the journey of life very beautiful and enjoyable. If the ultimate goal is achieved in the life, no charm will remain to live the rest of life. The charm of life is only in living mysteriously so that every day we may come into contact with something new and unknown. After solving each and every mystery; after achieving the goal; after attaining the enlightenment or spiritual awakening; after reaching the destination, the life will stop and then the journey of our life will become dull and boring. Therefore, in order to avoidance of dull and boring life, ultimate goal should never be achieved.

Actually, the life automatically stops at the time of death. If you achieve everything during the life, the meaning of remaining life will finish. Moreover, it will be like die before death because in that case, life will stop before death. Thus, everything can be enjoyed in the journey rather than at destination. Therefore, I am talking about such means that goes nowhere but they are themselves an end. Therefore, I emphasize on thoughtlessness without concentration on one point or any deity.

That's why the translation of the term 'thoughtless awareness' is *Nirvichara Samadhi*. Here, my aim to be thoughtlessness is to attain only a tranquil mind or internal peace and bliss rather than seeking any Eternal Entity. I think that Eternal Truth should remain mysterious forever.

How to achieve the state of thoughtless awareness

Incessant thoughts are going on constantly in our mind. According to a research from the University of Southern California's Laboratory of Neuron Imaging that a human being experience every day up to seventy thousands of all varieties of thoughts positive and negative, caring and hurtful. So it is really a difficult to be thoughtlessness. Due to one reason or another, our mind remains busy in thinking throughout the day, and during sleep through dreaming. Mean to say, our mind never rest. Thus, as it has been already written that meditation is the effective way to rest the mind while thoughtlessness is even more effective.

Actually, living in present, living mindfully, meditation and thoughtless awareness seem to same phenomena due to overlapping of one another. Though there is very slight difference among them, they are interrelated to one another. For example, if living in present routinize in our chorus, we also start to live mindfully, then meditation practice and achieving thoughtlessness will also become easy. On the other hand side, practice of sitting meditation will also helpful for mindfulness meditation and for living in present moment. Mean to say, practice of any one from all of them can become the base of others.

Thus meditation practice, living in present moment or living mindfully all are means to achieve the state of thoughtlessness. You can start with which you think easier and suitable for you. Even you can experiment with all. Anyway, how much the exercise may be easy, at beginning it seems too difficult but persistence patience makes it easier. Actually, to attain thoughtless awareness is a long process; even it may take whole life. Therefore, patience is very essential in the practice of thoughtlessness.

There are some other techniques also in common use to achieve thoughtlessness state. One of them is 'counting sheep'. Actually, this mental exercise issued in some cultures as a means of putting oneself to sleep. Though this idiomatic term associated with insomnia; it is also effective to achieve thoughtlessness state. In this technique, numerals are counted reversely. For example, starting the counting from hundred and end to one. Actually, by counting in such a way we can resist the thought while in straight counting from one to hundred, our mind functions under autopilot mode. So the autopilot mode will not fulfill this purpose.

In addition, focusing the concentration on any part of the body and shifting it on another part, after a moment sifting it again on another part and this process is going on, is also a way to achieve the state of thoughtlessness. For example, focus your concentration on toe then shift it to knee, naval, nose, eyes, forehead etc. Buddhists focus their concentration on breathing, thus they count their in-breathing and out -breathing up to nine. Then again start counting from one. The purpose of all techniques is only to resist the thoughts so that concentration may not be distracted.

Actually, thoughts do not stand alone or separate. Mean to say, thoughts are not independent rather they depend on other stuff such as feeling, emotion, sensation etc. to survive. Thus thoughts are completely dependent on such stuff which either has been already filled in your mind since your infancy or you are filling it now by day-to-days various sources. However, you are increasing this mind stuff each and every moment by reading Newspapers; surfing net; engaged in social media and watching news, movies, TV shows, serials etc. Therefore, your thoughts gain momentum from this unwanted information and emotional stuff.

Thus thoughts are directly triggered by external stimuli. Even a door bell or phone ring may trigger your thought process. Actually, thinking involves interaction between signaling pathway that are carrying information about world and neurons that are representing information in working or short memories. When our brains receive new information, it may be that it comes in improper order. Thus such information needs to be recognized and presented to us in a form so that we may understand.

Therefore, sensory information works as input for our brain to start thought process while outputs are the processes of organizing that information and controlling of our motor system. As new information require reasoning and cognition, our thinking process increases. Thus these inputs are not simply information rather they convert into feelings and emotions. Therefore, emotions and sensations exert much effect on human thinking. Anyhow, by avoiding external stimuli, the thinking process can be reduced.

Therefore, in order to avoid these external stimuli, their sources, such as—social media, TV shows, serials, News and other unnecessary information, may be minimized. In addition, social circle may be reduced and unnecessary activities should also be minimized. Actually, I experienced that whenever I remain free from all such inputs during the day, I become thoughtless easily during meditation practice in the evening otherwise it takes time.

Sensory organs, in fact, are gateway of input for our brains. Mean to say, we receive all worldly information through our senses. However, if there will be less input to our brain, there will be less thinking process. Thus, we can minimize these inputs to the brain by organizing our day-to-day schedule and activities.

Actually, reasoning or cognition is main ingredient of thinking process. Our brains take whole bunch of information from our senses and organize it in a way that makes sense before we perceive it. So, our reasoning is going on to complete this process. As our five senses are main source of input, meditation practitioners require such place for meditation which is free from noise and distraction, and they also close their eyes. Thus closing the eyes during meditation and lonely quiet place for its practice help practitioners to avoid inputs for brain so that thinking process may be minimized.

In addition, there may some stuff in subconscious which had been accumulated there since our infancy. Mean to say, unconscious mind has great roll in generating the thoughts. So, before one experience a conscious thought, unconscious brain processes work behind the scenes to generate the thought. Generally, this stuff is more negative than positive. So the stuff of unconscious mind is also big input to generate the thoughts. Anyhow, this unconscious stuff can be cleared by consistent meditation practice.

When your mind remains empty, only necessary and wanted thoughts enter in it. That's why empty mind is always peaceful mind. Thus, to avoid the thinking, all such suppressed emotions have to be released by one way or another. There are many ways to release the emotions from your conscious as well as unconscious mind. Some of them are mentioned here so apply which is most suitable for you.

You can disclose your emotions and feelings to some near and dear verbally or by writing; you may maintain diary; you may write them on a piece of paper and torn, then throw away; you may write any article in magazines or daily newspaper; you may write any book etc. Dancing, yoga, gardening, jogging, walking etc. also help in releasing the emotions. You can also express your emotions by drawing or painting.

Mean to say, pull away the dependent variables of thoughts by one way or another so that thoughts may not survive. When the input of the brain will be removed, naturally there will be no output in the form of thought. Thus the existence of thoughts will also come to end.

How do thoughts dissipate the energy while state of thoughtlessness conserves it?

Actually, thought process dissipates energy thus our energy is being constantly depleted that's why we feel tiredness in excessive thinking. On the contrary, the state of thoughtlessness conserves the energy this is the reason we feel freshness when our mind is calm and quiet. Therefore, when there is much thinking process, you dissipate more energy even it is much more when you think something negatively. In other words, negative thoughts such as anger, hatred etc. cause a great amount of energy to be dissipated. Thus, your blood pressure and rate of heart beat increase; mouth dry up and you feel more excited, when you are angry.

Even positive thought processes also affect your physical well-being. During the thinking, your breathing pattern change i. respiratory rate goes fast as brain needs more energy in the thinking process. On the contrary, when mind is at peace or in thoughtless state, our respiratory rate is less compared to other situations. These are such experiences which have been experienced by every one of us. However, what are the functions of our brain; how the neurons behave in the process of thinking: how they communicate with one another and how they transmit the thoughts is a very complex and complicated process.

Actually, human being has explored the Universe and its origin time; even Manhas calculated the age of the Universe. However, human's brain is still unfathomable. Neurologists and cognitive scientists are still probing how the brain generates the thoughts, emotions etc.

Norman Weinberger a neurologist at the University of California Irvine said, "If we understand the brain, we will understand both its capacities and its limits for thoughts, emotions, reasoning, love and every aspect of human life."

Scott Huettel Professor of Psychology and Neuroscience at Duke University also has similar views. He said, "The human brain is the most complex object in the known Universe. Even more pernicious factor is that we all think we understand the brain—at least own—through our experiences. But our own subjective experience is very poor guide to how the brain works."

Thus, even psychologists, neurologists and cognitive scientists are not claim to be the expert of our brain. Anyhow, on the bases of knowledge whatever has been known to me so far about the function of brain in thinking process, I am going to explain how thinking process deplete the energy and how thoughtlessness conserve it.

Actually, thoughts are experiences as an idea, an image, a vision or awareness of knowing something. Thus thought is simply a process of the mind playing with our mental energy. Thought itself, in fact, is a reverberation and energy. When mind receive any input for thoughts, brain cells called neurons activate known as neuronal firing in neurological term. So, distant brain's regions communicate with each other using brain wave oscillations of different frequencies which are produced by synchronous firing of large numbers neurons in each area. Thus, it can also be said that brain cells communicate with each other through an electrochemical process. In other words, cells communicate with one another through transmission.

Anyhow, when our thinking process is intense, the frequency of neuronal firing is also high. The higher the frequency, the more energy is required in firing process of neurons. Thus the higher is the frequency; the higher is the consumption of energy. It can also be said that at the time of crowded thoughts, neuronal firing is also intensive. Thus more mental energy is required in the neuronal firing at the time of intense thinking. Therefore, thought can neither be generated nor be transmitted without energy. In other words, energy that is characterized by our mind is the key factor of arising in the thoughts.

According to the Charles Jenning at the MIT Mc Govern Institute for Brain Research, hundred billons of neurons are interconnected by trillions of connections, called synapses. Moreover, on average each connection transmits about one signal per second while some specialized connections send up to thousand signals per second.

Therefore, it can be easily estimated how much energy is dissipated in thought process. Even we can discern and feel the flow of energy if we remain fully aware. Thus, thought process dissipates the energy. That's why we feel fatigue and exhaustion when we are busy in serious thinking.

On the contrary, it has been observed through EEG of Buddhist meditation practitioners that as they go towards the thoughtless state, the neuronal firing decreases and frequency also decreases which affect the whole network of brain. Thus, decreasing in thinking process, decrease not only the frequency of neuronal firing but the function of whole brain also changes and this whole process effects the dissipation of energy. Therefore, different kinds of feelings and their associated thoughts are transmitted with different frequencies.

Actually, brainwaves are directly controlled by thoughts and emotions. That's why brainwaves are transmitted at various frequencies according to the variety of emotions and thought pattern. Thus, if we become capable to control our thoughts, we can also control our emotions. Then regulated thoughts and emotions can control the frequencies of brainwaves. Mean to say, by regulating our thoughts and emotions, we can regulate the dissipation of our energy. Energy consumed in transmitting the thoughts and feelings is, in fact, directly proportional to frequencies of brainwaves.

In other words, the more the agitation in thoughts and feelings, the higher the frequency of brainwaves and the more the consumption of energy in transmitting process. Whilst the lesser the agitation in thoughts and feelings, the lower the frequency and lesser the consumption of energy in the transmitting process. Thus consumption of energy is in your hands. Either you may waste it in unnecessary thinking or you may save it by regulating your thoughts.

Thus by reducing our thoughts, we can conserve our mental energy which is being consumed in thought generation and transmitting process. However the transmission of brainwave is going on persistently irrespective of our waking state or sleeping. The consumption of energy can be comprehended by knowing the following classification of frequency of brainwaves on the bases of our emotions and thoughts pattern.

Generally, the frequency of brainwave is classified into five categories. When due to too much anxiety or high stress our thought process is very intense, the frequency of brain waves is between thirty one Hz to hundred Hz known as Gamma waves. Thus, these are the fastest of the brainwave because in this state mind is fully busy in processing information from different areas of brain. So perception is also high.

The second category of frequency is somewhat slower than Gamma waves, these waves are measured when one's mind is engaged in reasoning in the process of problem solving and decision making. Thus, in this state one is unable to relax due to crowded thoughts. In this state the frequency of brainwaves remain between fourteen Hz to thirty Hz known as Beta waves.

In the third category, when we live mindfully or just after yoga practice, the frequencies of our brainwaves remain between nine Hz to thirteen Hz known as Alpha waves.

Whilst during sleep and in sitting meditation when our thinking process is very minimum, the frequencies of brainwaves remain between four Hz to eight Hz known as Theta Waves. And Theta waves are placed in fourth category.

Finally, when our mind is fully calm and quiet either due to thoughtlessness or during dreamless sleep, the frequencies of brainwaves remain between one Hz to 3 Hz known as Delta Waves.

Delta waves have been measured through electroencephalogram (EEG) of the brain of Buddhist monks when they are in very deep meditation and have attained almost thoughtless state.

Thus, it is evident from the classification of frequencies of brainwaves that when thoughts are racing in our mind, we are almost in agitated state. Then frequency of transmission of brainwaves is also highland in this state the consumption of energy is more.

On the contrary, when either the crowed of thoughts in our mind is very less or we are in the state of thoughtlessness, we are calm and quiet. Then in this calmness state the transmission is also occurred at low frequency so the consumption of energy is also less.

How does the state of thoughtlessness enhance positive emotions and provide calmness and bliss?

For centuries, Buddhists believe that the state of meditative absorption, make people calmer, happier and more loving, and they are less and less prone to destructive emotions. Anyhow, due to non-availability of any measuring system of brain activities in olden days, it could not prove earlier. However, after invention of new technologies such as fMRI, MEG and EEG, neuroscientists became able to measure the activities of brain. Among these methods, EEG is the most versatile which generally used to measure the electrical activity generated by the neurons when they are activated.

Dr. Richard Davidson at the University of Wisconsin has been able to study of Buddhists practitioners for cultivating compassion, equanimity or mindful. By using the imaging device that shows what occurs in brain during deep meditation, Dr. Davidson found that emergence of positive emotions may be due to this thoughtless awareness. Persistent deep meditation practices strengthen the neurological circuits that calm a part of the brain that acts as a trigger for fear and anger. Thus, our violent actions can be controlled by controlling the brain violent impulse through thoughtlessness.

Dr. Davidson also measured brain waves of practitioners by EEG. He found that the abbot had highest amount of activity in the brain centers associated with positive emotions that had ever been measured by his laboratory of neuroscience. After eight weeks, Dr. Davidson found that in those people, the parts of their brains that help to form positive emotions became increasing active. Thus, persistent practice of meditation which helps to become thoughtlessness, enhance the positive emotions.

Additionally, when we proceed towards the state of thoughtless awareness, the activation of neurons start decreasing. Simultaneously, chaos and disordered neurons start falling in order. As the activation of neurons reach at minimum level, a state of calmness is perceived. As a positive feedback, these progresses further the neurons became synchronous. Actually, this is the state of complete thoughtlessness where the mind attains absolute calmness state. In this state the neurons no longer remain activate.

So in this state of absolute calmness, the neurons neither modulate nor amplifying any incoming signal. They just resonate in harmony. As this orchestra gets more in synchronize, we experience great joy even ecstasy and thus we achieve the state of bliss. In this state of thoughtless awareness, all thoughts, concepts, images and reasoning cease and a vacuum creates. Actually this state of thoughtlessness is such a wordless prayer which enables the practitioner to achieve highest level of spirituality where coincidences and synchronicityincreases in favor of practitioners. In other words, it is the state where practitioner feels presence of Divine.

However, the scientific reason behind this hypothesisis that when there are lesser thoughts in our mind, the frequency of transmitting the thoughts in the Universe is also lower. The frequency and amplitude are inversely proportional to each other. Mean to say, the higher is the frequency, the lower is the peak of amplitude while the lower is the frequency, and the higher is the peak of amplitude. Therefore, when the frequency of transmission is the lowest, the peak of amplitude is the highest. Thus when there is no crowed of thoughts in our mind, our mind becomes calm and quiet and in such state of tranquility, our thoughts reach everywhere in the Universe because the frequency of transmitting the thoughts is lowest and amplitude is highest. Thus being highest peak of amplitude, our thoughts connect to the Universal Soul. This is the reason that practitioners connect to Higher Power and feel presence of Divine.

After attaining absolute bliss by Buddha, he explained about the bliss to his brother Ananda, "I suffered a great deal over the past thirty years because of the aberrations of the mind. It was the mind that stood between me and Self-Realization. Today, I am free from hold of my mind. That is the cause of my bliss. When the mind is absent, there is bliss".

Actually, any happiness experienced through mind is not real bliss rather it is only a transient physical pleasure. Thus, the seekers who pursue spiritual practices with reasoning cannot attain actual bliss. Logic is concerned with the thoughts of one kind or another. Therefore, eternal happiness cannot be attained by thought process. Even a slightest of thought pushes you toward sorrow and crowded of thoughts leads you towards insanity. On the contrary, in the state of thoughtlessness, you may enter in the realm of great joy, peace and bliss.

Thus, it is only the state of thoughtlessness where true Self emerges and we can enjoy the beauty of life much better. Actually, peace likes to dwell in space and that space can be created within ourselves after attaining the state of thoughtlessness. Moreover, nothing is more valuable than tranquility.

The energy field around the body, known as aura in spiritual terms, becomes stronger when you attain tranquility and bliss. As this state progress further, the energy field not only increases in strength but its circumference also becomes wider. Thus, this sacred invisible field becomes like a temple where every person who comes under this circle of energy field feels peace and comfortable.

Chapter Twenty-two

Go within yourself

"You have no need to travel anywhere. Journey within yourself, enter a mine of rubies and bathe in the splendor of your own light"—Rumi.

Actually, contentment, peace and joy lie within yourself. So, don't waste your time and efforts to search them in the outer world. Remember that there is no true happiness in the worldly objects. Life rushes from within rather than without so happiness is subjective rather than objective. Therefore, we can attain the bliss and feel the beauty of Nature when we dive within ourselves because the source of everything is within ourselves. Therefore, bliss cannot be attained in materialistic things.

However, when the pleasure arises from external experience, the pleasure lasts only as long as the impression of that experience lasts. Even such pleasure eventually pushes you towards more sufferings. Therefore, pleasure achieved by worldly objects such as wealth, entertainment, wine, sex etc. are temporary and gives you joy only instantly. However, ultimately such pleasure leads you to mental agitation, depression and sorrow while joy and happiness spring from within. Thus in order to achieve peace and bliss, we have to go within ourselves.

Actually, it is human's tendency to feel safe and secure in external identities because Man is brought up in such environment. Even we are continuously being encouraged by society that safety and happiness comes from outside, such as—in clinging to the money, success, relation, material possessions etc. Thus we believe that the more we have name, fame, power, wealth and other materialistic things, the happier we will be. In fact, to seek happiness in materialistic things is a mirage that can be never achieved. Therefore, instead of trapping in the web of materialistic things, go within your inner source of happiness.

Thus, we spend our whole life in chasing the things which, we think, are being missed in our lives. A few people able to realize that materialistic things never bring them true joy, peace and fulfillment. Therefore, stop chasing the materialistic things in order to achieve permanent happiness, rather peep within yourself to attain it.

Meaning of going within yourself

Actually, the term 'within' is used generally for spiritual or non-physical aspect while the word 'without' is concerned with external worldly affairs. In other words, the term within is used to deal with soul, spirit, conscience etc. while the term without is used for materialism. In spiritualism, the term 'going within' is considered as a method by which we discover ourselves such as—who we really are; from where we came; where we will go after death; what the meaning of life is etc. However, I am not much concern about such questions.

Therefore, I believe that there is no need to know who you are; no need to probe or enquiry about your Inner Self; no need to seek Eternal Truth or God; no need to explore the depth of your spirit. For the reason, how much you try to know about such things, you will become mad but you will never know who you are, where you came from and where you will go. However, whatever you will find that will be your own beliefs. Anyhow, beliefs may be wrong, after all, they have developed on the basis of either as you are taught or as you read in scriptures. So, on the basis of prejudices, you cannot reach up to reality.

Actually, like other flora and fauna, human spices also take birth, flourish and die. Let it be star, galaxy or microbe everything follows this natural law. Everything in this Universe generates, operates and destroys after a certain period. After death of everything including human being, comes to end forever and nothing remains behind. Mean to say, death is ultimate annihilation of everything including soul or spirit.

Actually, all our experiences are associated with consciousness, and spirit or soul is nothing more than set of experiences. Therefore, all experiences are experienced due to consciousness. Therefore, without consciousness there is no experience of 'within-ness' or any soul or spirit dwelling in the body. Anyhow, our consciousness also comes to end when we die. Therefore, when there is no consciousness, no experiences. Thus no experiences, no existence of soul, spirit or self whatever you may call it .Therefore, everything related to ourselves is only existed till we survive because our whole being is existed due to a specific energy of life. And when that inner flame drops away, nothing is left behind.

The existence of human being, in fact, is not different from plant. When a tree fall down, its stem, branches, leaves etc. dries very soon and the existence of whole plant vanishes forever. Thus, everything in the Universe is perishable and nothing remains afterwards. Therefore, nothing is permanent in the Universe including Universe itself.

Anyhow, Man is not considered special by Cosmic Forces so cosmic system follows this law of survival in the context of human being too. Even abbreviation of GOD is also denoted this universal law of perishable. In the term of GOD, G stands for generator, O for operator and D for destroyer. Thus, everything in the Universe is generated (creation), operated (evolution) for a certain period and ultimately destroyed (demise) forever after that certain age. Everything has to follow this process of three stages.

Even this cosmic law is being also followed in the context of God. In Hinduism, trinity of gods is also symbolic of GOD and has a similar meaning. *Brahma* is Creator; *Vishnu* is Preserver and *Shiva* is Destroyer. In similar way, the goddess *Maha Sarsvati* stands for creation; the goddess *Maha Lakshmi* stands for flourishing the life on earth and *Maha Kali* stands for destruction, and like cycles of all other entities, this cosmic cycle also completes. Thus, trinity of gods and all three goddesses represent the same universal law of creation, preservation and annihilation.

In fact, everything including Nature generates, prosper, and ultimately destroy after completion of its lifecycle which is decided by Cosmic Forces in order to govern the Cosmos. Therefore, nothing can be spared from this universal law in the Universe where everything is ephemeral. Thus, God is a simply name of that Cosmic Forces which regulate the cosmic system according to cosmic law rather than a living entity, sitting somewhere in higher location or dwells in the sky behind the cloud, descends from sky to meet the person who pleases Him. In fact, every object/entity of the universe including God is bound to work/function according to cosmic law.

Therefore, set aside your all curiosities. Life can be analogue with an onion. The onion is nothing but bundle of layers. If you start to peel the layer one after another, you will find nothing. So it is better to accept the onion as it seems. Thus, in the process of seeking the life, you will lose your whole life but you will get nothing. So, stop peeling the skin of life rather accept each and every thing and situation as it is. Therefore, instead of splitting the hair, enjoy the ever-changing life in each moment as it comes.

Anyhow, still I advise to go within yourself because for me, the meaning of going within is somewhat different. For me, going within means, to live with yourself completely; feel yourself by ceasing the thoughts and by calming the mind; live in the world but don't attach with it emotionally; listen the voice of your inner guidance rather than guidance of any other master; withdraw your senses from the world and turn them inwardly. Additionally, going within means, forget about gaining the support, approval and any other expectation from friends, relatives, collogues and other members of society. In other words, detach yourself from the people, material possessions and beliefs. By living so, in fact, is true meaning of going within yourself.

In addition, let go of the daydreaming and accept the present moment as it is; stop to chase the mirage and embrace the reality; in spite of thinking 'what should be', accept 'what is'. Thus, enjoy with what you have already rather than desire what you have not. Celebrate the moment as it is 'now' and face whatever befalls on you. Mean to say, rejoice in the way things are, and enjoy the life more and more without any external support. If you will rely to bring joy and fulfillment on external support which itself is bounded to change, your joy will also stay for short period.

Thus, remove the conformity, justification, conditions, identities etc. from your being. Mean to say, what you are, you are already with your true being. No any external identities are required to prove your own being. Remain in the state of joy without any reason because the happiness which is associated with the specific reason cannot last long.

As and when the reason of happiness will fall away, the happiness will also cease to exist. Therefore, no needs to be spend the life in searching the source of peace and bliss in outer world rather look within your inner source. Whatever you are searching outside already exists within you.

Therefore, go within yourself so that you may be able to recognize your own true valve, wisdom, power, beauty etc. Everything exists within you so go within yourself to enhance your self-trust and for recognition of your true worth. Therefore, I advise to go within yourself to experience the everlasting peace, joy and bliss that come from within your inner self rather than external world. Thus, as and when you realize that nothing is lacking but you yourself are a treasure, you become the center of the world. Then you realize that everything is revolving around you. Thus, by governing yourself, you can govern the world. Therefore, in order to taking your life in your own hand, go within yourself.

However, it is another matter that what you are seeking such as Higher Self, Eternal Truth or Supreme Power, it may be sought spontaneously. Every mystery of Nature unfolds according to its own process, and that process cannot be short. How much you try makes no difference, every process has its own way. So follow the procedure rather than searching shortcut. Anyhow, you will get all your answers at accurate time because Nature Itself unfolds its mysteries to those who become capable to know them.

Therefore, go within yourself only to enjoy the life rather than any other reason. Enjoy the journey and forget its destination. So go within yourself in order to ceasing your all types of desires so that you may get peace and bliss during living this life.

Going within yourself as source of peace and bliss

Our desires never fulfill and we remain dissatisfy in spite of consuming of all type of materialistic goods. After fulfilling of one desire, we feel pleasure. Then we take current standard of living for granted however after some period our pleasure stays no longer due to our adaptive nature. Then our aspirations ratchet up and we aspire to the next level of living standard. Anyway, after achieving this next level living standard, our pleasure comes to an end in this level also due to our adaptive nature. Then we aspire something more and more and even after achieving higher and higher stage we remain dissatisfy due to adaptive nature of human being. Thus we become adaptive of every higher and higher living standard, and every pleasure proves ephemeral and so on……Thus in spite of fulfilling our desires one by one, we remain thirsty. In fact, neither our aspirations come to end nor we become able to satisfy ourselves.

Thus, we always remain unsatisfied and this phenomenon of hedonic treadmill is going on forever. Therefore, in spite of achieving lots of wealth, qualification, status, power, position, post, portfolios etc. Human being remains restless and feels boredom. It can be said that human being always feels emptiness in spite of having everything. Though we try to fill this emptiness by indulging in the ceaseless pursuit of materialistic things, getting involved in one after another unsatisfactory relationship or dissolving in wine drugs etc., but still feel emptiness from within.

Then we start searching *guru* in order to listen religious discourses so that our emptiness can fill. We start seeking religious places for pilgrimage for mental satisfaction even we start doing different kinds of rituals in order to achieve peace. However, after failing in all above efforts, we renounce our duty (*karma*) and run away to fill this emptiness, but every effort goes futile. In spite of indulging in sensual pleasures or emotional joy; participating in sermons or religious discourses; performing rituals; etc., our search for happiness seems unending.

Actually, for attaining the peace and bliss there is no other option remains excepting going within. Anyhow, after knowing the life style of King Solomon and his understanding about life and human nature, everyone will certainly agree that peace and happiness cannot be attained with the support of materialistic things.

King Solomon was the ruler of Israel about three thousand years ego. According to Old Testament Bible, he was the richest and wisest man who ever lived. In addition, he was poet, scientist and prolific writer. Apart from some other books, he had written three books of modern Bible which are: - a book of proverb which is collection of about three thousand proverbs; songs of Solomon which is collection of thousand and five songs and Ecclesiastes which is part of the Bible. He was so wise that kings from all over the world came to hear his wise deliverance.

King Solomon handled many projects; built several cities; numerous harbors; marvelous palaces and temples, out of them one temple was laden with gold both sides, even floor and door were made up from gold. Mean to say, he made silver and gold as common in Jerusalem as stone. King Solomon reigned for forty years in one of the highest and most prosperous periods in Israel's history called by many 'The Golden Age' of Israel. In other words, he had accumulated enormous wealth and control the entire region west of the Euphrates.

Additionally, King Solomon had seven hundred wives of royal birth and three hundred concubines. There were many luxurious things were available in his palace. In spite of all type of luxuries; marvelous palaces; beautiful gardens and huge harem, what the king wrote in the book of Ecclesiastes will definitely surprise you.

King Solomon wrote, "I amassed silver and gold for myself, and the treasure of kings and provinces. I acquired—a harem as well—the delights of hearts of man" (Ecclesiastes 2.8). "But harem did not bring happiness to me. Everything was meaningless a chasing after the wind; nothing was gained under the sun," (Verse11) he said further.

Then he elaborated his dissatisfaction. "I have seen all the things that are done under the sun; all of them are meaningless, Meaningless! Meaningless! Utterly meaningless. Everything is meaningless, a chasing after the wind." (Ecclesiastes 1.2)

King Solomon said that all possessions are meaningless; harem is meaningless because they mean nothing and offer no comfort to sleepless, restless soul. "Possessions become a striving after wind. Even wisdom was meaningless because wise and fool die in the same way", he explained further.

Thus, in his old age, he found everything in this world empty and void of meaning. As he had lost interest in God in those days so he said that religion is also meaningless.

Actually, saying 'meaningless' is not represented king Solomon's depression but it was, in fact, his understanding about the life and world. However, king Solomon previously thought that having thousand wives and concubines, lot of wealth, status, popularity, trade, business etc. would provide happiness but whatever pursue he derived was not worth the price he paid. So, he concluded that all materialistic things are meaningless, and happiness cannot be attained by external support including religion.

In other words, it can be said that nothing was beyond his capacity to achieve but he was still dissatisfied. He utilized and consumed each and every luxurious thing of the world as he mentioned as 'under the sun'. Therefore, in spite of all the possessions king possessed, he was dissatisfied. Thus Solomon was unable to achieve happiness with the help of all his materialistic things and call it 'striving after wind'.

If King Solomon could not attain happiness, contentment and peace in the materialistic world then how can you think to achieve satisfaction, peace and bliss with the help of materialistic things?

Thus, there is no other way to attain the bliss and peace except going within yourself. Therefore, you should look within your inner source rather than outer sources because true happiness lies within you. Do not waste your time and efforts searching for peace, fulfillments and joy in the world outside. Thus stop chasing the source of happiness in external world rather go within yourself because the source of happiness lies within yourself like source of fragrance of musk lies within the musk deer itself.

Meaning of vacuum within us and ways of its creation

Actually, our thought process is going on constantly. Our mind is incessantly busy in thinking without halting even a fraction of second. Anyhow, when we start meditation practice, a slight gap occurs between two thoughts and this gap between two thoughts is termed vacuum or void. However, as our meditation practice increases, the thoughts start to disappear; suppressed emotions starts releasing and our false ego starts to fall away, the gap starts increasing. Thus the empting the mind from its all type of stuff create vacuum in the mind where nothing remains.

Mean to say, the state of thoughtlessness is a state of void or vacuum within you. Thus, vacuum is a state of mind where nothing is exists except purity. It can be said that after achieving the state of thoughtlessness, you reach in your inner most core of self which is also known as Higher Self. Mean to say, it is such vacuum where everything vanishes except Higher Self. And Higher Self cannot be bind in any definition, even description of this vacuum is unlimited.

That's why I separated this content from the content of thoughtlessness and wrote in a separate chapter so that the term within or vacuum can be explained clearly and thoroughly whatever I have experienced so far and knew from the experiences of prominent spiritual people.

Thus, as your thought process start decreasing, a space starts creating within you. As your thoughtlessness state increases, your inner space also increases. After achieving complete thoughtlessness state, the inner space extends infinitely. It is also known as mini Universe because it is a space in our own mind like the space in the Universe. However, when we experience our inner space, we feel tranquility and realize bliss.

Actually, this void is already exists very deep within all of us but it is fully covered under our thoughts and vanity. When we start meditation, not only our thoughts start to disappear but our vanity also starts vanishing. In fact, as and when you accept that you are nothing, you become the whole at the same moment. Mean to say, you become the knower of Eternal Truth just after accepting your ignorance. So it can also be said that our own conceit is the last obstacle in the way of realizing the Eternal Bliss.

However, it is really very difficult to define the void inside us. In the context of its definition, Chinese monk Huang Po said, "If you try to define the term void, you are contaminating it". Therefore, great sages and Buddhist monks have different views regarding its definition although they have realized the Absolute Peace and Eternal Bliss.

However, according to Hinduism, it is known as Eternal. According to their beliefs, it is existed when there was no 'before' and it will survive even after when survival ceases to exist. So in the beliefs of Hinduism, it neither takes birth nor dies. That's why they call it Eternal. Mean to say, it is Spirit or Soul which is beyond birth and death.

On the other hand, Buddha call this as 'no self' or *anatta*, dissolution or disappearance. It is non-being or it can be said that our inner most being is non-being. Nothing is there, only vacuum is there where self, individuality etc. everything has dissolved.

Thus Terry Murphy describes the Buddhist view and says that we imagine we experience a self, because we are told we do. If you really look inside you, without concepts, all you will find is a vast, vast emptiness and no 'self' at all. This is void, Non-existence, the Tao, the Unconscious, mother of all phenomenon.

Whilst in Sufism, the void is known as *funa* or dissolution. According to them, it is the inner-most core which is empty, pure space or it can be called 'nothingness'.

However, it makes no difference whatever we call it, but it is sure that we experience absolute peace when we go within ourselves.

About this void space within us, the neuroscientists are also busy in conducting experiments with the help of modern technologies. However, till now, they are only able to know that the firing of neurons comes to almost at end and subject perceives nothing but only peace and serenity.

However, regarding the methods of going within yourself, there is no any special technique rather than meditation practice. After getting rid of all types of shackles which had tied you so far such as—releasing your suppressed emotions; letting go of your ego and beliefs; accepting the present moment as it is, detaching yourself etc., when you start to live in the state of thoughtlessness, you enter in the realm of the vacuum within yourself spontaneously.

So there are no separate ways for going within you. There is no other path rather it is pathless. Thus after completing all the stages sincerely, you can enter into the door of that void space which lies within yourself. However, for completing all these stages, I advise only one technique and that is—practice meditation. After lot of meditation practice, when you will attain the state of complete thoughtlessness, you may be able to enter the void within yourself. However, after going within yourself, you will realize yourself that you have been transformed.

Experiences of Transformation:

Actually, when we start meditation and go towards the state of thoughtlessness, we start to realize that something new is happening in ourselves such as—changing in our schedule, attitude, feelings etc. As we go further we realize somewhat calmness, cheerfulness and happiness without any reason which we have not realized so far. Co-incidences and synchronicity in our life also start to increase.

However, when meditation practices increase and meditation routinizes in our day-to-day schedule, we start to stay in thoughtlessness state. Then our circumference of vacuum also increases and we experience such a serenity which is, in fact, beyond explanation. However, this state of serenity is varied time to time. Mean to say, sometimes it increases at higher level while sometimes descend at lower level.

Actually, serenity and bliss are directly proportional to our state of thoughtlessness. Though the state of serenity varies according to the state of thoughtlessness, it always remains there. Mean to say, once we achieve this joy and peace, we usually remain with it whatever its degree may be. Anyway, whatever I have experienced in my life about this serenity and bliss, I would like to complete the book with those experiences.

After achieving the tranquility and attaining the bliss, we begin to realize our multidimensional existences which separate us spontaneously from the conflicted situation and people whose resonations are no longer match with ours. Moreover, we feel connected with everyone and everything; even we realize that we are connected with the Whole or Universal Self.

Thus we not only realize this connection with each and every other thing but our creativity also increases manifold. Actually, this vacuum within us is like the womb of female mammal which generates new life. Means, unexpected answer of unsolved questions are emerged from nowhere, in this state of tranquility. Thus, as the circumference of inner vacuum increases, our creativity also increases accordingly.

Our aura becomes so strong that people are attracted towards us; like us and try to make connection with us, even though we have not done anything special in favor of them. Additionally, Not only friends and colleagues but strangers also express their pain and woe even they disclose their secret themselves to us when they come in our contact. Mean to say, everyone trusts on us when we attain this state of peace and bliss.

Generally, we feel detached from worldly affairs, and this detachment, in fact, soothes us. Most of the time we feel comfortable without company and we have no intention to reunite with this chaos world. Our sensitivity resist us to go in crowd and in case, if we have to go in the crowd, we feel dizziness and suffocation. Mean to say, we like to live in solitude rather than with companions.

Though we have already released our suppressed emotions, we have become so compassionate that sometimes we feel overwhelmed. In that state of compassionate, sometimes we sacrifice our own valuable things in order to make comfort to the needy. Mean to say, we start to care needy even on the cost of our personal requirement.

Anyway, when we achieve somewhat higher stage of peace and bliss, we start to feel intense joy without any reason. Mean to say, we start to live in such state of euphoria where nothing more is required. Thus all desires come to end spontaneously. In other words, in this state of bliss, outer world completely vanishes.

Actually, it is such a state of peace and bliss where we feel nothing except Higher Power. It seems that Divine Power remains present with us in one form or another irrespective of our sleeping or waking state.

Additionally, Nature seems very pretty. Every blade of grass and every leaf of plant seems greener than ever before. Fragrance of flowers feels more pleasant than ever before. Every particle of sand looks shinning and every rock or structure seems very holy and sacred. Chirping of sparrows and tweeting of other birds can be heard clearly and distinctively which, in fact, soothe us. Moreover, melodiousness of birdsongs increases. Mean to say, we start liking flora and fauna than ever before.

Sun rising and setting seem more beautiful and more scarlet than ever before. Sunshine seems brighter; calmness of moon and brightness of stars also seem increasing than ever before. Every blow of wind seems very cool and provides pleasure to us. Various types of clouds fascinate us towards sky.

Nature seems to be very excited for conversation with us. It seems that whole Universe is composing melodious music for us.

All these realizations of Nature, in fact, are experienced due to the mindfulness rather than self-hypnotism or any other illusion. Actually, when you hear, look, watch or feel something with full awareness, your focus of attention reaches at higher level on that particular object. Mean to say, your concentration increases manifold. In this mindfulness state, your concentration can be analogue with the legend of Mahabharata when the main aim of Arjun was bird's eye at the time of practice of bow and arrow. Though there were many things on the tree such as branches, leaves and bird itself, Arjuna noticed only eye of the bird because his focus of attention was only the eye of the bird. So due to his intense concentration, the eye of bird seems bigger than all surrounding objects. This is the reason that branches and leaves remained out of his sight.

Therefore, if you live mindfully then every object of your discerning seems big and bright due to your concentration and fully awareness. Thus you can ignore external disturbances by increasing your awareness and attention, and your senses become so capable that they can discern the object more clearly. As in the state of tranquility and serenity, your awareness increases manifolds so as your attention and concentration. That's why Nature and its objects seem brighter, bigger and clearer in comparison when you are not living mindfully. And the reason of increasing the mindfulness is the state of thoughtlessness.

When you achieve the highest state of bliss due to going within, you enter in the realm of such state of elation which is really beyond explainable. Actually those persons who have already experienced this state can understand better this highest state of bliss. In this state, it seems that nothing exists except yourself and Nature. You become so intoxicated that you forget all your worldly relations. All materialistic things seem superficial. You do not want to come out from that intoxicated state even not to earn for livelihood.

In this state of bliss, every object of the world seems to stand still at its place quietly; faces of people seem very innocent like children and their behaviors and activities make you comfort rather than create irritation. Mean to say, in this state, you shift your attitude from blaming to appraisal. You immerse in your ecstasy at such a level where difference between friend and foe; relative and stranger come to end. In this state of bliss, difference between sorrow and joy has also been vanished, even grief seems as blessed.

It seems that your inner space has been merged with outer space. Thus, resonations of your vibration reach up to Universe. So no need to be wandering anywhere rather all your requirements will be fulfilled in a miraculous way at suitable time.

Thus, set aside all outer source of happiness such as power, prestige, fame, wealth etc. Actually, these all factors of happiness work as a cage to trap in. Therefore, there is one and only one source to attain the Absolute Peace and Eternal Bliss and that exists within you. So dive within yourself.

ABOUT THE AUTHOR

The Author is the eldest son of a very simple farmer of Haryana. After matriculation, he could not study further due to differences among the members of the family so he joined the Indian Army as Telecom Mechanic in EME Corps at the age of eighteen. During his service, he completed BA, MA (Pol Science), and B Ed as private or correspondence courses. After serving sixteen years of service, he took a medical board pension from Army in 1986 and had also run his own business successfully for six years.

Being passionate for the teaching profession, he joined the Delhi Education Department as TGT in

1992. After witnessing the critical condition of Gujarat Earthquake's victims and bad management of the system, he took up M Sc. Degree in Disaster Mitigation in 2003. Later on, he wrote a book on the Environment *"Man towards Its Own End"* which was published in 2010 by Raider International Publisher New York.

After serving for twenty two years as a teacher, he retired in 2014 and shifted to Nainital. Now he is conducting a programme to improve the education of needy children of tribes in Uttrakhand.